Her Kama
Women, Intimacy and Identity

Edited by
Jaganniwas Iyer

Vitasta

Published by
Renu Kaul Verma
Vitasta Publishing Pvt Ltd
4348/4C, Ansari Road, Daryaganj
New Delhi-110 002
info@vitastapublishing.com

ISBN: 978-81-19670-73-4
Originally published in 1924 as *Kama Kalpa* or *The Hindu Ritual of Love* by D B Taraporevala Sons and Company Limited.

First Edition 2025
MRP ₹ 795

Edited by Vichitra Goel
Layout & Cover Design by Rohit Gautam
Printed by Chaman Enterprises, New Delhi

Contents

Publisher's Note

When *Kama Kalpa or The Hindu Ritual of Love* was first published in 1924 by D B Taraporevala, it stood out as a groundbreaking survey of Indian customs, beliefs, and rituals around love, marriage, and morality. A century later, we at Vitasta Publishing are proud to reintroduce this rare and remarkable work to a new generation of readers.

Far from being a mere treatise on sexuality, *Kama Kalpa* is a bold exploration of gender and society across millennia—tracing the arc of Indian womanhood from the empowered Vedic era to the oppressive customs of medieval times.

P Thomas, a scholar of Indian epics and folklore, draws richly from Sanskrit classics like the *Kama Sutra, Ananga Ranga, Rati Rahasya,* the Mahabharata and Ramayana, as well as works by Kalidasa and Kautilya, to paint a vivid picture of love and its many dimensions—spiritual, social, and sensual.

What makes this book valuable is its honest chronicle of the decline in the status of women—from choosing their partners in *swayamvars* to being denied basic rights like education or consent. The pages shed light on disturbing practices like child marriage, sati, and the stigma around literacy among women, while also acknowledging the colonial reforms that slowly reversed some of these injustices.

This passage from the book sums up the plight of women in medieval India:

> Knowledge of letters was considered disreputable for respectable women. Some ladies of the aristocracy, of course, had the benefit of a sound education; but as a rule, the art of reading and writing was considered the undesirable accomplishment of a courtesan.
>
> It was believed that 'It is a shame for a young woman or girl to hold a paper or book in her hand, or to read in the presence of others in her husband's house. It is a popular belief in high caste women that their husbands will die if they should read or hold a pen in their fingers.'

A belief was generally entertained that intrigue is facilitated by a knowledge of letters on the part of females.

Child marriage was another outcome of false beliefs in this dark, medieval period—and the superstition connected with Ritu. Quoting from the book, 'Ritu, the few days immediately following the menstrual flow, was considered the fertile period in women and it was thought a crime to let it go waste. The Aryans, who were then yearning for many sons, made copulation compulsory during this period.

'To ensure copulation in the first Ritu, it was binding on a man to get his daughter married before she reached puberty. A grown-up girl was considered more difficult to guard than a child, and a father was quite anxious to get his daughter married before she became too troublesome for watching.

'The proper age for marriage of a girl was believed to be

between eight and twelve. Manu says that if a girl remained unmarried after reaching puberty, then her father had failed in his duty towards her, and she could resort to the unsavoury action of choosing a husband for herself. Parasara, the law specialist went so far as to say that the parents or guardians of a girl in whose house a girl had reached puberty before marriage would assuredly go to hell.'

We may curse the British for robbing India's unlimited wealth, but we can also thank them for raising awareness of the pitiable plight of Indian women who often voluntarily jumped into the funeral pyre of their husbands because an even worse fate awaited them in society if they chose to live on after their husband's death.

It was Governor-General William Bentinck who abolished Sati after he became aware of the inhuman practice after Raja Ram Mohan Roy's campaign against it. The same foreign invaders also brought educational institutes into the country that opened their doors to both girls and boys, men and women, treating them as equals in the pursuit of education.

Kama Kalpa is exactly the kind of book Vitasta Publishing stands for—one that dares to challenge convention, provoke thought, and illuminate forgotten truths. In reprinting this work with updated editorial framing, we hope to present not a relic, but a reminder: that the way a society treats its women tells us everything about its moral compass. We gave the book a new title, as well, one that the present generation can identify with: *Her Kama: Women, Intimacy, and Identity.*

Editor's Note

Excavations in the Indus Valley region carried out in early twentieth century trace civilisation to at least 5,000 years ago, but subsequent discoveries and research put India's antiquity firmly back to a period, several thousand years before.

There are seeming contradictions of Indian attitudes towards gender and sex and these can be best explained through the context of history. How it treated its women can also be gleaned through the pages of Vatsyayana's *Kama Sutra* that not only outlined the history of sex, but also gave more than ample glimpses of the society of those times.

India is a multiethnic and multilingual society with wide variations in demographic situations and socioeconomic conditions. In a nation as religiously and ethnically diverse as India—often commonly described as 'a jumble of possibilities'—people follow a wide variety of customs, and have varied beliefs that ultimately mold their lifestyles and sexuality.

Sexuality means different things to different people. For some people, it could mean the act of sex and sexual practices, for others, it could mean sexual orientation or identity and for some others, it could mean desire and eroticism. Sexuality encompasses many ideas and has many facets. The definition of sexuality has been evolving along with our understanding of it. Sexuality is experienced and expressed in almost everything—in thoughts, fantasies, desires, beliefs, attitudes, values, behaviours, practices, roles and relationships.

The first evidence of attitudes towards sex comes from ancient Hinduism, Buddhism and Jainism texts. These texts are also, perhaps, the oldest surviving literature in the world. These most ancient texts, the Vedas, reveal moral perspectives on sexuality, marriage and fertility. It appears that polygamy was widely practised during ancient times, mostly by royalty, with common people maintaining a monogamous marriage. It is common in many cultures for the ruling class to practise both polyandry and polygamy as a way of preserving dynastic succession.

Let's get on to the subject of nudity in art. It seems to have been acceptable in southern India, as paintings at Ajanta and the sculptures of the time in various temples show. It is equally likely that in most regions with tropical climates, some tribes did not wear clothes, and other than for fashion, there was no practical need to cover the upper half of the body. This is supported by historical evidence, which shows men in many parts of ancient India covered only the lower half of their bodies with clothes and the upper part of the body by gold and precious stone jewellery, while women wore traditional sarees of silk and expensive clothes as symbols of their wealth.

Vatsyayana's classic work *Kama Sutra* (*Aphorisms of Love*) written somewhere between the first and sixth centuries includes the three pillars of the Hindu religion: Dharma, *Artha* and *Kama* representing religious duty, worldly welfare and sensual aspects of life, respectively. The main theme here appears to be the expression of the Indian attitude toward sex as a central and natural component of the Indian psyche and of life.

The *Panchatantra* states that the human obsession with shyness, friendship, melodious voices, intellect, brilliance of youth, sensuality of men and women, equanimity within species, absence of sorrow/misery, carnal pleasure, religion, scriptures, intelligence of Brihaspathi (the teacher of Gods and Devatas), hygiene, concerns about good behaviour—all occur only when a human's hunger is satiated.

A historical analysis of Vedic India, as revealed by its literature, shows that women were treated with grace and consideration. However, in the post-Vedic age, there was a slow but steady decline of their importance at home and in society. The decline, indeed a distinct degeneration in their status, is visible in medieval India. The *purdah* system of female seclusion, too, began around this time, including the sati tradition of immolating the widow on the husband pyre. Dowry and child marriages were also obvious in the pre-Independence period.

In India's male-dominated tradition, and everywhere in Vedic, classical, medieval, and modern Hinduism, paradigms in myths, rituals, doctrines, and symbols are masculine.

Her Kama: Women, Intimacy, and Identity by no means claims to present the comprehensive literary history and/or tradition of India's exploration of the most fundamental of human instincts. The vast world of *kama* demands a study that commands extensiveness, rigour, analysis and eclecticism. This is understandable once the reader factors in the *Kama Sutra* itself. The text is much more than just a guide to sexual positions and techniques. It is, quite amazingly, also a comprehensive guide to virtuous and gracious living that covers various aspects of life, including relationships, social practices, and the art of living well. It also delves into the nature of love, finding a life partner and managing relationships and explores the social practices of its age, including detailed courtship, marriage, and the roles of men and women. All of this is captured in *Her Kama: Women, Intimacy, and Identity* with plenty more quotes from other noted works and writers of that time.

Ultimately, in this book, you have a text that emphasises the importance of living a virtuous and gracious life, and balancing sensual pleasures with ethics and spiritual seeking.

In its choice of content, this book seeks to present a microcosm of the ancient *Kama Sutra* but also expands its gaze to encompass the social world of the contemporary age it is supposed to countenance. In this respect, it may be said to be a humble endeavour to present ancient Indian thought on an important element of human living and interaction for the benefit of the present generation.

Chapter 1

From Matriarchal to Patriarchal

The role of women in society has always been a reflection of the evolving values, power structures, and cultural norms. From early matriarchal societies, where women were central figures in both family and community, to the gradual rise of patriarchal systems, the status of women has fluctuated dramatically. Let us explore the changing nature of women's position across different eras and cultures, focusing on how their societal roles have been defined, revered, and sometimes diminished over time. Through a lens rooted in ancient scriptures and societal practices, we examine how the feminine has been perceived, celebrated, and suppressed, setting the stage for a deeper understanding of the forces that have shaped women's lives and identities through history.

A scrutiny of traditions and ancient literature of the world would arguably reveal that all nations have passed through what is known as the matriarchal phase of social development. The mother—or matriarch—exercised the same authority in domestic and social matters as the father or patriarch does in contemporary society. The father in a matriarchate is subordinate to both the mother and the property inherited through her; the home and children belong to the mother, and the father is more or less economically dependent upon her. In the ancient Hindu world, the progeny would acquire its name and *gotra* (lineage) through the mother in a matriarchate.

Any notion of a matriarchate would appear strange to our current notions about social order which are largely patriarchal. However, a matriarchal way of life, if not a proper order, was fairly common to primitive people. Contrary to the general conception of masculine tyranny in savage society, the male savage, with rare exceptions, is found to be a tame animal so far as his mate is concerned. In fact, the position of women seems to have deteriorated with time. With this, though materially advancing, civilisation too began dissipating in its emotional and empathetic quotient. Come the medieval age, the woman degenerated into a chattel. It is now that she has just begun to uplift herself from this fallen state.

It could also be argued that a matriarchate is the natural state of society; the rationale being that the savage male was essentially nomadic, a wild wanderer. The love of his mate alone could keep such a being fixed to any abode. The female, on the other hand, is inclined towards a more settled dwelling, that is, a home, mainly because of her lesser abilities with regard to the maternal function of operating a family. Yet, the chief factor in civilised life becoming a reality was the maternal instinct of the woman and her domestic interests.

Modern sociologists, or at least a segment among them, believe the prevalence of the matriarchate in ancient times to be the evidence of primitive man's ignorance of paternity—the primitive ancestors of today's humans were unaware of their sexual activity as the cause of pregnancy in women. In other words, men and women mated solely for pleasure and had not the slightest idea that mating was responsible for the reproduction of the species. Women were thought to become pregnant as they came of age, just as trees bear fruit in their time. The male had no right over the children of his mate. He had, of course, some attachment to her offspring because of constant association with their mother. The brutally minded of the male species, however, saw children as an impediment to pleasure and did not hesitate from killing them on occasion, a cruel trait observed in certain, mostly carnivorous, animals even today. Even in the present age, we come across mated groups of primitive people who have no idea of paternity. Their concepts of marriage and morality are directly opposed to what mainstream society holds as civilised norms.

It is reasonable to conclude that the status of women in all ancient civilisations was definitely high when compared to medieval ages. Ancient Egyptian society, for instance, was well-known not only for the freedom women enjoyed but also for the economic dependence of its men on women. The Greeks, the civilisations inhabiting the Levant, the Persians, and indeed almost all the patriarchal nations of the ancient world, had a matriarchal ancestry. That the mother right once prevailed even among Vedic Hindus is borne out by sufficient indications in their literature and traditions.

The Rig Veda, humankind's oldest body of literature, has little to support the theory of the overriding right of the mother. Rig Vedic society was essentially patriarchal. The deities worshipped were mostly gods, and the father was rightfully the head of the family. Goddesses like Ushas, Aranyani and Saraswati were indeed worshipped, but more for bestowing light and knowledge. The worship of the Great Mother as the deity of power is an essential feature of mother cults. The people of the Vedic civilisation worshipped male deities more. The Aryan/Hindu marriage ceremony, which emerged from Rig Vedic times and is followed by the orthodox even today, is a strong pointer to the patriarchal nature of society in those days.

For traces of a mother's rights among the Hindus, we have to look for guidance in the Mahabharata rather than in early Vedic literature. The Mahabharata is a repository of Hindu *itihasa* (history) and tradition. In this voluminous work, we come across several passages that reveal segments of Hindu society as being matriarchal. These references are probably to the pre-Vedic periods and communities inhabiting regions coterminous with ancient *Bharatavarsha*; but there are indications that some post-Vedic communities also followed ancient matriarchal traditions.

A significant episode in the Mahabharata tells us that there was a period in the Aryan society when married women could legally enter into sexual congress with other men for begetting progeny if the husband was incapable of siring children. Surrogacy of this nature was known as *niyoga* in ancient society and could be entered into only with the express consent of the lady's husband; else, it would be a mere satiation of one's carnal cravings. In a highly interesting moral situation, the virtuous Kuru monarch Pandu tells his wife Kunti to seek another man for the sake of progeny. Pandu, forbidden by a curse to have relations with his wife and thus disabled for the propagation of his line, confided to his wife that it is not sinful for a woman to have relations with another man for progeny. He reveals the moral law of a bygone age to the revolted Kunti:

> O Kunti! I shall now tell thee the practice of old, indicated by illustrious rishis fully acquainted with every rule of morality. Women formerly were not immured with their houses and dependent on husbands and other relatives. They used to go

> about freely, enjoying themselves as they wished. They did not then cling to their husband faithfully, and yet they were not considered sinful; for that was the sanctioned custom of the times. This practice sanctioned by precedent is applauded by great rishis. The practice is yet regarded with respect among the Northern Kurus. Indeed, the custom so lenient to women has the sanction of antiquity.

This ancient law was revised by the sage Svetaketu, son of Uddalaka, who forbade any relationship between a married woman and a stranger. The custom apparently had a life in the Vedic age too. The *Chandogya Upanishad* has the episode of the learned Brahmin Satyakama Jabali who, as a young child, sought instruction in the *shastras* at the feet of a learned *acharya* (teacher). Before accepting the boy as a disciple, the teacher wished to know his father's name and clan. Ignorant of both, he returned to his mother to enquire his father's name. The lady acutely confessed her ignorance:

> Son, I know not of what gotra you are. During my youth when I begot you, I was engaged in attending on many guests who frequented the house of my husband; I had no opportunity of making any enquiry about this. I therefore, do not really know of what gotra you are. All I do know is that Jabala is my name and yours is Satyakama. Tell the world that you are Satyakama, son of Jabala.

Satyakama returned to his teacher and faithfully reported to him what his mother had said, upon which the latter accepted the young lad as a pupil declaring his caste as Brahmin, on the lofty principle that only a noble Brahmin could speak the truth unfettered and unhesitatingly even in a situation as sensitive as this.

Vedic history is replete with individuals and clans who took their names and gotras from their mothers. Kadru and Vinata were sisters. The former is the mother of the species of all serpents called Kadraveya, while Vinata is Garuda's mother, of the eagle clan, known as Vainateyas. Clans and races today categorised as demonic were predominantly matriarchal. The Daityas are the progeny of Diti, and the Danavas are of Danu. Both Diti and Danu were wives of the sage Kashyapa. Their younger sister Aditi was another of the sage's wives, from whom the Adityas or Devatas were born. Buddhist tradition too speaks of individuals who took on their mother's gotra and were known by them—there is Mantaniputta, son of the lady Mantani, and Sariputta, son of Sari, as mentioned in the *Majjhima*. However, this eulogy of matriarchal lineage should not be taken as the complete absence of paternity or patriarchal society. Paternity was certainly known and recognised in matriarchal societies; it is just that in these societies, men and women were known by their mother's names.

The Daityas and Danavas were particularly noted for their strict adherence to and advocacy of maternalism. The Daityas and Danavas, as mentioned earlier, were the offspring of Diti and Danu respectively, both of whom were the wives of the sage Kashyapa. The children and descendants of both took their names and gotras from their mothers. Ravana, the demonic ruler of Lanka vanquished and slain by Shri Rama in the epic *Ramayana*, was a Daitya by lineage, his forefathers having descended from Diti. In *Ramayana* and Hindu tradition, Ravana, his family and followers are known by the more popular name of Rakshasa, which, historically speaking, originated towards the end of the Vedic age.

As mentioned earlier, the Daityas and Danavas were staunch about their matriarchy; the Daityas more so. Ravana's sister

Shurpanakha fell in love with Vidyujjiva, a Kalakeyan ruler of Ashmapuri, an island kingdom in South-East Asia in the Javan Sea, off the coast of Sumatra. The Kalakeyas, though a demonic community, were patriarchal in their societal life and, as such, a misfit among the then non-celestial Asuric communities and hence were seen as both outliers and challengers. Though women in the Daitya, Danava, Rakshasa and Asura clans enjoyed the freedom to choose their partners, both for life and companionship, Ravana outright refused to his sister marrying a Kalakeyan as the clan was patriarchal and adhered to the gotra lineage of the male parent. It also did not help that Vidyujjiva, an intrepid warrior, had challenged Ravana's imperial domain over the South-East Asian Ocean (today's Indo-Pacific region) and declared his kingdom of Ashmapuri to be independent, a direct challenge to Ravana himself. Shurpanakha chose to defy her mighty brother and went ahead to marry her lover, which, unfortunately, brought Ravana and the Lankan navy to the shores of Ashmapuri. Despite resolutely standing up to the Lankan invaders, Vidyujjiva was killed in a one-to-one combat by Ravana, who thus made his sister a widow. Shurpanakha is the same woman who earned notoriety in the southern Indian forest of Dandakaranya for trying to unsuccessfully woo Rama and Lakshmana. Failing this she tried to physically harm Sita and had her nose and ears chopped off by Lakshmana. This in turn triggered off a chain of events culminating in the Rama-Ravana war in Lanka, Ravana's eventual defeat and death at Rama's hand and the end of the Lankan Rakshasa Empire.

In the Mahabharata, the Uttara Kurus, living further north of Hastinapura, are mentioned as people living in an exalted moral realm, free of jealousy and bonds. By the time of the Mahabharata, i.e, the Dwapara Yuga, most clans practised polygamy and, in a few instances as mentioned above, polyandry too. However, the latter was less prevalent and was even fading away by the age of Shri Krishna and the Pandavas. Patriarchy was firmly ensconced in Hindu society; matriarchy was apparently on its last legs as far as mainstream society was concerned, though it had not vanished completely. Polyandry survived in a few pockets among the Uttara Kurus, as exemplified by Draupadi, daughter of King Drupada of the Panchala region. There are passages in the Mahabharata that express patriarchal dissonance and even intolerance of the right of the mothers' clan(s). Arguments, however, run both ways. Those brought up in a patriarchal tradition are conditioned to view women of matriarchal societies as laxer in morals, while supporters of a matriarchal order could argue that it is a well-balanced social system conducive to the flowering of individuality in men and women alike, and that the freedom of the sexes acts as mutual restraint, which is lacking in a patriarchal system.

The age of the Mahabharata, the Dwapara Yuga, had stronger views derived from patriarchal ideas, though one comes across many deviations, too. Polyandry had no approval; Draupadi's marriage to the five Pandavas was exceptional though it was only Arjuna, the third Pandava brother, who had won her hand in the *swayamvara* displaying his archery skills. In the case of Draupadi's swayamvara, King Drupada had fixed a near-impossible contest as the condition to win her hand. The contestants had to hit the eye of a fish sculpture fixed atop a pole through a revolving wheel by looking at its reflection in a small pond of still water below. Obviously, the test was designed to ensure that only the best bowman could win, which, then, turned out to be Arjuna. However, Arjuna had two older brothers, Yudhisthira and Bhima, who were still unwed. The shastras forbid a younger brother from marrying so long as an older brother, who is free of vice or physical deformity, remains unwed. A violation of this norm is called *parivedan* and the offender is called a *parivetta*.

Vyasa's epic also reveals another important reason behind Draupadi's polyandrous marriage with the five Pandavas. Their mother Kunti was responsible for bringing up the five brothers after the untimely demise of their father, King Pandu of Hastinapura. The Pandavas had a tough and hostile childhood deprived of their rightful inheritance of the throne because of the greed of their older uncle Dhritarashtra, who had become the regent owing to Pandu's absence, and the jealous machinations of their *adharmic* cousins, the Kauravas (Dhritarashtra's sons). However, their mutual bonding and unity was unshakeable and Kunti was particularly concerned at preserving it at any cost. She had insisted that any achievement or accomplishment by any of the brothers ought to be shared equally by all five brothers. Arjuna's resounding success in the bow contest at Kampilya (capital of Panchala, Drupada's kingdom) was undoubtedly a feat, but Kunti was worried lest it set off a discord among the brothers. Though the five brothers were united and obedient to their eldest, Yudhisthira, Draupadi's beauty was such that jealousy could easily take root among the five.

Besides the obvious suggestion of a matriarchal antiquity, the episode of Draupadi wedding all the five Pandavas sheds light on an interesting institution prevalent among the ancient Aryan communities. So was the practice, or tradition, of *niyoga* (surrogate parentage). Nor is polyandry entirely gone, although it is spoken of as a dying tradition. Several hill tribes in contemporary India openly practice polyandry, while other seemingly more respectable communities follow it secretly.

Traces of matriarchate in society are more discernible in the religious, literary and cultural worldview and practices of the Hindu world. Other than Hindus, no other civilised community in the world reveres God as both male and female. Moreover, no community other than the Hindus worships the divine as goddess, too. The Shaktas are a powerful sect that worship God as the Mother and not Father. Though they may not be the most widespread form of Hindu worship, the Shakta thought and outlook has permeated Hindu society to the extent that even the most stringent phases of patriarchy have been unable to dislodge the respect for, and worship of the Mother Goddess from the Hindu mind. The *Mahabharata* says that a spiritual guide deserves ten times as much reverence as a private teacher, a father as much as a hundred spiritual guides, but a mother merits reverence more than a thousand fathers. This sentiment is reiterated in almost all Hindu scriptures—something even no supposedly modernist Hindu can dare contradict or deny.

It is in Hinduism that the female deity is accorded preference when a goddess and her spouse are mentioned—Sitaram, Radhakrishna, Umashankar, Lakshminarayan, and the list continues. Moreover, it is the goddess who is first addressed while invoking the blessings of deities.

The Nairs of Kerala

Patriarchy is the reality of today's age, not just in India but in most of the world. Matriarchy is likely to be thought of as a thing of a distant past, but this is hardly the case. Today, Hindus from the three castes of Brahmin, Kshatriya and Vaishya follow the code of patriarchy, which, though not originating with Manu, were given a codified status by him. Yet, there are communities in India who even today adhere to a matriarchal social system. Presently, matriarchy is prevalent more among the tribal communities mostly in the country's Northeastern region. But, the Nair community of Kerala also offers a glimpse of a well-developed matriarchate. Regarded as one of the more cultured and progressive castes among Hindus, the Nairs (originally of Kshatriya lineage) also have a virile matriarchal tradition. Though matriarchal traditions of this community might seem loose in the towns and cities of present-day Kerala, it continues to hold sway in the villages. A closer look at some of the salient features of the social life of Nairs should help dispel some of the distorted notions held about matriarchy.

Marriage among Nairs is not a sacrament, but a mundane and worldly affair which includes scope for divorce and remarriage. A married woman does not hesitate before leaving her home; it is generally the same with a married man. Marriage in this community hardly brings any significant domestic disruption. The husband visits his wife in her house for availing his conjugal rights, and returns to his house in the morning to live with his sisters and their children. Children live with their mothers and uncles, and are dependent upon them. The men manage the estates belonging to the household while the women look after the household. The eldest male is the head of the family, but he cannot dispose of moveable property without the consent of his brothers and sisters.

Historically, Nairs lived in large family units called *tharavads* with descendants of one common female ancestor. These family units and their unusual marriage customs are no longer practised though they have been much studied. For a Nair, bringing his wife and children to his house is considered 'bad form', except as guests for a few days' stay. Moreover, he is not supposed to give anything of worth to them. Transgression of this rule generally brings his sisters up in revolt to curb any tendency he might develop to help his wife and children. Respectable women even refuse to accept presents from their husbands; accepting presents is looked upon as a characteristic of courtesans.

When a Nair lady's husband is divorced, he merely stops visiting her. The termination of a marriage does not involve any economic or domestic compulsions. The man simply starts looking for another wife and the woman for another husband. However, despite the ease of divorce in a Nair matrimonial bond, permanent union is the rule and divorce an exception.

Nairs usually marry their first cousins. A distinction though, is made between maternal and paternal cousins. It is considered the right of a young man to marry the daughter of his maternal uncle, but he is not permitted to marry the daughter of his mother's sister. The reason for this taboo is obvious. Children of sisters are brought up in the same house and are believed to be of the same blood, but the maternal uncle's children are brought up elsewhere and are not treated as belonging to the same blood.

Arguably, the matriarchal social system of the Nairs can claim advantages over mainstream patriarchy. With husbands and wives not regularly living in the same dwelling, interminable quarrels and discords between husbands and wives are avoided. Ladies in the Nair community, with considerably more economic freedom, hold their heads higher than their counterparts in the patriarchal world. However, no system is devoid of flaws. In the matriarchal world, a tortuous and inseparable nexus between sex and economics has marred the Nair social system too. Women of families whose matters have fallen into a bad way often exploit their husbands, especially if the latter happen to be wealthy, leading to quarrel and litigation.

Though the matriarchal way of life is still prevalent in parts of India, many find that it is not easy to live by its rules in today's times. It is easy for a man in the village to live in his own house and visit his wife at night. But a Nair living and working in Delhi, Bangalore, Mumbai, or abroad certainly cannot adhere to this age-old matriarchal system. On a practical plane, pockets of matriarchy are surrounded by the ocean of patriarchy and are slowly succumbing to it.

The Mahabharata, too, mentions a certain community in South India, ruled by king Nila (blue-black in complexion). Prince Sahadeva, the youngest of the Pandava brothers, visited their kingdom and found the women exceptionally good-looking and enjoying almost unfettered freedom in moral matters. This could be a reference to the Nairs.

Woman, said to be the ultimate of God's creation, has been worshipped, venerated and adored in the Hindu world. Despite medieval outlook turning against her and all adverse laws and rules targeting her, the woman remains an enigma worthy of both reverence and even submission. A woman's goodwill enhances the reputation of not only her immediate family, but also of her clan; conversely, her fall is the fall of her clan. An erring man brings affliction upon himself, but an erring woman draws trouble upon herself, her relatives and her clan. A man may marry below his caste, but a woman cannot demean herself thus. A woman's defilement is the defilement of her race. Ironically, the very greatness of the woman has been the cause of her troubles. Considered a precious possession, she had to be constantly guarded lest the entire race be contaminated through her defilement.

Chapter 2

Marriage in Vedic Times

The Vedic culture celebrated vitality, strength, and the pursuit of pleasure, all while upholding *dharma* and spiritual duty. Marriage was viewed as a sacred, balanced partnership between equals, where both men and women shared spiritual and material responsibilities. The wedding rituals emphasised this mutual bond, marking a journey together in life and duty. Through these unions, women were recognised as central, powerful figures in Vedic society, laying the foundation for the evolving narratives of love, duty, and power that continue to shape Hindu thought and culture.

The Indians, that is the Hindus of the Rig Vedic Age, were highly evolved people, spiritually, materially and even metaphysically. They had an active, energetic existence characterised by their zest for life; they loved and worshipped free, healthy and beautiful women. These women would share their domestic lives, establish families with them, take care of their home, and be of help in the farm, camp and even in the battlefield. Vedic Aryans were hardy, warlike people with a well-founded dharma and a profound love for the healthy pleasures of life. The meta speculations that later led to the degeneration of the Hindus into stay-at-home people given to ascetic leanings had not yet developed. Most hymns and prayers of the Vedic Aryan people were for long life and mighty, illustrious and victorious progeny. Their main occupation was either agriculture or war with hostile tribes inimical to the Vedic way of life and its values. For such virile people, women were equal assistants and partners in daily life and not mere ornaments, articles of pleasure or subservient stay-at-home maids.

Child marriage was not prevalent in the Vedic age, certainly not in the early period. All accounts speak of the married girl as a youthful maiden and that marriages consummated on the fourth night of the ceremony.

Widow-burning was unknown. Some anecdotes in the *Vedas* mention an ancient rite wherein kings and chieftains had their wives and cattle buried with them. The practice was not widely popular and was even abolished though its memories might have lingered among the ancient Aryans. There are many instances of widows marrying the younger brother of the deceased husband. The Hindu custom of niyoga (surrogacy) also supported this practice. The custom of sati definitely came later.

Monogamy was mostly the rule in Vedic times, though wealthy clan leaders often had many wives. Though we come across learned sages having more than one wife, polygamy among rishis was, contrary to popular perception, not a norm. The plight of multiple wives of a single man was not always enviable. Polyandry is mentioned in Vedic literature, but was not widely practised.

Women of Rig Vedic times lived an active life, sharing with their husbands, the labours of the fields and the hazards of a hardy life. There is mention of Mugdalini or Indrasena, wife of Sage Mugdala, who helped her husband in the pursuit of robbers who had stolen their cows. She drove the car (a horse-drawn chariot) to help her husband when he was in a tight corner, and taking up her husband's bow and arrows, defeated the robbers in battle, and recovered the stolen property.

The Vedic age also saw women of learning. A large number of the hymns of the times were composed by women rishis such as Lopamudra, Mamata, Apala, Surya and Visva.

Vedic literature shows families in those days were similar to the present-day Hindu joint families (even this is increasingly becoming a thing of the past). As a rule, things change slowly in India and many of the ancient Vedic practices still exist. The father was the head of the family, exercising supreme authority and familial rights over the younger members of the household. The mother-in-law had considerable influence in the Vedic family, though probably much less than in present-day Hindu families.

Since child marriages did not exist in Vedic times, young men and women had ample opportunities for courtship. Matches and matrimony resulting from love between couples—which has also given birth to the Indian colloquialism of 'love marriage'—were common, though not a norm. Fairs, festivities, social gatherings, bathing ghats, accidental crisscrossing of paths while visiting places of worship, and the like provided the lovesick with opportunity and space to meet and exchange glances. Marriages were arranged by parents (as they are in traditional Hindu society even today), but the concerned parties weren't without a say in their own future married life.

Variations apart, marriage in the Vedic period was sacramental. Since the ceremony established in this period is to this day performed in its orthodox form, it merits a detailed description as it throws light on the status, dignity and age of the bride.

The marriage ceremony now, as in times of yore, is performed in the bride's house. Usually, a temporary hall is constructed or taken on rent, either at plush hotels or specially built marriage or conference halls for the ceremony and for accommodating the guests. The chief witness is Agni, the deity of fire, purity and truth—a sacrificial fire is lit in an altar and the ceremony is performed in the presence of the sacred fire. The guests and the relatives of the bride and groom serve as the witnesses.

The first step towards the ceremony is the groom's *sankalpa*—an avowal of determination to direct one's energies in attaining the object in view. The groom recites the verse: 'This woman I now marry to acquire the wealth of *dharma* (religious merit) and *praja* (progeny).' After having thus prepared himself for the solemn ceremony and its commitment for life, the groom then addresses the bride: 'Look upon me with no angry eye; be not hostile to me; be tender to animals, be amiable, be glorious; be the mother of males; be devoted to the gods; be the bestower of happiness; be the bringer of prosperity to our bipeds and quadrupeds.'

The bride's father then extracts a promise from the groom before surrendering his rights over his daughter. He proclaims: 'In the attainment of *dharma, artha* and *kama*, she is not to be transgressed.' The son-in-law-to-be responds: 'Transgress her I will not.' This solemn promise is extracted thrice, indicating that the Vedic wife was not a mere chattel of her husband, but his *swamini* (one who owns her husband, just as a husband owns his wife). Other items of the marriage ceremony too confirm this Vedic injunction and rule.

The girl is now given away by her father to the groom. This relinquishing of parental authority over the little darling, lovingly brought up among her parents, brothers and sisters, and now to be taken away for good to another household, is an occasion for much sorrow. During this culmination of the wedding ceremony, the girl's parents, sisters, and relatives usually well up with tears, a scenario that Hindu families solemnising their wedding according to traditional rites are all too familiar with.

The groom then speaks:

> First Soma (the deity of the *soma* plant, a herb that yields an intoxicating juice; *soma* juice is widely used in Vedic rites) had thee for bride; Gandharva (celestial beings from whom music has originated) thee next; Agni (the presiding deity of fire and the purifier of all things) was thy third husband; thy fourth husband is myself, born Soma gave thee to the Gandharva, the Gandharva gave thee to Agni, and Agni thee to me for wealth and sons.

This verse symbolises the growth of the girl. In childhood, a girl is believed to be guarded by Soma, in girlhood, (after attaining puberty) by the Gandharvas, and after puberty till marriage, by Agni. According to Vedic literature, the girl's association with these three celestial beings does not corrupt her, and the man is enjoined to accept the girl from Agni without any hesitation. The verse also clearly reveals that at the time of marriage when a man receives his bride from Agni, she is a young woman who has reached puberty.

The *Dharmashastra* mentions the next ceremony is the *panigrahana* or the groom accepting the bride's hand. He takes the hand of the bride, and the presiding priest chants verses to be repeated by the groom. After the *panigrahana* comes the ritual of *saptapadi* or seven steps. The groom leads his wife around the sacred fire seven times, each time repeating a vow. After the seventh round, which seals the irrevocable union, the bride is thus addressed by her husband:

> Now, we have taken seven steps together; be my companion. Let us be companions. Let me have your companionship. May I never part from you, nor you from me. Let us be united; let us always take counsel together with glad hearts and mutual love. May we grow in strength and prosperity together. Now are we one in mind, deed and desires. You are Rik, I am Saman; I am the sky, you are the earth; I am the semen, you are its bearer; I am the mind, you are speech. Follow me faithfully, that we may have wealth and children together.

After the *saptapadi* and the repetition of this verse by the groom, the priest offers a concluding *ahuti* (oblation) to the sacred fire, ratifying the union, and blesses the bride, the groom and the guests in due order. He proclaims:

> May Pusa (the Vedic deity who blesses the smooth conduct of a wedding, and protects travellers, pilgrims and animals, especially domesticated ones, is also invoked for protection from accidents, mishaps and sudden deaths) lead you hence, taking you by the hand; may the Ashwinis (twin gods, who are also the physicians of the devatas) convey you away in their car; go to the dwelling (of your husband), as you are the *swamini* (lady) of the house; you, while being submissive (to your husband) give orders to his household. In this (your husband's family), may affection increase with offering; be watchful of the fire in the house; unite your person with this your husband; and both growing old govern your household.... Let not the robbers who approach the husband reach them; may he by easy roads bypass the difficulty; may enemies keep aloof. Fortunate is this bride; approach, behold her....Having given your congratulations, depart to your houses.

After this, the priest collects his *dakshina* (fee) and wedding garment as a gift, and the guests are treated to a feast. This concludes the main function of the marriage ceremony in the orthodox form.

As the bride reaches the husband's, and now, also her home, several minor ceremonies are performed. When the bride with the party arrives at the threshold, she is thus hailed:

> Be you supreme among father-in-law, supreme also among brothers-in-law; be you supreme over sisters-in-law, supreme also over mother-in-law.

Also notable is:

> Let this fair wife, with aspect bright,
> And honied words her lord delight.
> Let brothers' mutual rancour shun,
> And sister, sister kindly treat,
> Let each the rest with accents sweet
> Address, and all in heart be one.

After reaching the groom's house, the newly-weds in Vedic times had to observe continence for three nights. This was a test of endurance. The husband and wife were to sleep on the same bed, but not touch one another. A celestial being called Visvavasu Gandharva was to be a witness to their continence. A stump of *udumbara* (the ficus fruit, considered auspicious for ceremonies), dressed in silk and coated with sandal paste, representing this divinity would be placed between the husband and wife, and neither was to cross this holy barrier.

Upon the termination of the three-night-ordeal, the couple were permitted to indulge in sexual congress on the fourth night. The nuptial bed was decorated for the occasion and

Visvavasu Gandharva was ceremoniously asked to depart. Before initiating the sexual union, the groom addressed Visvavasu thus: 'Rise up from hence, Visvavasu, we worship you with reverence; seek another maiden with large hips; leave the bride to me, her husband.'

The *udumbara* stump which had stood between the couple for three nights would then be removed with reverence; the newly-weds were now in a position to embrace each other. But sensuous thoughts were not to mar so holy an act. We are told:

> There must be no lascivious thoughts, and the idea of animal gratification must be pushed entirely to the background. Both must consciously and deliberately *will*, with all their might that progeny shall be spiritual.

In keeping with the Hindu conception of the superior sex nature of woman, it was the bride who took the initiative in the bedroom. Before the union, she was to address her husband: 'Know I what you have in your mind, you that have had your birth in *tapas* and enriched in *tapas*. Here in my house, may you enrich me with progeny and wealth, being born in your son, that has a desire for sons.'

The husband would willingly respond: 'Know I what you have in your mind; lovingly do I view you as one seeking impregnation in your body during the Ritu period, you who have had me in your mind. A youthful woman you are...and may you be born in your son, desirous as you are for a son.'

It isn't as though it was all by mutual consent. The groom would say a final prayer to the gods:

> May the Vishvedeva unite our hearts; may the Udaka Devas, Vayu and Dhatr unite our hearts; may Saraswati vouchsafe to us appropriate speech. O Prajapati! Enter my body. O Tvastr,

> fashioner of forms, enter thou my body with Vishnu and other Devas. O Indra, come thou with thy friends, the Vishvedevas, and enter thou our bodies with them to grant us our wish. Parents of a numerous progeny are we to be. May Prajapati grant us progeny till we grow old. May Surya make us each love the other. O bride, live thou long in the house of thy husband; and enjoy the companionship of thy husband ever more. May we be happy in the wealth of our big and quadrupeds.

After this fervent last prayer, the couple could sleep together without further ado.

It can be easily seen that the Vedic marriage had been highly idealised, the emphasis being on desirable progeny and the attainment of dharma or religious merit through sacrifices by the couple. The essential features of the Vedic rite have come down to us in the orthodox form of the present-day marriage ceremony. However, it is only the form that remains now, the meaning having long become obscure. The priest chants the mantras in Sanskrit, a language barely known to the young. Occasionally, the priest translates some Sanskrit mantras on the spot, though this is not the norm.

Marriage was sanctified and idealised towards the later Vedic period when the Brahmins' ascension in religious ceremonies and the ritualism of the *Brahmanas* began to influence the Hindu way of life. The extreme spiritual emphasis, and the near-total divorce of marriage from carnal desires might even point to a later date, probably the period of the *smritis*. The sages who instituted these ordinances probably interpolated the Vedic texts and the *Grihya Sutras* freely. The marriage ceremony, as it stands at present, points to progeny and performance of the *Agnihotra* as its main objectives. Any desire for pleasure in marriage was deprecated as unbecoming of the sacrament. The *Agnihotra* was a daily domestic ritual performed by householders in ancient India and was performed in the presence of the consecrated fire brought from the marriage hall by the husband and wife and perpetually maintained in the husband's home. Considering the importance given to the Agnihotra in the ancient texts, it would appear that a married couple lived solely for the sake of performing the holy rite.

However, not all marriages during ancient times were treated as sacrosanct. The *Rig Veda* contains the beautiful story of king Pururavas, the progenitor of the illustrious lineage of kings known by his name, and his marriage with the celestial *apsara* (nymph), Urvashi. This marriage was more of an understanding between the two lovers with no officiating priest to sanctify the matrimonial bond. As it was not entirely divorced from carnal desires, it would be worthwhile to know the episode in some detail.

Urvashi was the main apsara of *Swarga Loka* or heaven and was known to be irresistibly beautiful. She was blessed by Indra, king of the *devatas* and performed every evening in the celestial court. No one had known her as a girl, teenager or mother and it was believed that she had never offered her heart to anyone. She was known to be the female friend of all the devatas.

Once, she and her apsara friend Chitralekha, visited the earth. A *rakshasas*, who saw them, abducted both of them and carried them off in his chariot. The loud wails of the two damsels in distress drew Pururavas, king of the Purus (of the same lineage that later became the Kuru dynasty). Pururavas, fearless as a lion, attacked the rakshasa without any hesitation and slew him with sword in a one-to-one combat.

Urvashi fell in love with the victorious Pururavas and he too became the lover of that beautiful apsara. But, she had to return to heaven even as Pururavas got restless for her. Not knowing what to do, he narrated his plight to his childhood friend Rajvidusa. One day, he was sitting in his garden talking to his friend about Urvashi when his beloved arrived and stood behind him, although not visible to him. She made Pururavas aware of her presence and they embraced each other. Just then, a messenger came from heaven to convey Indra's message. The lord of the celestials had ordered her to reach heaven immediately and participate in a special dance drama. Helpless, Urvashi had to return to her celestial abode.

But the heavenly apsara could not concentrate on dance and drama. Unknowingly, she called out to Pururavas and with that, Bharat Muni, the creator of the dance drama, got angry and immediately cursed her. 'You did not enjoy my drama. Go to earth and live there with Pururavas, like a human being,' he told her.

Undoubtedly, Urvashi loved Pururavas, but did not want to live in the mortal world. She, therefore, reached out to Indra and pleaded on her knees to free her from the curse. Indra felt pity on his beloved apsara and said to her: 'Urvashi, proceed to earth, but you shall not stay there for long.' Urvashi thus united with Pururavas. He was happy to get her, but was also sad that his beloved would be deprived of all heavenly joys.

The damsel, however, was not going to unconditionally submit to her earthly lover, laying down a strict condition, 'King, I will live with you; I will become your bride, but on one condition.'

'What is that? Know with certainty that I shall follow it,' said Pururavas.

'May I never see you undressed.'

'So be it! I accept this condition,' Pururavas promised.

A year later, Urvashi gave birth to a son named Ayu.

Urvashi had kept two lambs. She loved them so much that she used to keep them tied to her bed even while sleeping and waking up. Meanwhile, the Gandharvas were finding their art incomplete without her. They were aware of Urvashi's condition imposed upon Pururavas. Wanting to get the apsara back to the celestial abode, they arrived at midnight and noisily stole a lamb, so that Urvashi would wake up. She nudged Pururavas and told him, 'You're sleeping; the Gandharvas are stealing my lamb.' A sleepy Pururavas merely yawned and turned to the other side. The next day, Urvashi remained angry and her consort could not assuage her.

After a few days, the Gandharvas once again returned at midnight. Urvashi again shouted, 'The Gandharvas are going to steal my other lamb!' An aroused Pururavas immediately stood up to chase the Gandharvas. His night clothes fell from his body and he was bereft of attire. The Gandharvas immediately caused lightning. Urvashi saw her husband without his clothes and was stunned. In strict adherence to the condition laid down, she left him.

Pururavas searched the entire earth for his beloved, wandering in the mountains and valleys. When he finally became mad, he would sometimes embrace the vines and creepers in the forest, considering them to be Urvashi. When drops of water fell from the leaves of the forest trees, he would hear Urvashi's footsteps in them. When the sky was clear and the birds were chirping, he would think that Urvashi was laughing and singing. When the sky was cloudy, he felt that Urvashi was hidden and he would suddenly discover her, but his search would be in vain. After many years, Urvashi finally appeared before Pururavas.

Yet, this meeting was with a condition. She said to the king,

'You will find me only on the last day of the year.'

And, in this way, Pururavas could obtain her for only one day in the year. He would feel the pain of separation from her for the remaining days of the year; he would search for her, but could not find her.

'You did not do what I had told you; hard to catch am I for you, go to your home again, she said.' To this, Pururavas replied, 'Then will I rush away this day, never to come back, to go to the farthest distance; I will lie in *Nirriti's* (Nirriti is an evil spirit; also used allegorically to mean a state of disorder or ruin here) lap, fierce wolves will devour me—nay, your companion will hang himself or rush forth; or the wolves or dogs will devour him.'

Urvashi said, 'Pururavas! Do not die. Do not rush away! Let not the cruel beasts devour you! Truly, there is no friendship with women and theirs are the hearts of hyenas...Do not take this to heart! There is no friendship with women. Return home...When, changed in form, I walked among mortals and passed the nights there during four autumns, I ate a little ghee once a day and even now I feel satisfied therewith!'

We certainly do not find the heart of a hyena in Urvashi's words, but instead, tenderness mixed with love and pity. In spite of all her persuasion, Pururavas refused to leave her, and Urvashi was so moved by his love that she confided to him a plan by which he could convert into a Gandharva and live with her.

Such marriages, or unions, born of love were confined to the earlier Vedic period; later, marriage became strictly sacramental. After the Vedic age, the rigour of the patriarchal code bore its natural consequences, Women were found unequal to the ideal preached by the pious. Adultery was not uncommon, and birth of illegitimate babies and their exposure are mentioned in ancient literature. Later, as the ages wore on, with incursions of alien and hostile cultures into India, women soon became a cumbersome responsibility and trouble for the parents, and the birth of daughters came to be looked upon as a misfortune. Hence, in some texts, we come across fervent prayers by parents to give them sons and to 'give daughters elsewhere.'

For the present, we will confine ourselves to the general spirit of love and esteem for women discernible in early Vedic literature. The poet who sang hymns to Ushas, the virgin goddess of the dawn, certainly had an adequate conception of the charm, grace and dignity of women. One particular hymn of the *Rig Veda* eloquently speaks of the esteem the Vedic Hindu race had for women.

> उष: प्रतीची भुवनानि विश्वोर्ध्वा तिष्ठस्यमृतस्य केतुः I
> समान्मर्थ चरणीयमाना चक्रर्मिक नण्यस्या ववृत्स्व II

> *Ushah Pratichi Bhuvanani Vishwordhwa Tisthasyamrutasya Ketuh I*
> *Samamartha Charaniyamana Chakrarmik Nanyasya Vavrutsva II*

> O goddess, Usha! says Sage Vishwamitra, You are one who traverses towards all the worlds and enables the realisation of the power and domain of the Sun, who is devoid of perishability. You reside in the sky, above all the worlds. O Usha! You are ever young, one who can never grow old. Just as the cycle of the Sun always circumambulates (the Universe), may you too traversing a constant path, remain ever present.

Chapter 3

Womanhood, Marriage, Love and Sex

The Ramayana and Mahabharata are not only the pillars of Hindu mythology but are also the key to understanding the evolving role of women in marriage and society. Through the stories of Draupadi, Sita, Savitri, and others, we see women navigating complex relationships that intertwine duty, power, and love. The customs and rituals portrayed in these epics reflect a society in transition, where women were both revered and constrained by their roles in marriage, offering profound insights into the balance of love, duty, and the position of women in ancient times.

The Ramayana and Mahabharata are undoubtedly the two most important epics of the Hindu world, the Mahabharata being the greater and more voluminous. Both represent Sanatana Dharma, Hinduism and the Hindu ethos, in all its glory as well as diversity. They represent the Aryan culture and civilisation, particularly at the zenith of its glory.

The events of the Mahabharata are more or less spread over the Gangetic plains of India, with most events of that era concentrated around Hastinapura (the ancient capital of the Kurus in present-day western Uttar Pradesh, a small, nondescript town) and Indraprastha (today India's capital, Delhi). But, the Hastinapura-Indraprastha belt was not the only scenario of action; eastern, western and southern India too figure with varying degrees of prominence in the Mahabharata. Girivraja, later known as Rajgriha (today's Rajgir in Bihar), then the capital of Magadha, Pragjyotishpura in Assam (still existing near Guwahati and the proposed site for its futuristic capital), Avanti (modern-day Madhya Pradesh), Manipur of the Northeast, Kalinga in Odisha, Vidarbha in Maharashtra, Dwaraka and Prabhas in Saurashtra (Gujarat), Tungabhadra in Karnataka, the kingdoms of Kerala and the Cholas in today's Tamil Nadu also figure prominently in the Mahabharata. Gandhara (in today's Afghanistan), Kamboja (Central Asia), Siam (Thailand) and Madra (in West Asia), among others, are the regions that figure in Bhagawan Veda Vyasa's account of the events of the Dwapara Yuga. The Arya culture and civilisation extended well beyond the Vindhyas into the southern part of the Indian peninsula.

Originally called *jaya* (victory), the Mahabharata is the narration of the struggle of the virtuous and dharmic Pandavas against their evil cousins, the Kauravas, who were wedded to *adharma*. Today, Mahabharata is the world's longest epic, which speaks of the supremacy of dharma and the threats to it, along with one's duty to adhere, sustain and, when called upon, fight for. The Mahabharata is an entire world of *itihasa* (history), geography, rules and norms for a life and sociopolitical structure based on the principles of dharma, moral precepts, descriptions of myriad customs and practices—many of which have become outdated long ago—besides scientific treatises on war and warfare. It is about statecraft, philosophy, an exposition on human nature and an interplay of divinity and the human world, besides being a repository of spiritualism and metaphysical reflections. The undercurrent of Arya spirit and the zest for life and the attainment of material prosperity and well-being is an innate part of the Mahabharata. It is the epitome of the cultural heritage of the Hindus.

Coming to womanhood, marriage, love and sex, the teachings of the Mahabharata are generally in conformity with the moral precepts of the *Grihya Sutras* (domestic rules of conduct) and in some respect, the laws laid down by Manu, arguably humanity's foremost lawgiver. When one talks of a marriage ceremony in the era of the epics, one generally refers to the Vedic ceremony as the prime form of matrimonial ceremony. This was further cemented with the solidifying of the *varna* system. The Vedic ceremony of marriage became more important among the upper castes, particularly the Brahmins.

The importance of marriage, however, wasn't any less among other communities. The Kshatriyas attached equal, if not more, importance to marriage and its ceremony. Only, the hardy warrior spirit of the Kshatriyas manifested in the form of the *swayamvara* (literally meaning 'groom of one's choice') when it came to matrimony. The Kshatriya girl who had come of age was free to choose a husband from among the many suitors assembled. The prospective bride, mostly a princess of a royal dynasty, would garland one of the invited princes and young men of worthy royal lineages, who she found worthy of becoming her married partner for life. Her choice of the groom was final, without any parental or elderly diktat. The right of the maiden to choose her husband from among many suitors is the most important aspect of the swayamvara.

Occasionally, each suitor had to fulfil a test or condition laid down to qualify for obtaining the young girl as his wife. The tasks could range from performing a feat of valour or meeting a pre-determined condition laid down by the princess's father, brother or family. Such a feat was referred to as *viryashulka* (fee to be paid in the form of a valorous feat). The swayamvara, itself, was an elaborate and lavish ceremony, and not for commoners. With the princess coming of age, her father, the king, would send formal invitations to other kings and royal dynasties, informing them about his intention to hold his daughter's swayamvara. The invitations also depended on the existing state of political relations between monarchies and royal lineages, as also striking up new alliances or strengthening the existing ones.

The distinguished royal guests were seated in a specially constructed hall, lavishly decorated for the occasion. At the appointed hour, the princess would appear, splendidly attired, holding a garland in her hands. With the princess came a couple of intelligent attendants, well-versed in the lineage and genealogies of the royalty present at the swayamvara. As the princess passed each one of the royal suitors, her attendants described heir names, titles and lineage, and the princess placed the garland on the neck of the suitor she wished to wed.

A marriage, or any other important gathering, could easily turn into an occasion for a quarrel as guests often considered a social function the most suitable for settling a dispute. The presence of a large number of people is an incentive to complain because of the publicity it would bring in its wake. The great warriors of the epic period were no exceptions to this norm. The swayamvara in ancient India often broke up in a trial of arms. It was not unusual for the rejected suitors to aggressively argue that the choice of the princess was ill-advised, and to violently vent their feelings. More so since they wanted to show the princess their skill in arms and how great a husband she had lost through her folly. The host king, however, would be well aware of the proclivities of

Kshatriyas on such occasions and keep an adequate army ready to drive away turbulent guests. There are many instances in India's ancient history where the outcomes at swayamvaras weren't that happy for both the princess and her father.

A famous swayamvara described in the Mahabharata is that of Damayanti, the princess of Vidarbha. Though Damayanti is not the main character in the epic, she is the heroine of the story narrated to the Pandavas, by a sage. Damayanti loved Nala, a virtuous king of Nisadha, and the king, too, reciprocated her love. The lovers had never seen each other, but knew enough about each other to ignite love. Bhima, Damayanti's father, declared the date of her swayamvara and sent special invitations to all the kings of India so that his daughter could have a wide choice. Nala was one of the specially invited guests. But even uninvited people were welcome on the occasion. Hence, the celestials—Indra, the lord of the Devatas, Yama, the deity of death, Varuna, the deity of the oceans and Agni, the fire deity—the four guardians of the Universe decided to attend the swayamvara as they had heard of Damayanti's beauty and accomplishments. On their way to Vidarbha, the gods happened to meet Nala and learnt that he was also going as a suitor. Nala's personality impressed the celestials so much that they thought the princess was likely to prefer him. The jealous gods then cunningly worked on the prince and made him promise to run an errand for them. They asked him to go as a messenger to Damayanti and plead their cause.

To save his honour, Nala proceeded on his awkward mission and pleaded with the princess on behalf of the Devatas. Though he was in disguise, princess Damayanti could recognise him. She put him on oath and asked him to disclose his identity, which the prince did after much reluctance. He was even forced to tell her the strange circumstances that had made him perform the duty of a messenger for the gods. The princess pleasantly chided her lover for getting himself involved in such a situation and asked him to attend the swayamvara.

Nala faithfully reported how events had unfolded to the gods. Fearing the worst, the gods decided to frustrate the plans of the princess. All of them assumed the form of Nala and sat near him in the hall. As a result, Damayanti couldn't ascertain whom to garland, and even her omniscient attendants were unable to guide her. In this predicament, the princess prayed to the gods themselves, invoking their honour, and asked them to help her distinguish Nala from them. Upon this, the helpless devatas floated mid-air and Damayanti placed her garland on Nala's neck. It is said the four Devatas themselves were so struck by the suitability of the match that they departed for their heavenly abode after blessing the couple.

The better-known swayamvara described in the Mahabharata was a less happy occasion, raising acrimony and sprouting the seeds of a future strife in the Kuru Dynasty that culminated in the Kurukshetra War. This was the swayamvara of Draupadi, the daughter of King Drupada of Panchala, who later became the wife of all the Pandava brothers. In Draupadi's case, the principle involved was not love. She could not wed anyone she liked (or loved) among the assembled guests—but only an archer with the requisite skill in wielding a divine bow. She was, more or less, the prize in a contest of martial skill, a viryashulka.

To appreciate the implications of the situation, the events leading to Draupadi's swayamwara must be studied in some detail.

Drupada, king of the Panchala kingdom, wished to give his lovely daughter Draupadi in marriage to Arjuna, the third of the five Pandavas. Arjuna was a renowned archer. The Panchala monarch had been humbled in battle by Arjuna, who, on behalf of his guru Dronacharya, had defeated Drupada in single bow-combat and brought him as a prisoner to Drona. Drupada, who hailed from a powerful and prominent Kshatriya dynasty of that era, was not going to forgive his humiliation by the Brahmin. He seethed with vengeance, and nothing less than slaying Drona would now satiate him.

Drona and Drupada had been *ashrama*-mates and thick friends at the ashrama of Drona's father, Sage Bharadwaja. As pupils, the much more affluent Drupada had promised his friend, the son of a rather impoverished Brahmin, 'Half of whatever I have, will be yours.'

Boyhood transpired into adulthood. Drupada and Drona completed their education and their adolescence took them on different courses of life. Drupada succeeded his father Prisata as the king of the Panchala kingdom. Life, however, was less kind to his Brahmin friend. Despite being an immensely learned scholar of the *Vedas* and of the science of weaponry, Drona remained impoverished, his condition becoming more acute after his marriage to Kripi, the twin sister of Kripacharya, who served as the preceptor with the Kuru Dynasty in faraway Hastinapura and after the birth of his son, Ashwatthama. He remembered his childhood friend, Drupada and, in the hope of improving his financial condition, travelled to the latter's capital, Kampilya. Drona reminded him of his childhood promise, but Drupada rather bluntly told Drona that their respective stations in life had changed. Moreover, something spoken in childhood could not carry the weight of a promise made by mature adults, and it was naïve of Drona to expect Drupada to share 'half of what he had' with his boyhood companion.

Drupada was willing to help Drona in overcoming his material destitution, but this would by no means be a relationship of equals. This was, of course, a worldly truth, but Drona, perceiving this to be a slight, strode out of Kampilya, vowing to teach his friend a lesson. He sought and obtained employment at Hastinapura with the Kurus, becoming the famed guru of the Kuru princes, teaching them the art and science of weaponry. His greatest disciple was the legendary Arjuna, who humbled Drupada. Drona let the defeated Drupada go, but not before exacting revenge for his perceived humiliation at Drupada's court. The Brahmin took away half of Drupada's kingdom. Drupada became the ruler of half of Panchala with Kampilya as his capital, while the other half that had Ahicchatra as capital, fell into Drona's possession.

Though forced to make peace with his once boyhood friend, Drupada seethed with vengeance and awaited the day it would be a reality. He also performed a *yajna* to beget a mighty son who would slay Drona, and a daughter who would bring about the end of the Kuru Dynasty. The yajna deities blessed him with Dhrishtadyumna and Draupadi.

Drupada's daughter, though dark in complexion, outshone other women of her age in beauty. Her father made up his mind to give her in marriage to Arjuna, who, though instrumental in satiating Drona's pique, had left an indelible imprint on Drupada as an archer and bow-warrior par excellence.

By the time princess Draupadi became of marriageable age, the struggles of the Pandavas for sheer survival had entered a serious phase. Their evil cousin Duryodhana, a sworn enemy, along with his friend Karna, conspired to burn down the palace of wax (which Duryodhana himself had got built) in which the Pandavas were residing, and were reported as burnt alive.

Drupada came to hear of this tragedy and was distressed for having lost Arjuna, whom he had intended to make his son-in-law. He, however, decided to get Draupadi married to a marksman as skilled as Arjuna. With this end in view, he arranged for her swayamvara. An arena was constructed for receiving the guests and in the centre, a high pole with a revolving wheel on top was fixed. To win Draupadi's hand, the candidates had to shoot five arrows in quick succession through the ring to hit the eye of the image of a fish fixed atop the pole, but only by looking at its reflection in a pond of still water kept below. Moreover, the candidates had to be of 'noble birth, beauty and strength to qualify to compete for the princess's hand.'

All in the gathering of mighty and proud Kshatriya dynasties failed this near-impossible test; some of them failed to even lift the bow. In fact, the only bowman who won the princess's hand was an uninvited vagabond Brahmin.

Even in a viryashulka swayamvara like that of Draupadi's, the bride could refuse to wed a person of low birth, lacking in beauty and strength of person. Karna's deadly hatred for Draupadi was born in the Kampilya swayamvara hall. He harboured lifelong jealousy and rancour towards Arjuna because of the latter's superiority in archery. He considered himself a better archer than Arjuna—a dubious claim at best, considering his track record later against Arjuna, both in the Kurukshetra War and on other occasions—and had come as a suitor with his friend, Duryodhana. Karna was Kunti's son (Kunti was also mother of the Pandavas) by Surya, the sun-deity. But, his divine origin was a secret and he was publicly known as the son of a charioteer who had brought him up, after Kunti was forced to send him away. Becoming a bow-wielding warrior of some repute, he was befriended by Duryodhana who saw in him a potential counter to Arjuna, whose prowess in archery, Duryodhana feared.

Duryodhana ceremonially made Karna the king of Anga.

When all the assembled Kshatriya kings and contestants failed to hit the target, Karna strode into the arena and, taking the bow with ease, tested the string with admirable grace. The assembly was sure he would win the princess. But, Draupadi interrupted him announcing, 'Halt! I will not wed the son of a charioteer.'

Thus, openly humiliated, Karna threw down the bow and returned to his seat and thus remained the most relentless enemy of Draupadi and her five husbands, whom he hated anyway. Years later, when she was dragged by Duryodhana's lecherous brother, Dusshasana into the Kaurava hall in Hastinapura, Karna was quick to seize this opportunity to vent his hatred for her and display his vile nature. He declared that Draupadi, being the common wife of five men, was not to be treated with the courtesy due to her gender. Rather, she was to be treated as a shameless and fallen woman living beyond the pale of ordinary morality. In other words, he described her as a harlot.

After all, the Kshatriyas had failed to shoot into the revolving ring, and the prize for the archery contest was well-nigh being declared unclaimed, when a young Brahmin rose from the crowd of spectators and entered the arena. This was the third of the Pandava princes, Arjuna, who had come to Kampilya with his brothers in the guise of Brahmins and was seated in the hall. The brothers had not perished in the flames as reported, but had escaped with their mother into the forest. After overcoming many hardships, they had settled down in an obscure village in the guise of Brahmins. It was here that they heard of Draupadi's swayamvara. When Arjuna found that none of the Kshatriyas could claim the princess, his royal blood rose in his veins. He stood up, strode forward, and sought permission from Drupada's son and crown prince, Dhrishtadyumna. After being solemnly assured that there was no objection to a Brahmin participating in such a contest, he reached the platform where the bow was kept. Picking up the mighty bow with ease and stringing it, to the dismay of the failed competitors, he shot five arrows in quick succession, piercing the eye of the fish's image. Arjuna's identity was not revealed, but a delighted Draupadi accepted this young, handsome, and powerful-looking Brahmin as her husband.

Very few Kshatriya swayamvaras are simple, trouble-free and straightforward. Draupadi's was certainly not one of those. The Kshatriya community was infuriated that an unknown Brahmin vagabond had emerged out of nowhere and achieved a feat that the much-fancied figures from royal dynasties hadn't. Karna, seeing this as both a personal humiliation as well as a challenge, had appealed to the other princes and kings to take up arms and offered to lead them; Duryodhana had supported him. The fact that the groom was a Brahmin was also an incentive to the Kshatriyas to fight and abduct Draupadi if possible, so they sided with Karna and rushed to confront Arjuna. But Karna, despite his self-perceived dexterity with the bow, had to soon retire from his combat against Arjuna, who quite easily was able to rout out the other combatants. The giant Bhima did not even need a weapon to put out the other hostile invitees. The Pandavas had little trouble in chasing their foes out of Kampilya city.

Another unusual swayamvara was the wedding of Savitri mentioned in the *Vana Parva* (shloka 295) of the Mahabharata. Savitri, the daughter of King Ashwapati, was so full of splendour that no one dared to ask for her hand. Hence, she remained unmarried for a fair length of time after adolescence. Her father did not, however, arrange a swayamvara in the conventional manner, but sent her with a royal escort to visit the neighbouring kingdoms and select a husband for herself. The princess wandered into many lands but found no one to her liking. At last, she came to a forest and, in an ashrama of hermits, found the young Satyavan and fell in love with him. Satyavan was a royal prince, the son of king Dyumatsena of Madra. His father had been overthrown by an unscrupulous underling and forced to spend his days in exile in the forest. He lived with his old parents in the forest.

Savitri returned to her father and told him of her desire to wed Satyavan. She was firm on her intent to marry Satyavan, despite the celestial sage Narada predicting that the virtuous prince would not live long after his marriage. Savitri dwelt in the forest, dutifully serving her husband and in-laws, until Yama, the Deity of Death, arrived on the ordained day to take away her husband's life. The never-say-die Savitri not only refused to part with her husband, but also overcame Yama in debate, forcing him to restore her husband's life, and her in-laws' kingdom and well-being. For this, she is renowned as *Sati Savitri*.

This romantic episode stands alone in Hindu sacred literature. This instance of a respectable maiden of royal blood leaving her father's house in search of a husband is unique in Hindu history. It has not occurred elsewhere in any historical record of Vedic, post-Vedic, classical or medieval ages.

The conventional swayamvara is a historical institution since the Kshatriya dynasties receded towards the end of the classical period making this institution all but disappear. However, in the medieval period, the swayamvara was revived by the Rajputs, the lineal descendants of the Kshatriyas of the epic age. The last recorded swayamvara is of the princess Samyogita, daughter of Jaichand of Kannauj. Samyogita secretly loved Prithviraj Chauhan, emperor of Delhi, but being an enemy of Jaichand, he was not invited to the swayamvara. The Chauhan king, who also loved Samyogita, made a surprise raid on Kannauj, swept into the swayamvara hall and carried away his bride, resulting in a vain chase and fighting.

Sadly, Prithviraj's clash with Jaichand not only weakened intra-Hindu relations, but also left northern India seriously weakened during the second Islamic invasion by Muhammed of Ghori, which proved fatal.

That brings us to the topic of marriage by capture. The abduction of a maiden, especially from the swayamvara hall in the manner described here, was considered in epic times as highly becoming of a bold Kshatriya and was known as *haran* or kidnapping. A similar incident occurred in the Mahabharata age, throwing light on the institution of marriage by capture among the Arya communities, mainly Kshatriyas. The incident was all the more worthy of attention and scrutiny since the brides were abducted by the revered Kuru grandfather, Bhisma himself, one of the more morally scrupulous characters of the Dwapara Yuga.

The king of Kashi (Varanasi) had three daughters—Amba, Ambika and Ambalika, who were to be betrothed in a swayamvara on the same day. Bhisma's half-brother, Vichitravirya, was the then regent on the Kuru throne. Bhisma had given up his royal inheritance to fulfil his father Shantanu's desire of marrying Satyavati, a beautiful fisherfolk girl, whose father had laid down the condition that his daughter's progeny alone would inherit the Kuru throne. Satyavati bore Shantanu two sons, Chitrangada and Vichitravirya. The older prince perished in a mortal duel with an enemy king, while the younger was sexually impotent and hence no royal family was consenting to give its girl to this Kuru prince. Satyavati saddled Bhisma, as her son's guardian, with the responsibility of finding wives for him. Hearing of the beauty and accomplishments of the daughters of the king of Kashi, Bhisma decided to abduct them for his half-brother.

Accordingly, he visited Kashi at the time of the swayamvara. The assembled Kshatriyas viewed him with scorn as years ago, he had vowed to remain a celibate in deference to his father's amorous desire. Nonetheless, Bhisma made light of the spitefulness, declared the abduction of the three princesses, and made them mount his swift-moving war chariot. Meanwhile, Shalva, the king of Saubha, had been secretly betrothed to Amba as they both loved each other. For Amba, this swayamvara was a mere formality, as she had already decided who she would garland and wed. Fate, however, intervened in the form of the son of Ganga.

Such a haran was a direct challenge to the manhood of any Kshatriya. Other kings and princes, though, were wary of confronting Bhisma, whose prowess as a warrior had spread to all corners of Jambudwipa (Asia) and, therefore, only put up a show of combat. But, the humiliated Shalva gave hot chase to the captor and engaged him in action, only to be eventually routed by Bhisma, who spared his life.

On the three princesses being taken to Hastinapura, the Kuru capital, Amba told Bhisma that she would not wed Vichitravirya as she dearly loved Shalva. The other princesses married the incumbent Kaurava king as they had no other choice.

The abduction of Amba was to have unforeseen and long-term consequences for not only Bhisma but for the Kuru dynasty and empire. Although Bhisma had acted within the ambit of Kshatriya law in abducting Amba, he could not force a marriage on her against her will. He, therefore, allowed her to return to Shalva. But, when Amba returned to her lover, she was shocked to find him in no mood to accept her.

He bluntly told her that he would have nothing to do with a woman captured by another man and taken to his palace. Moreover, the humiliation Bhisma had heaped on him—of vanquishing him, but not slaying and sparing his life instead—was unbearable. For a Kshatriya warrior in that age, a battle had to have only two outcomes—*vijay* (victory) or *virgati* (a glorious death on the battlefield). Bhisma had deprived him of either, and a defeated Shalva wasn't going to touch someone's leftovers, particularly that of an enemy. Neither Amba's protestations of innocence nor her pleas helped—instead, she was turned out of the kingdom of Saubha. Thus abandoned, Amba could not return to her parents for shame, and left for the forests where she sought counsel with the holy sages and wished to know from them who was responsible for her miserable plight. After much deliberation and argument, the sages, in conjunction with the mighty Brahmin sage-warrior Parashurama, concluded that Bhisma alone was to blame for this sordid turn of events, since he had no business abducting a maiden from her father's house without first ascertaining her intentions.

Amba avenged her wrong and brought about the destruction of Bhisma, but that is another chapter to be discussed later. The moral of the tale of Amba's abduction is that though such an act was permissible for Kshatriyas, the lady's willingness to marry the abductor, or his ward, had to be previously obtained to give it full moral authority. This is amply proved by other similar episodes in the epic. Most of the abductions mentioned in the Mahabharata were contrived through the connivance of the fair victim, the necessity for haran arising out of the stubbornness of parents or guardians who wished to give the maiden in marriage to a person of their choice against her wishes. The abduction of Rukmini by Krishna is of interest in this regard. Rukmini was betrothed by her older brother prince Rukmi to Shishupala, the ruler of the Chedi kingdom. Both hated Krishna, and Shishupala was Krishna's mortal enemy, although Rukmini loved Krishna.

Krishna, with her full collaboration, took her away from her parents' palace in Vidarbha and married her.

Another interesting marriage after abduction mentioned in the Mahabharata is that of the beautiful Subhadra, sister of Balarama and Krishna, by the third of the Pandava brothers, Arjuna. Balarama being the elder brother was Subhadra's guardian and he was an ardent admirer of the Kaurava prince, Duryodhana, whereas Krishna, the younger brother, was a staunch friend of the Pandavas, Kaurava's cousins, and of Arjuna in particular. Balarama did not much fancy Arjuna as a possible brother-in-law, but he had a high opinion of Duryodhana, a lifelong adversary of the Pandavas.

Arjuna was highly enamoured of Subhadra, and Krishna, too, wanted his sister to marry the Pandava prince. But, it was difficult to conventionally arrange a match between the two because of Balarama's objection to Arjuna, and his excessive fondness for Duryodhana. To overcome this predicament, Krishna advised his friend, cousin and pupil to take recourse to the bold law of the Kshatriyas. Arjuna was happy to demonstrate his Kshatriyahood and while Subhadra visited the temple in the morning with her companions, he made away with her in his chariot. Balarama was furious and was bent upon chasing the couple, but Krishna tactfully soothed him by reciting quotations from holy texts. Krishna told his brother that the act was already done and, therefore, there was no sense in fuming and fretting, and the best thing they could do was to reconcile themselves to an accomplished fact—a view grudgingly accepted by the fierce Balarama.

Marriage by either mutual agreement, or following a promise to adhere to laid down precondition(s) such as the tale of Pururavas in the Vedas, is mentioned in the Mahabharata. Shantanu, Bhisma's father, was the Kuru ruler in Hastinapura.

Once, while hunting in the forest, he met a maiden of celestial beauty bathing in a stream. The king fell madly in love with the nymph and wished to marry her. The fairy-like lady agreed to wed him provided he would raise no objection to whatever she did; if he objected, she would leave him. King Shantanu was so besotted that he accepted the condition and married her.

Ganga, the celestial beauty, lived as Shantanu's queen and bore him seven sons. But, every time a son was born, the mother took the infant to the Ganges and drowned it. Shocked, Shantanu was beside himself with grief, but said nothing because of his promise. When the eighth son was born and Ganga took him in her hands and proceeded towards the holy river, the father, unable to bear it any further, stopped her. Ganga left him and returned to her celestial abode along with her eighth child, promising to return him to his father in due course of time. Shantanu's eighth son, Devavrata, born of Ganga, was none other than the renowned warrior, Bhisma, the grandfather of the Kauravas and the Pandavas.

The conduct and origin of most of the heroes of the Mahabharata age did not exactly conform to the Brahminical morality contained in the epic.

Take the case of Draupadi, who was married to all the five Pandava brothers. Arjuna won her hand in a tough, near-impossible contest of archery. He and his four brothers then returned to their mother in the village of Ekachakranagari in the guise of Brahmins. The brothers told their mother that Arjuna had won something precious that day. On hearing this, Kunti, the mother of the Pandavas, not knowing the exact nature of the precious possession, told her sons to share it among all the five. Thus was Draupadi shared by all the five brothers, in order to uphold their mother's word.

This is the justification given in the epic for Draupadi's polyandrous marriage to the Pandavas. However, one has to traverse beyond the superficiality of the narration and understand the entire gamut of circumstances that led Kunti to plead with her sons to arrive at such an arrangement.

The five Pandavas—Yudhisthira, Bhima, Arjuna, Nakula and Sahadeva were sons of Pandu, monarch of the Kuru Dynasty because his older brother, Dhritarastra, being blind by birth, could not become king. Pandu's children through his wives Kunti and Madri were born in the Himalayan forests where he lived with his wives. Dhritarastra's sons, including the eldest Duryodhana, were Hastinapura-born, but Yudhisthira was still the eldest among all by birth. Naturally, only the king's son could succeed him to the throne, and Yudhisthira was the eldest. Duryodhana though, felt that fate had cheated his father and when Dhritarastra got to sit on the throne following Pandu's absence and, later, untimely death, he became the de facto king of the Kurus.

According to Duryodhana, the Kuru throne was his natural inheritance, and his cousins, the Pandavas were unwelcome interlopers. The five Pandavas were virtuous, upright, and staunch adherents of dharma and loved by all, while Duryodhana and his brothers were the exact opposite. Moreover, the Pandavas excelled in both Kshatriya vocation of arms and in their Brahmanical duty of learning. Jealousy and discord arose from the very outset between both sets of cousins. Duryodhana hated and feared his cousins, particularly Arjuna, whose ability and prowess in archery was unmatchable, and the gigantic Bhima, whose superhuman physical might was a cause of mortal fear to the sons of Dhritarastra. Even in their childhood, he had attempted to poison Bhima twice and later tried to burn the Pandavas along with their mother Kunti in a palace constructed of wax and other combustible material.

Kunti's life, having single-handedly brought up her sons following the tragic demise of her husband Pandu, was a saga of struggle. She was more than aware of her situation at Hastinapura under the shadow of Dhritarastra and his wife, Queen Gandhari, the mother of the Kaurava princes. She was acutely aware of the ill-will of Gandhari's sons towards her children, and of the perils they would face in life. Kunti had instilled the values of dharma, truth, valour and piety in her children and knew that their strong bond with each other would protect them from external harm. This drove her to impress upon her sons the importance of equally sharing any success they would attain in the future.

Sharing material accomplishments was justified, but Arjuna winning the bow-contest, and thereby Draupadi's hand, presented Kunti with a dilemma with no apparent solution. It was Arjuna who had won Draupadi in the test of skill and, therefore, he ought to have wed her. The *shastras* however, forbid the marriage of a younger brother so long as a faultless older brother remains unwed. In Arjuna's case, Yudhisthira and Bhima were older to him. Bhima had already taken on a wife during the Pandavas' brief sojourn in the forest after their escape from the palace of wax. This sojourn was apart from the twelve-year exile of the Pandavas after the fraudulent game of dice. Bhima's wife was the *rakshasi* Hidimba, who bore him a son, Ghatotkacha.

However, Yudhisthira was still unwed. A younger brother marrying while the elder remained unmarried was a sin, a *parivedana* in the *shastras*, and the sinner was called a *parivetta*, something Arjuna was not willing to become. Yudhisthira wouldn't stand in his brother's way; all the brothers rejoiced in Arjuna's achievement, but could not suppress or deny their own infatuation for Draupadi, who was blessed with a goddess-like beauty. The situation carried all the potential to sow discord among the five, and Kunti was well aware of this. She turned to her eldest son, Yudhisthira for a way out of this vexatious predicament.

Yudhisthira and Krishna, thus consulted learned Brahmins, including Sage Vyasa. They quoted many precedents of polyandry that seemed to have the sanction of the scriptures. Jatila, of Gautama's race, had seven learned Brahmins for her husbands; Varkshi had wed ten brothers. This quietened Yudhisthira's conscience and he agreed to Draupadi's polyandrous marriage with all the brothers.

While there is the opinion and counsel of learned sages on matters of marriage and morality, one often reads in the Mahabharata that several individuals in that age weren't too concerned about adhering to sex-related taboos that later bound Hindu morality. The institution of *niyoga* (progeny through surrogacy; levirate) was prevalent. When a man or woman was incapable of raising progeny, due to impotence or any other cause, both were permitted to have relations with another chosen partner to beget children. Such surrogacy had to be approved by the other partner. A near kin was preferred for this; if not available, a worthy partner would be recommended to further one's lineage.

Though illegitimacy is a heinous sin today, it wasn't so in the times of our great epics. Though children born illegitimately were usually exposed, the woman was not abandoned as was done in later, medieval times. She even found extremely desirable husbands. Almost all the heroes of the Mahabharata were born outside the confines of conventional morality.

We have already noticed the polyandrous marriage of the Pandavas to the Panchala princess, Draupadi. The Pandavas were born outside the bounds of conventional morality as their father, King Pandu, could not biologically beget any children because of a rishi's curse. Kunti, the venerable mother of the Pandavas had, before her marriage to Pandu, begotten a son through the celestial Surya, the Sun deity. While still a maiden, she had to attend on Sage Durvasa, a quick-tempered ascetic. Pleased by her devotion and dedication to serving his ritual needs, Durvasa granted her a boon whereby she could summon any Devata (celestial being) by chanting the mantra dedicated to him.

After Durvasa's departure, Kunti, full of adolescent curiosity, wished to know whether the mantra could be really effective and invoked Surya, the Sun God, to appear before her. The mantra given by Durvasa worked and the Sun God asked her why she had called him. Kunti confessed that she was curious and had nothing particular to ask of him. However, Surya told her that the divine mantra she had used was so powerful that the celestial god was bound to deliver progeny through her. Moreover, the Sun deity himself was enamoured of her beauty and earnestly solicited her embrace. The virtuous maiden pointed out the immoral nature of his demand, but Surya, bursting with passion, maintained the divine right of gods, who do not conform to the laws of humans.

Kunti had to yield to his embrace, and of this union, was born Karna. She was unwed and had to conceal her child by handing him over to a *suta* couple, (a particular caste which entered multiple vocations in administration, soldiery, charioteering, and bookkeeping among others—some sutas even became kings and rulers) Adhiratha and Radha, who brought him up as their son. Karna went on to become a skilled bowman and obtained a kingdom owing to his close friendship with Duryodhana. He was indebted to Duryodhana for elevating him to the ranks of kings and nobles, and thus remained a staunch friend and ally of his benefactor, who happened to be the sworn enemy of his five half-brothers, the Pandavas.

The birth of Karna did not, however, disqualify Kunti from marriage. She was honourably married to King Pandu, even though she could not have children as he had been cursed by a sage. While hunting, Pandu had accidentally shot at a sage who had been making love. The dying sage cursed Pandu that he too would die like him, if he ever yielded to amorousness. Fearing this calamity, Pandu abjured the company of his two wives and lived as a celibate. But he wished to have sons and advised his wife Kunti to take recourse to the sanction of niyoga. Kunti suggested an alternative and revealed her secret power to call the gods whenever she wished. Pandu agreed and Kunti obtained three sons, Yudhisthira from Yama, the deity of death and dharma, Bhima from Vayu the wind god, and Arjuna from Indra, the lord of the celestials. Pandu desired more progeny, but the wise Kunti, quoting the *shastras*, forbade him. Instead, she generously taught the secret of the divine mantras bestowed on her to Madri, Pandu's second wife. This clever lady prayed to the twin Ashwini Kumaras to favour her, and was blessed with the twins, Nakula and Sahadeva.

Pandu himself and his half-brothers, Dhritarastra and Vidura, their third sibling, were born through levirate. Vichitravirya, the second son of Satyavati, the second wife of Bhisma's father Shantanu (and thus Bhisma's stepmother) was the husband of Ambika and Ambalika (two of the three Kashi princesses whom Bhisma had abducted from the holy city for his half-brother). After he died childless, his mother Satyavati was obstinate that the illustrious Chandra lineage should not end with his untimely death (her first son, Chitrangada, had met his death in a duel with another king). She insisted that Bhisma renounce his vow of celibacy and marry her two widowed but young daughters-in-law to further the Kuru lineage. But, the son of Ganga, steadfast in his oath, refused. Satyavati, therefore, requisitioned the services of her first-born son, Vyasa (begotten following her romantic interlude with Parashara, an ascetic of the illustrious solar, Suryavansha lineage), who had become a sage and lived in uninhabited forests.

The great sage agreed to fulfil his mother's wish and arrived in Hastinapura and got introduced to the inner chambers of his deceased half-brother Vichitravirya. Vyasa's physical appearance was, however, far removed from his spiritual illuminance. He was abnormally tall and of disproportionate muscular build, of dark complexion with red hair bound in matted locks and a flowing red beard; his countenance was startlingly unnerving. The elder princess Ambika closed her eyes in shock when the sage embraced her; as a result, her son Dhritarastra, born of this union, was blind from birth. Ambalika, the younger daughter-in-law, was somewhat bolder but even she turned pale when the holy man approached her. Her son, Pandu, had no congenital defect, but had a pale complexion. Satyavati, highly displeased when she learnt of her elder daughter-in-law's experience, forced her to enter niyoga with Vyasa one more time. Not having the courage to disobey her irascible mother-in-law, but not desirous at all of undergoing the experience a second time, Ambika made her maid take her place and meet Vyasa. The sage was of course, not deceived. He blessed the attendant maid with a son who, he predicted, would go on to become the upholder of dharma in a dynasty whose slow but steady descent into adharma was just beginning. This son was known as Vidura.

The story of the birth of Bharata, from whom India is said to take her name Bharata, is noteworthy. Bharata was the son of Dusyanta, born of Shakuntala—the offspring of a liaison between the heavenly nymph Menaka and Sage Vishwamitra. Dusyanta married Shakuntala in her foster father's Kanva hermitage according to the Gandharva rite which, strictly speaking, is no rite at all. Lovers in a Gandharva *vivah* (marriage) agree to be united in matrimony by mutual consent and exercise their conjugal rights straightaway. There need not be any priest to conduct and preside over the ceremony, as there isn't any ceremony in the first place. There are no witnesses to bless the union, and no invoking the gods to ratify the marriage.

The Middle Ages saw the Gandharva rite fall into disrepute, though in the epic era, the Gandharva interpretation of morality in matrimonial matters was highly acceptable to kings and sages. Let us understand the disadvantages of the Gandharva way of marriage in a patriarchal community, especially for the woman.

Marriage brings definite economic and social responsibilities for the male in a patriarchate. But, a youthful lover may forget his obligations once the thirst of love is quenched. In Shakuntala's case, something similar happened—the loyal, impregnated woman was first disowned and disgraced by her husband before being, through divine intervention, accepted by Dusyanta as his wife.

Ambivalence about conventional morality is conspicuous enough in the Mahabharata. This will seem less surprising when we delve further into the origin of its author, Krishna Dwaipayana Vyasa, already mentioned as the first-born son of Satyavati.

Satyavati was the daughter of Dasharaj, the chieftain of a fisherfolk community, and was then known as Matsyagandha (of fish odour) because she smelt of fish. In spite of the obnoxious smell, she was good-looking. One day, an anchorite sage Parashara happened to meet the youthful beauty on his journey through the forest where Matsyagandha was then living. The holy man was immediately overcome with an intense desire to enter into an amorous relationship of matrimony with her. The maiden too, was in her *ritu* or fertile period and on realising this auspicious time, the sage declared his love. Matsyagandha put forward some feeble objections, including that of her smell, which the holy man instantly converted into a pleasant fragrance through his yogic powers. The maiden, now convinced of his greatness and desiring a son like him, surrendered to him. But, she was still an unwed maiden, and, as such, under the protection and wardship of her parents. Parashara explained to her that it was a woman's right to choose her life partner, and a girl who had reached puberty was mature and free enough to choose him. More than Parashara's logic, it was the power of his character that drew Satyavati to him.

After their union reached its culmination, Parashara went his way, but Satyavati chose to live with the consequences of her wilful act. Her father was crafty as well as ambitious. A reclusive, forest-dwelling hermit wouldn't suffice for his daughter—he was after a bigger catch. Satyavati conceived in due course, but her father kept her confined to an island till she gave birth to her son, Vyasa. Because of his birth and life on an island, he was known as Dwaipayana (of an island) and also as Krishna because of his dark complexion. He became a great ascetic and a learned sage, authoring the Mahabharata and editing the four Vedas.

The birth of Vyasa did not prevent Satyavati from getting married to the great Kuru king, Shantanu. The King had previously fallen in love with Goddess Ganga and married her after agreeing to her conditions. His marriage with Satyavati was the outcome of similar circumstances. While engaged in the pursuit of game, he had happened to see the maiden and intoxicated by her heavenly fragrance and beauty, had approached her with a proposal of marriage. Satyavati, having learnt a worldly lesson from her liaison with Parashara, requested the royal suitor to ask her father for her hand in marriage. Shantanu had to seek out her father Dasharaj for permission to wed his daughter. The fisherman, already saddled with an unwanted grandson, was not going to take chances and demanded the king to promise that Satyavati's son would inherit his kingdom. Shantanu already had a son, the mighty prince Devavrata, by Ganga, whom he loved dearly. Disinheriting him was out of the question, so he returned to Hastinapura.

Torn between his passion for the fisherman's daughter and his duty towards his son, Shantanu could neither eat nor drink. Devavrata saw his father's plight and ascertained the cause of his misery. He then secretly proceeded to the forest abode of the fisherman and promised him that he would renounce the crown if Satyavati were given in marriage to his father. The fisherman, true to the trade of his community, drove an even harder bargain. While he had little doubt that the Kaurava prince would live up to his promise, he knew that future progeny was not bound to do so. What would be the fate of Satyavati's sons and their lineage, if Devavrata's sons refused to abide by their father's promise? Wouldn't there be a fratricidal war among the Kurus if such a situation came about?

Bent upon fulfilling his father's wish, Devavrata now resolved to remove all impediments in his father's way. In the presence of his Kuru elders, he swore an oath to remain a lifelong celibate, thus eliminating every possibility of his future progeny clashing with Satyavati's offspring.

The earth shook and the heavens gasped to the accompaniment of terrifying thunder and lightning when Devavrata uttered his oath, much to the consternation of his Kuru elders. For this terrible oath, prince Devavrata came to be known as Bhisma, one who makes an unthinkably tough vow and lives up to it. Shaken by Bhisma's oath, the fisherman handed over his daughter to the Kuru prince and the latter took her to his delighted father.

The marriage of a girl by payment to the bride or her family was also a practice in epic times. The people of Madra, a prominent kingdom then in West Asia, close to India (now North-West India), practised this code of matrimonial morality. Bhisma procured Madri from her brother Shalya, the ruler of the Madra kingdom, as a bride for his nephew King Pandu. The price for obtaining this bride was 'Wrought and unwrought gold, and many kinds of jewels in thousands; elephants, horses and chariots, apparel and ornaments, precious stones, pearls and coral that shone.' On receiving this treasure, Shalya gave Bhisma his sister.

The Mahabharata, like all ancient Hindu works, deals mainly with the doings of kings and sages, and it is arguably difficult to find out from the epic the moral standards of the common people. Each community presumably practised its own traditional morality conforming with the Hindu view that traditional practices should always be treated with respect. Brahmins, undoubtedly followed the Vedic marriage ritual, though sages with unique powers and learning practised exceptional morality.

Sati was uncommon in these times. However, there are instances where wives perished on the funeral pyres of their husbands. Madri, in whose arms her husband Pandu died, immolated herself on the funeral pyre of her husband. She did not do this as a matter of course, but as a penance for inadvertently bringing about the death of her husband.

There was a firm belief among ancient Hindus that interruption of the sex act was cruel. In Pandu's case, death before completing the sexual act was thought to have left his unsatisfied soul midway to the hereafter, yearning for the company of his spouse. It might have been due to this belief, in addition to her own sense of guilt, that Madri decided to accompany her husband to the other world.

Kunti, Pandu's elder wife, did not perish with her husband and Madri. Many other noble ladies of the Mahabharata age also outlived their husbands, and did not think it obligatory to accompany the souls of their husbands by ending their lives.

The central point of morality in these epic times, as in the Vedic age, was the need for begetting sons, and marriage was considered a means for achieving this end. When this end could not be gained, deviation from what was strictly orthodox was permitted.

Indiscriminate asceticism is also condemned in the epics. An illuminating tale of the famous ascetic Jaratkaru says that even in childhood, this Brahmin had a strong other-wordly leaning and so he leaned towards asceticism. He once entered a huge cave, deep as a well in a forest. From the side of the cave, a tree branch stuck out from where several men were hanging head downwards from a feeble thread, while a mouse gnawed at the thread. Jaratkaru enquired about the nature of the sin which had condemned these men to such a terrible punishment. The hapless creatures told Jaratkaru that they were his own ancestors about to be consigned to hell, not because of their sin, but because Jaratkaru, their only surviving progeny, had taken to asceticism, leaving none to perform the periodical rites of the dead, and thus prevent their fall into hell. Jaratkaru immediately stopped his wanderings and started looking for a wife.

The principle that a married woman was her husband's property can be found in the Mahabharata period as well. But whatever their status, the women of the epic exercised considerable influence in social, domestic and even political affairs. Bhisma always consulted Satyavati on important affairs. Gandhari, wife of Dhritarastra, was a forceful woman who alone could generate respect even in her wayward and rough son, Duryodhana who always dominated his blind father.

Similarly, Kunti, the Pandavas' mother, had a say in all their political deliberations. The most interesting, assertive and forceful character that arrests the reader's attention in the Mahabharata is its central woman character, Draupadi. She is truly lifelike and represents the diverse characteristics of a woman—her strength, weakness, egoism, loyalty, pride and vanity.

Draupadi, the ideal wife

Though, technically the common wife of the Pandava princes, especially of the eldest, Draupadi always commanded them and the way she controlled her turbulent warrior husbands attracted admiration and curiosity of her friend Satyabhama, Krishna's wife, who wished to know the secret of her power.

Satyabhama asks:

> Draupadi, by what behaviour is it, that you are able to rule the sons of Pandu—those heroes endued with strength and beauty and like unto the *Lokapalas* themselves? Beautiful lady, how is it that they are so obedient to you and are never angry with you? Without doubt, the sons of Pandu are ever submissive to you and watchful to do your bidding! Tell me, dear, the reason for this. Is it the practice of vows, or asceticism, incantation or drug at the time of the bath (in season), the efficacy of science, the influence of youthful appearance, recitation of particular mantras, or *Homa* (sacred herb), or *collyrium* and other medicaments? Tell me now of that blessed and auspicious thing by which, O Krishna (Draupadi), Krishna may ever be obedient to me.

Draupadi's detailed reply to Satyabhama's questions can serve as a guide for today's housewives. Telling Satyabhama that only foolish women would try to win their husbands' love and esteem through drugs, charms and witchcraft, Draupadi adds, 'You ask me, Satyabhama, of the practices of women that are wicked. How can I answer you, dear, about the cause that is pursued by wicked females? It does not become you, Satya, to pursue these questions, or doubt me, after this, for you are endued with intelligence and are the favourite wife of Krishna. When the husband learns that his wife is addicted to incantations and drugs, from that hour he begins to dread her like a serpent ensconced in his sleeping chamber. And can a man that is troubled with fear have peace? And how can one who has no peace have happiness? A husband can never be made obedient by his wife resorting to incantations. We hear of painful diseases being transmitted by enemies. Indeed, they that desire to slay others, send poison in the shape of customary gifts, so that the man that takes the powders so sent, by tongue or skin, is, without doubt, speedily deprived of life. Women have sometimes caused dropsy and leprosy, decrepitude, impotence, idiocy, blindness and deafness in men. These wicked women, ever treading in the path of sin, do sometimes (by these means) injure their husbands. But the wife should never do the least injury to her lord.

'Now listen to the behaviour I adopt towards the high-souled sons of Pandu. Keeping aside vanity, and controlling desire and wrath, I always serve with devotion, the sons of Pandu with their (other) wives. Restraining jealousy, with deep devotion of heart, without a sense of degradation at the services I perform, I wait upon my husbands. Ever fearing to utter what is evil or false, or to look or sit or walk with impropriety, or cast glances indicative of the feelings of the heart, do I serve the sons of Pritha—those mighty warriors blazing like the sun or fire, and handsome as the moon, those endued with fierce energy and prowess, and capable of slaying their foes by a glance of the eye. Celestial, or man, or Gandharva, young or decked with ornaments, wealthy or comely of person, none else does my heart like. I never bathe or eat or sleep till my husbands have bathed or eaten or slept—till, in fact, our attendants have bathed, eaten, or slept. Whether returning from the field, the forest, or the town, hastily rising up, I always greet my husband with water and a seat. I always keep the house and all household articles and the food that is to be taken well-ordered and clean. I keep the rice carefully, and serve the food at the proper time. I never indulge in angry and fretful speech, and never imitate women that are wicked. Keeping idleness at a distance, I always do what is agreeable. I never laugh except at a jest, and never stay for any length of time at the house-gate. I never stay long in places for answering calls of nature, nor in pleasure-gardens attached to the house. I always refrain from laughing loudly and indulging in high passion, and from everything that may give offence.

'Indeed, Satyabhama, I always am engaged in waiting upon my lords. A separation from my lords is never agreeable to me. When my husband leaves home for the sake of any relative, then renouncing flowers and fragrant paste of every kind, I begin to undergo penances. Whatever my husband does not drink, does not eat, does not enjoy, I ever renounce. Decked in ornaments and ever controlled by the instruction imparted to me, I always devotedly seek the good of my lord. Those duties that my mother-in-law had told me of in respect of relatives, as also the duties of alms-giving, of offering worship to the gods, of oblations to the diseased, of boiling food in pots on auspicious days for offer to ancestors and guests of reverence and service to those that deserve our regards, and all else that is known to me, I always discharge day and night, without idleness of any kind. Having with my whole heart, recourse to humility and approved rules, I serve my meek and truthful lords ever observant of virtue. I think that the eternal virtue for women is based upon a regard for the husband. The husband is the wife's god, and he is her refuge. Indeed, there is no other refuge for her. How can, then, the wife do the least injury to her lord? I never, in sleeping or eating or adorning any person, act against the wishes of my lord, and always guided by my husbands, I never speak ill of my mother-in-law.

'(Therefore) Satya, my husbands have become obedient to me in consequence of my diligence, my alacrity, and the humility with which I serve superiors. I personally wait every day with food and drink and clothes upon the revered and truthful Kunti—the mother of these heroes. Never do I show any preference for myself over her in matters of food and attire, and never do I reprove in words that princess equal unto the Earth herself in forgiveness. Formerly, eight thousand Brahmins were fed daily in the palace of Yudhisthira in plates of gold. Ten thousand *yatis* with the vital seed drawn up, had their pure food carried unto them in plates of gold. All these Brahmins that were the chanters of the Veda, I used to worship duly with food, drink, and raiment taken from stores only after a portion thereof had been dedicated to the Vishwedeva.

'And while Yudhisthira lived in Indraprastha, a hundred thousand horses and a hundred thousand elephants used to follow in his train. These were the possessions of Yudhisthira while he ruled the earth. It was I, however, Satya, who regulated their number and framed the rules to be observed in respect of them; and it was I who had to listen to all complaints about them. Indeed, I knew everything about what the maid-servants of the palace and other classes of attendants, even the cow-herds and the shepherds of the royal establishment, did or did not. It was I alone amongst the Pandavas who knew the income and expenditure of the king and what their whole wealth was. And those bulls among the Bharatas, throwing upon me the burden of looking after all those that were to be fed by them, would, pay their court to me. And this load, so heavy and incapable of being borne by persons of evil heart, I used to bear day and night, sacrificing my ease, and all the while affectionately devoted to them. And while my husbands were engaged in the pursuit of virtue, I only supervised their treasury that was inexhaustible like the ever-filled receptacle of Varuna. Day and night bearing hunger and thirst, I used to serve the Kuru princes, so that my nights and days were equal to me. I used to wake up first and go to bed, last. This, Satyabhama, has ever been my charm for making my husbands obedient to me! This great art has ever been known to me. Never have I practised the charms of wicked women, nor do I ever wish to practice them.'

More than Draupadi's domestic virtues, it is her pride and spirit of independence that holds our attention. She was in no way responsible for the bitterness between the Kauravas and the Pandavas that led to the Mahabharata War. Rather, she was caught up in the politics of the Kuru Dynasty, becoming its victim only to later metamorphose into the goddess of vengeance that eventually consumed the Kuru Dynasty, itself. She was won by Arjuna in a near-impossible archery contest fixed as the condition for her swayamvara. Most accounts of this incident of the Mahabharata recount how she stopped a much-hopeful Karna in his tracks, bluntly declaring that she wouldn't marry a *sutaputra* (son of a charioteer). Modern-day eulogists of Karna make a big song and dance about this 'insult' to their newly-crowned champion of 'empowerment of the downtrodden', but Draupadi was well within her rights to refuse to wed a suitor with whom her own life, would at best, be uncertain. However, the original Mahabharata does not mention Karna as having strung the bow before shooting at the target. Instead, it states that Karna was among the unsuccessful suitors as the mighty bow jerked and jumped out of his hands when he tried his luck at winning Draupadi. Moreover, given his actual record, vis-à-vis his incessant boasts about his prowess and his constant outpourings of scorn regarding his adversaries' capabilities, it is unlikely that Karna had been able to string the bow. Talk of Draupadi insulting him with reference to his caste is thus, most likely an interpolation that happened much later in history.

Draupadi's swayamvara was not just an open-and-shut affair. In addition to fulfilling the condition laid down for her hand—stringing the mighty bow and hitting the target, the suitor also had to come from a noble background. Dhristadyumna, Draupadi's brother, who was in charge of the swayamvara ceremony, unambiguously declared after escorting his sister to the hall, amidst the assemblage of kings:

'*Etanmahatkarma Karoti Yo Vai Kulena Rupena Balena Yukta* I

Tasyadya Bharya Bhagini Mameyam Krsna Bhavitri Na Mrisa Bravimi II'

[*Mahabharata*, *Adi Parva*, chapter 184, shloka 36. (He who accomplishes this mighty feat and is of noble birth, endowed with looks and befitting strength; of him shall my sister Krishna become the consort, and I speak not the untruth)]. The suta caste (in which Karna was raised by his foster parents, Adhiratha and Radha) was not generally considered low. But Karna was not a known Kshatriya (by his birth to Kunti). His status among the Kshatriya kings and princes of his age was solely due to his friendship with Duryodhana, who had befriended and elevated him as King of Anga, so he could have a formidable ally in his confrontation with the Pandavas. Duryodhana himself ardently desired Draupadi, but had failed in the bow contest at her swayamvara. Assuming Karna had succeeded in hitting the target, Draupadi would have had to be the wife of someone who was not even a reasonable vassal, but a mere dependent on another king's favour. Karna's outsized status depended solely on Duryodhana's continued animosity with his cousins. Minus that, his relevance to the Kauravas was dubious, at best. He was, by his own admission, beholden to Duryodhana for just about everything in life—the kingship of Anga, status, a position in Hastinapura and the opulent, privileged life of a vassal (Karna himself did nothing to acquire it). In return, he not only swore lifelong loyalty to Duryodhana, but also came to hate his rivals, the Pandavas, more than Duryodhana did himself.

It is inconceivable that Karna would have retained Draupadi for himself, given his utter servility to Duryodhana and his willingness, rather readiness, to do the latter's bidding in everything, fair or foul. Karna, who unhesitatingly played a part in Duryodhana's every evil plot to murder his cousins and usurp the Kuru throne, wouldn't think twice before handing over Draupadi to his master. Moreover, Karna's attitude to women can be rightly termed as a mini-text of misogyny. While Duryodhana always talked of Karna as his excellent friend, it is undeniable that this was never a relationship of equals. And Duryodhana would in no way have tolerated Draupadi, the most beautiful and desirable among the Kshatriya women of his generation, to be his subservient friend's wife after winning a contest which Duryodhana himself had miserably failed. What if Karna had simply handed over Draupadi to his benefactor under the pretext of winning her for Duryodhana? The Kauravas were never shy of resorting to subterfuge of this nature. One can recall the deceitful game of dice where Duryodhana, having tricked an unsuspecting Yudhisthira to play the game, suddenly declared that his maternal uncle Shakuni would play on his behalf. The disaster it bore is too well-known.

One cannot brush aside the possibility that such misapprehensions would have weighed heavily in Draupadi's mind as Radheya (Karna; son of Radha, his foster mother) got up from his seat, approached the dais where the bow was placed, and put his hand to it in an attempt to string it and hit the target. Karna was happy being a minion of Duryodhana, but why would Draupadi, a fiercely independent woman with a mind of her own, settle for being a minion's wife? She did the only thing she could have—stop Karna in his tracks. The vainglorious Karna was never one to forgive a humiliating takedown, particularly by a woman. Though he did not react on the spot, he later fought the eventual victor of the bow-contest, Arjuna, only to sustain defeat at the latter's hands. He simply could not stomach the fact that anybody could be better than him in wielding the bow! Karna also had his revenge upon Draupadi later in the hall during the game of dice, where he instigated Dusshasana, Duryodhana's younger brother, to publicly disrobe a hapless Draupadi. But, Karna had aroused the wrath of Yajnaseni (Draupadi, so named as she was born of the sacrificial yajna). She would go on to consume the Kuru dynasty itself, including Karna.

Enmity between the Kauravas and Pandavas had been ongoing long before Draupadi's arrival in the Kuru family, and it is not only meaningless but utterly false to blame her for it. Duryodhana was consumed by jealousy and hatred for his dharmic cousins, especially since his own worldview had no place for things like dharma. He could not tolerate them becoming independent rulers having built the new capital, Indraprastha (today's Delhi) from the desolate forest ruins of Khandavaprastha. He coveted the Pandava domain, and, knowing it was impossible for him to defeat them in battle, finally resorted to trickery on the instigation of his evil maternal uncle, Shakuni. A game of dice was arranged and Duryodhana had his father, the ever-doting Dhritarastra, invite an unwilling Yudhisthtira to play along.

A game of dice

Yudhisthtira had been apprehensive right from the outset—a dice contest, though a favourite of Kshatriya rulers, was known to lead to undesirable outcomes. However, kingly etiquette in those days demanded that an invitation to gambling should not be declined.

But, the reasons for Yudhisthira accepting this challenge, that was against the counsel of his brothers and Draupadi, are to be found in his excessive deference to elders borne of the Pandavas' tough and troubled childhood, and his own pacifist nature. He did not wish to say a firm 'no' to the family elders, particularly his elder uncle, Dhritarastra, although he knew of the latter's blind affection for his obdurate and evil son, Duryodhana. When the orphaned Pandavas had arrived in Hastinapura as children from the Himalayan forests with their widowed mother Kunti, they had faced an uncertain future. Their late father Pandu had been the Kuru emperor, but he was no more. His older brother Dhritarastra had become the occupant of the Kuru throne and his son Duryodhana who believed that his father was cheated of his right to kingship, was not prepared to tolerate even the existence of the Pandavas.

The Pandavas' childhood was an almost daily battle for survival in the face of unrelenting hatred, hostility and active, but secret, attempts to murder them. In Yudhisthira's mind,

Dhritarastra was still his elder who must be obeyed. And so, he agreed to the game of dice despite being aware of its potential to unleash viciousness.

In that ill-fated game in which Duryodhana appointed his uncle Shakuni as his proxy, Yudhisthira lost heavily—he gambled away his kingdom, his four brothers and, finally, himself. The five princes thus became the slaves of the Kauravas. 'You have but your common wife Draupadi left, now,' said Shakuni tauntingly, 'Why not offer her as a last stake, Yudhisthira? You may possibly win back everything you have lost.'

A ruined gambler is maddened by his losses and Yudhisthira behaved no differently. He accepted and offered Draupadi as a stake. The dice were thrown, and Yudhisthira lost. Duryodhana, waiting for precisely an opportunity to take down his virtuous cousins, now decided to humiliate Draupadi—and her husbands—in the most shameful manner. He wanted to denude her in public!

He ordered Draupadi to appear before him in the royal assembly. When the messenger conveyed Duryodhana's order to Draupadi intimating to her that she had been wagered and lost in a gambling game and was, as such, Duryodhana's slave, the fiery Panchali told him to leave. She also raised a pertinent concern—when Yudhisthira offered her as a stake, she argued, he had already gambled himself away; hence he was not his own master and had no right to offer her as a stake. The messenger returned to Duryodhana and intimated to him what Draupadi had told him. Duryodhana, however, was drunk with power in his moment of triumph and was in no mood for niceties. He now sent his brutal brother Dusshasana to the ladies' inner chamber to fetch the Pandavas' wife. Dusshasana dragged a hapless Draupadi by the hair all the way from her quarters to the Kuru royal court. Though in the grip of a lustful molester, she did not lose her nerve and, in the court where all the Kuru elders were also present, she put up a strong case for her independence on the rightful plea that Yudhisthira had no right to offer her as a stake when he himself had become a slave to Duryodhana.

Duryodhana contended that Yudhisthira, in gambling away his brothers and himself, had already gambled away what belonged to him, including his wife who was but a chattel. He lifted his dhoti to beckon Draupadi to sit on his thigh. The vainglorious, jealous Karna, no less evil than his benefactor, didn't lose this opportunity to have his revenge on Draupadi. He expressed his view that a woman who was the common wife of five men was outside the pale of ordinary codes of morality and chivalry and therefore, there was no sin in even stripping her completely. It was Karna who exhorted Dusshasana to disrobe Draupadi to satiate his own burning desire to humiliate Arjuna, whom he knew he could never defeat in a battle.

Dusshasana, now even more eager to do this bidding, strode forward to disrobe Draupadi who watched disbelievingly while a momentary paralysis seemed to have taken hold over her warlike husbands. None of them raised a finger in her defence. The Kuru elders, Bhisma, Drona and others too, did not intervene because of their selective interpretation of rules of kingly conduct. Vidura, the younger uncle of both the Dhartarastrans and the Pandavas, was the sole sane voice in the wilderness as he helplessly appealed to his older brother, the incumbent monarch Dhritarastra, to stop this naked dance of evil in the Kuru court and stave off what could be the certain destruction of the Kuru race, itself.

Draupadi, now, appealed to Krishna; the moment she called out to him in her hour of despair, a ravenous Dusshasana froze in his tracks and sat down with a thud, as though felled by a bolt of lightning. Neither could Duryodhana, Karna or their minions move a muscle. All were aware of what Krishna did to evildoers; the fates of Kansa, Sishupala and Jarasandha were only too well-known. Such was the terror of Govinda's name for any violator of dharma, even if He weren't physically present on the scene. The Pandavas and Draupadi were under His protection. Moreover, the presence of the giant Bhima was another deterrent. He swore to smash Duryodhana's thighs and rip out Dusshasana's heart and drink his blood. Thus, by Krishna's intervention, Draupadi was saved from ultimate humiliation. The howling of jackals in the distance, the momentary disappearance of the sun and other ill omens foretold what was to come for the Kurus. A benumbing fear gripped Dhritarastra and in supersession of the outcome of the game of dice, he commanded Draupadi and her husbands to be released forthwith from bondage and freed.

Draupadi's molestation by the Kauravas cast the die for the eventual destruction of the Kuru dynasty. She swore she would not tie her hair except by anointing it with Dusshasana's blood. From then onwards, her only purpose to live was to seek vengeance. Draupadi had to go into exile with her husbands and during her long wanderings in the forest, she constantly reminded them of the terrible wrongs done to her and the necessity for avenging the humiliation and injustice meted out to the Pandavas, particularly the need to put down adharma and establish a state based on the values and ideals of dharma. At the end of their exile, the kind-hearted Yudhisthira offered peace with his adversaries if they would grant the Pandavas only five villages, and Krishna proceeded to Hastinapura on a mission of peace. Even Bhima and Arjuna thought of burying the hatchet, albeit reluctantly, and fell in line with their elder brother's initiative for a peaceful, but honourable, settlement. But Draupadi called Krishna aside and said to him, pointing to her unbound hair,

> Of this hair dragged upwards by Dusshasana's hand, shall you, O Lotus-Eyed One, think on every occasion if you even desire to make peace with the foes. If Bhima or Arjuna too wish for peace, O Krishna, then my old father will fight beside his sons, the great chariot warriors. And my five sons with the strength of heroes will fight with Abhimanyu (son of Arjuna by Subhadra, Krishna's sister) at their head against the Kurus. But if I do not see Dusshasana's black arm lying hewn off and covered with dust, my heart shall know no rest. Thirteen years have gone by me in hoping and waiting, while I have been fostering my anger within me like a burning fire!

Krishna consoled her assuring that just as she was weeping, the wives of her foes would weep for their dead husbands before long. 'The mountains of the Himalayas may move from their place, dear Krishna,' said Krishna, 'The earth will be shattered into a hundred fragments, the sky with its stars will fall down—but my words cannot stay unfulfilled.'

And Krishna's prophecy was fulfilled. None of the Kaurava brothers survived the holocaust that the world came to know by the name of the Kurukshetra War. Bhima bare-handedly hewed off the hand of the molester Dusshasana and tore apart his chest to drink his blood in the Kurukshetra battlefield, before the very eyes of a quivering Duryodhana and a stupefied Kaurava army. On the final day of the war, Bhima, the son of Vayu, dispatched his arch-enemy Duryodhana to his doom in the most gory manner, crushing not only his thighs as he had sworn to in the shameful hall of dice, but every limb in Duryodhana's body, leaving him to bleed a slow and painful death. Draupadi's burning thirst for vengeance was sated. It was true that her five sons, father

Drupada and brothers Shikhandi and Dhristadyumna along with many other relatives perished in the carnage and her triumph was accompanied by much grief; yet, it was a triumph and she suffered the loss like a true Kshatriya woman.

Sita of the Ramayana

Sita, the Ramayana's central woman character, was different from Draupadi. The Brahminical values and ideals were preponderant in Sita's age, and she herself adhered to those high ideals. Both Rama and Sita were strictly monogamist, and observed all the rules of conventional morality. Sita was won by Rama in a trial of the bow, although it was not a swayamvara.

Sita is regarded as the paragon of womanly virtue, particularly among the Hindus. To this day, the ambition of a traditional Hindu wife is to emulate the example of Sita. Her greatness lay in her complete self-surrender to her husband and in her readiness to suffer for and with him. When during his coronation, Rama was banished into the forests of Dandaka by a cruel twist of fate, Sita followed him as a dutiful wife. All, including Rama, tried their best to dissuade her from her decision. Rama spoke to her at length about the horrors of life in a forest, and warned her that, having been born and brought up in a palace, she would not be able to live with him in the jungle. Thus was Sita's reply to Rama, her husband:

> A wife must share her husband's fate. My duty is to follow you wherever you go. Apart from you, I will not dwell in heaven itself. Deserted by her lord, a wife is like a miserable corpse.
>
> Close as your shadow shall I cleave to you in this life and hereafter. You are my king, my guide, my only refuge, my divinity. It is my fixed resolve to follow you. If you must wander forth through thorny trackless forests, I will go before

> you, treading down the prickly brambles to make your path smooth. Walking before you, I shall feel no weariness: the forest thorns will seem like silken robes; the bed of leaves, a couch. To me, the shelter of your presence is far better than stately palaces, and paradise itself. Protected by your arm, gods, demons or men shall have no power to harm me. With thee I shall live on roots and fruits, sweet or not. If given by your hand, they will to me be like the food of life. Roaming with you, even hell itself would be to me a heaven of bliss.

Thus, young Sita followed Rama into exile and wandered with him in the forests of Dandaka, treading thorny paths and living on jungle fare.

Her absolute and unshakeable devotion to Rama gave her the strength to brave innumerable dangers. The Lankan Rakshasa ruler, Ravana, abducted Sita to avenge the destruction of his army and military base in southern India in the Dandaka forests, the slaying of his cousin Khara by Rama, and the mutilation of his sister Shurpanakha, who, failing in her amorous overtures to Rama, threatened to kill Sita and had her ears and nose chopped off by Lakshmana. Ravana kept Sita captive in the Ashoka Vatika in Lanka. But Sita refused to yield to Ravana. Neither his immense prosperity nor his demonic threats could shake her devotion to her husband and her faith that he would rescue her and slay her kidnapper. She was immune from harm by Ravana through the occult powers acquired through her constancy, and because Ravana himself was under a curse that would consume his life if he violated any woman against her wish.

Sita lived meditating upon the form of Rama. Her faith was vindicated with the coming of Rama to Lanka and Ravana's defeat and death at his hands. After the terrible war, Rama redeemed

Sita. When the couple met after their nearly year-long separation, Rama had a rather cold initial response to Sita, saying he could not accept her as she had been captivated by another man and had been forced to live in his domain. This response has become the topic of a lot of modernist calumny heaped upon the moral standards of that age. But the dictates of *Lok Dharma*, the moral standards and the code of governance of that age do not lend themselves to breezy modern-day presumptions and conclusions. Rama himself never doubted Sita's chastity and devotion, but had to bow to the demands of the populace. An even harsher episode awaited him after his return to Ayodhya when he had to banish a pregnant Sita to sage Valmiki's ashrama, where Sita's twin sons, Kusha and Luva, were born.

The *Ramayana* lays down strict monogamy as the ideal of marital life, though polygamy is permitted to kings and sages as an exception. Polyandrous practices are mentioned as existing among demonic and other communities. The practice was considered unworthy of Aryas.

Chapter 4

Medieval Morality

The medieval period in India saw the intertwining of rigid moral codes with the complex realities of women's lives. Social evils like child marriage, sati, and the devastating effects of Muslim invasions shaped the position of women in society. Practices like *jauhar* and sati highlighted the extreme lengths to which women were subjected in the name of honour, while continuously focusing on Hindu lineage and dharma. This chapter delves into the contradictory nature of medieval morality, where women's autonomy was curtailed, yet their roles in marriage and family remained central to societal survival.

European and Muslim travellers visiting medieval India found the status of Hindu women low. Every woman of the upper caste was married off in childhood. Polygamy was in full force. Every visitor to India has recorded harrowing tales of sati, an institution they found nowhere in the civilised world of the time. Those widows who did not burn themselves to death suffered a worse fate. The only free women in the country were the courtesans who dominated the social life of the city.

This state of affairs was certainly not in keeping with the

spirit of the Vedas and the Mahabharata. The reason behind the degeneration of women in medieval India must be looked for in the *Dharmashastras*—texts that lay down the social and religious laws of Hindus. The *Dharmashastras* enforced the patriarchal, priestly ideal on society, in general, and women, in particular. The flexible traditions of the Mahabharata were abandoned for a strict and rigid moral code. The spiritual conception of marriage was propagated and popularised which saw the downgrading of the status of women to that of an appendage of the man she married. This tendency was accentuated by the codifiers of Hindu law and the codes. They were tireless in their insistence on the need for women to be watched, guarded, and kept in a state of perpetual dependence on men.

Several factors contributed towards the engendering of this attitude. Following repeated Muslim invasions from central and West Asia, there were innumerable instances of forced abduction, rape and enslavement of Hindu women. A Hindu country and society fighting for its existence was naturally alarmed at this fate that had befallen their ancient nation. Hindus wished to maintain the purity of their progeny and future generations. Struck by the beauty and openness of the women of an open, liberal Hindu society, the Islamic invaders, whose prime objective was to spread their expansionist religion by sword and rapine, wreaked havoc with abductions, seductions and rapes—things hitherto unknown and unseen in India. The attitude of the invaders towards the genocidal crimes committed by their brethren was similar to that of the conquering White European settlers towards the indigenous people of the New World—the Americas, north and south. As with the Red Indians, so with the Hindus; the murder, abduction, enslavement and violation of the womenfolk of the defeated and subjugated people of either continent was not even a crime for the conquerors. It was not a surprise that the Hindu law became so strict in this matter that anyone abducted, forcibly converted and/or their womenfolk raped by the *jihadi* invaders was abandoned and never taken back. The remnants of those medieval attitudes can still be found among the orthodox communities in India. However, broader views began to prevail; people who were forcibly converted, abducted and/or violated could be taken back after undergoing a process of *Shuddhi* (purification). This view was widely popularised beginning from the eighteenth century with the collapse of Mughal rule in India and the rise of the Maratha and other Hindu powers. The nineteenth and twentieth centuries began to witness widespread communal riots in India that led to large scale abductions and conversions, bringing further responses from the Hindus, who perceived this social issue to be a matter of concern.

Another factor demanding exceptional vigilance on women was the Hindu insistence for male progeny of one's own blood for *shastra*-sanctioned performance of funeral rites which alone could ensure bliss in the hereafter. An adopted son, or one begotten in levirate too, is competent to perform the funeral obsequies, but a son begotten in adultery is not. With the vulnerability of women becoming a growing concern, it became the duty of every adherent of Arya dharma to guard his wife. Economic jealousy and property rights in women, the prerequisites of a patriarchate, also contributed towards the promulgation of strict moral codes to govern Hindu society.

Of the law books that fall in the domain of the *Smritis,* the *Manusmriti* (Manu's code) is considered the most authentic, besides being an ancient one. Other lawgivers drew mainly from Manu, while Manu drew from the *Grihya Sutras* (domestic rules of conduct) of Ashvalayana and other writers of the post-

Vedic period. The codes represent an epoch of intense priestly activity to spiritualise the whole conception of life and elevate the soul, though not at the expense of the body as is often grossly misunderstood. Possibly, earlier codes might have been interpolated by minor legislators who wrote later, giving rise to contradictory interpretations.

Manu's code, and the ones following his text, predominantly say that woman is incapable of looking after herself, and hence should not be given freedom beyond a limit. Manu himself says, 'In childhood, a father must guard his daughter; in youth, the husband shields his wife and in (old) age, a mother is protected by her sons. A woman should never lean upon her own self.' The marriage of a woman, interpreted by today's 'liberals' as the loss of her individuality, is like a river blending with the sea.

The medieval age propagated the greatness and salvation of a woman as depending upon nothing but her devotion to her husband. The sacred literature of the period is full of illuminating stories of women who obtained superhuman powers by their wholehearted devotion to husbands. One such story, narrated in the *Markandeya Purana*, is of Anasuya, wife of the sage Atri, and a paragon of wifely devotion. Once, the trinity of Brahma, Vishnu and Shiva appeared before her in the form of sages to test her. Through the sheer power of her *tapasya* (austerities), Anasuya changed them into infants. The divine consorts, Goddesses Saraswati, Lakshmi and Parvati, could not identify their husbands and had to plead with the supremely devoted Anasuya to restore their lords to their respective original forms.

The Hindu lawgivers have laid down detailed instructions on a woman's conduct to show her subordination to her husband, including strictures even in the matter of eating and drinking. She ought to give him precedence always. Some even enjoin that a woman who eats before her husband doesn't have a place in his house. According to Vasishta, another sage and lawgiver, if a man eats with his wife, his sons will be born without manly power. Baudhayana, however, mentions that in the South it was usual for a man to eat with his wife and that the custom was good enough for southerners.

The record of Western religions, whose advocates have unrelentingly targeted Hinduism over its alleged treatment of women, is hardly flattering in this regard. The general tendency of their law books is to treat women with contempt and categorise them with children and slaves. In fact, the much-maligned *Manusmriti* has passages that emphasise the need for honouring women. Sample the following passage:

> Where women are honoured, there the gods are pleased; but where they are not honoured, no sacred rite yields rewards. Where the female relations live in grief, the family soon wholly perishes; but that family where they are not unhappy ever prospers. The houses on which female relations, not being duly honoured, pronounce a curse, perish completely as if destroyed by magic.
>
> Hence, men who seek their own welfare, should always honour women, and on holidays and festivals bestow on them gifts of ornaments, fine clothes and dainty food.

In medieval India knowledge of letters was considered disreputable for respectable women. Some ladies of the aristocracy, of course, had the benefit of a sound education; but as a rule the art of reading and writing was considered the undesirable accomplishment of a courtesan. 'It is a shame for a young woman or girl to hold a paper or book in her hand, or to read in the presence of others in her husband's house. It is a popular belief in high caste women that their husbands will die if they should read or hold a pen in their fingers.' A belief was also generally entertained that intrigue is facilitated by a knowledge of letters on the part of females.

An institution supported by the Medieval laws and assiduously practiced by the people was child marriage. One primary reason enforcing child marriage was the medieval concerns connected with ritu, the days immediately following the menstrual flow, considered a fertile period in women; her family would be loath to let it go waste. The Hindu community's yearning for as many sons as possible in that period is understandable as it was engaged in a titanic struggle against the expansionist and often genocidal Islamic rule. Socially and from the familial point of view, it was binding on families to marry off their daughters before they reached puberty. Besides, a grown-up girl was more difficult to guard from predators of a hostile faith than a child, and fathers were anxious to get their daughters married before they became too troublesome for watching.

The adequate age for the marriage of a girl was believed to be between eight and twelve. Manu says that if a girl remained unmarried after reaching puberty, the father had failed in his duty towards her, and she could resort to the 'unsocial' action of choosing a husband for herself. Parashara, the law specialist whose codes are weighty even in the modern Kali Yuga, went so far as to declare that the parents or guardians in whose house a girl reached puberty before marriage would certainly go to hell.

These dire warnings have had a prolonged effect; no other social law has been so well respected among the Hindus for so long. From the time of the promulgation of the codes till recently when the Sarda Act was passed, every Hindu had been careful to get his daughters married in childhood. In fact, to have a grown-up unmarried girl in the house was considered a shame and humiliation; it continues to be an undesirable familial occurrence. While child marriage was a norm, the marriage of even infants was not uncommon. Marriage became a religious duty for all women, and an old maiden was an impossibility in medieval India, although in Vedic literature, we do find mention of some.

The ancient (and medieval) Hindu codes recognise eight forms of marriage. These are:

- Brahma,
- Prajapatya,
- Daiva,
- Arsha,
- Gandharva,
- Pishacha,
- Rakshasa,
- Asura.

Of these, the first four are approved forms of marriage, the fifth is considered undesirable and the remaining three are positively objectionable, though valid when performed.

In the Brahma form, (named after Brahma, the creator) a man invites a bridegroom of much learning and great repute and gives his daughter in marriage to him, having decked her out for the occasion. Considered the best form of marriage by the Hindus of the orthodox school, it is the most popular form of marriage to this day. However, the bridegrooms, or their parents, often interpret the phrase 'decking her out' differently and demand that the bride should carry a fortune when she steps into her husband's home. In the Brahma form of marriage, the bride and bridegroom are passive agents, the match being arranged and solemnised solely by their parents.

The Prajapatya form is named after the Prajapatis or celestial patriarchs. In this form, the bridegroom on arrival is worshipped with the prescribed rites, and the girl is bestowed on him with the injunction, 'Go, both of you, and jointly discharge the duties of a householder.' It does not differ materially from the Brahma form, except in name. Some lawgivers do not mention the Prajapatya form of marriage.

In the Daiva (celestial) form, a householder bestows his daughter on a priest officiating in a sacrifice, more or less as a gift, in recognition of his learning and piety. This was prevalent in the Vedic age, but now sacrifices have gone out of vogue, and with them, the Daiva form of marriage.

The distinguishing feature of the Arsha form is that a bull and a cow are given by the bridegroom to the father of the bride. Some commentators maintain that this amounts to the purchase of the bride, and as such the marriage is not completely free from commercial motives. However, others contend that the gift of a pair of cattle is purely religious and that this marriage is as meritorious as the other three. The Arsha is probably a modified form of the Asura marriage described below. Nonetheless, it is an ancient ritual, not prevalent today.

These four forms of marriage are said to be the best for the Aryas. Sons born of these marriages 'become possessed of the energy of Brahma and are recognised by honest men. Handsome, wealthy, renowned, possessed of fortitude and good qualities, virtuous and amply provided with all objects of enjoyment, these sons live for a hundred years.'

The Gandharva marriage is love marriage, pure and simple. For obvious reasons, this is secretly performed by the lovers without priests and spells. The marriage takes its name from the Gandharvas, celestial musicians, who are said to live in free love. Hindu lawgivers condemn Gandharva marriages citing that children born of such unions are sure to be feeble, unreliable and dishonest. However, this is not always the case. The renowned Bharata, one of the most illustrious rulers of the nation's kingly dynasties, whose descendants are named after him, was born of Dushyanta and Shakuntala after a Gandharva marriage of the two lovers.

Some commentators maintain that an appropriate ceremony is necessary to ratify the unsanctioned union of the Gandharva partners before they can be considered married. Others point out an insurmountable obstacle to the solemnisation of a wedding ceremony. In an orthodox ceremony, a bride always has to be a virgin. In the case of two lovers, taking advantage of the Gandharva rite, the girl might not be a virgin.

Pishacha means 'devilish' and Paishacha is its adjective form. As evident from the name, the ancient Hindu lawgivers did not easily accede to this form of marriage; they were probably forced to accept it having no other alternative. And they had good reason for their attitude. Paishacha is mere drugging and rape. The man doped the woman using drugs or intoxicants and while she was unconscious, took his pleasure. It is strange that a marriage under such circumstances should be considered valid. It was probably to be kind to the woman that the lawgivers recognised this rape as marriage, for a raped woman was an outcaste in Hindu society and her only chance of redemption was having the ravisher marry her. A Paishacha 'marriage' has no sanction in Hindu society, social or legal, although certain other faiths have accorded it a religious sanction; overtly skewed as they are, in favour of the male owning the female.

The Rakshasa form is marriage by capture. It is named after the powerful community of demons called Rakshasa. This form of marriage was quite prevalent among some Kshatriya communities in the epic age. Although the maiden is taken away by force, she remains blameless. However, a Rakshasa marriage is not without political consequences. The grandsire Bhisma abducted the three princesses of Kashi for his foster-brother Vichitravirya. The eldest among them, Amba, not only refused to marry the then Kuru king, but also had her revenge on Bhisma. She was reborn as Shikhandi and was the prime cause of Bhisma's death in the Kurukshetra War.

The Asura form of marriage, named after the Asuras or enemies of the gods, involves purchasing a bride for an adequate sum. In this case, the price of the bride is not a token gift of a pair of cattle as in the Arsha marriage, but a sum depending on the accomplishments and status of the bride. Many Arya communities practiced this form of marriage, especially in north-west India. As mentioned earlier, Princess Madri of Madra was given away in marriage to King Pandu of the Kurus upon the payment of a large sum to her brother Shalya (the maternal uncle of Nakula and Sahadeva).

Despite acknowledging the disreputable forms of matrimonial alliance, the ancient Hindu codes do not mention swayamvara, the pride of the Kshatriyas. The institution continued right down to the Muslim period and withered away only after the downfall of the Rajput ruling dynasties.

Of the eight forms of marriage, the Brahma is the only form widely practiced among Hindus at present. The Sarda Act of 1929 raised the age of marriage among girls and boys, and the subsequent legislations in post-Independent India followed. Modern India has moved much ahead on this score, and now many men and women take an independent decision in their marriage. However, this is not yet a norm in Hindu society which is still steadfast to its tradition of arranged marriage. Gandharva marriages have become fashionable among the more affluent classes. Though they do not go to extremes like Dushyanta and Shakuntala, they do express their choice of mates and get their parents to accede. Though the Asura form of marriage is largely a thing of the past, it might still be practiced in certain pockets of the country. Buying a bride is considered disreputable and those who do so are in for social censure. On the other hand, buying of bridegrooms has yet to be completely eschewed in Hindu society.

The status of the widow in Medieval India requires particular mention. We have discussed that in ancient India, a widow usually married her husband's brother. Even without marriage, the widow was permitted to bear children in levirate. Codes, however, prohibited the custom on account of being sinful. According to these codes, a respectable widow was to live in her husband's house as a nun, cherishing the memory of her lost spouse and observing the fasts and rites prescribed for such unfortunate women.

Some earlier lawgivers permitted the widow to beget children in levirate. Gautama, a liberal in this regard lays down that 'A woman whose husband is dead and who desires, may bear a son to her brother-in-law. Lacking a brother-in-law, she may obtain offspring by cohabiting with a Sapinda, a Sagotra, a Samnapravara (all relatives) or one who belongs to the same caste.' Similarly, a discarded wife, a woman whose husband had deserted her or had gone missing had the right of remarriage after waiting for a certain period. Manu, however, did not favour this view. According to him, a widow could not remarry because a woman was a gift given away to her husband, and 'the same thing cannot be given away twice.'

The followers of the codes were greater zealots than their

authors, and hence many things not ordained in the codes were enforced by society. Sati was one such institution. We have already referred to the sacred writ which lays down that a married woman has no life apart from her husband. It was believed that she should obviously perish with her husband on the funeral pyre. Male jealousy also contributed substantially to the spread of the institution. Kings were the worst culprits in this matter, and this was found more in the civilisations and cultures outside India than among Hindus. The monarchs of yore could not bear the thought of their beautiful women submitting themselves to the embraces of less worthy individuals. When Herod the Great went to see Octavius, he gave secret orders to his trusted agent to put his wife Herodias to death if he did not return from the fateful encounter with the Roman conqueror. The Rajputs were the most ardent in this regard. The Islamic invasion of India took a terrible toll on Rajput women; the feminine population of entire cities perished in the horrible mass suicide known as *Jauhar*. The iconoclastic zealotry of Muslim invaders roused hatred against them among Hindus, and Hindu women often preferred suicide to capture and slavery.

The practice established by the royals spread among other classes too, who tried to imitate them. Learned men found sacred texts to justify the institution, though the Vedas contain no trace of sati and afforded no sanction to the practice. The practice took such hold among Hindus that even the Sikhs to whom sati is prohibited, encouraged it; on the death of Maharaja Ranjit Singh, four of his queens mounted the funeral pyre.

The Shaktas, the worshippers of female deities, and other enlightened Hindus had revolted against this practice from early times. Bana, the well-known author of *Kadambari*, wrote in the seventh century AD:

> To die after one's beloved is most fruitless. It is a custom followed by the foolish. It is a mistake committed by infatuation. It is a reckless course followed only on account of hot haste. It is a mistake of stupendous magnitude. It does no good whatsoever to the dead person. It does not help him in ascending to heaven; it does not prevent him from sinking into hell. It does not at all ensure union after death; the person who has died goes to the place determined by his own Karma, the person who accompanies him on the funeral pyre goes to the hell reserved for those who are guilty of the sin of suicide. On the other hand, by surviving the deceased, one can do much good both to oneself and to the departed by offering prescribed oblations for his happiness in the other world. By dying with him, one can do good to neither.[1]

The *Tantras*, the scriptures of the Shaktas, also denounce sati. The *Mahanirvana Tantra* expressly prohibits sati and declares that a woman burning herself with her husband is sure to go to hell.

These views, however, did not obtain popular approval. The voice of the advocates of sati was dominant in medieval India and both sacred and secular literature is full of panegyrism of sati. The rite of sati was extolled as the supreme expression of a woman's love for her husband and she was held up as a goddess on earth. Some writers maintained that the law of Karma was inoperative in the case of sati, and even a dissolute woman could obtain eternal bliss by mounting the funeral pyre of her husband. The lawgiver Parashara maintained that sati was so powerful that

1 Dr A S Altekar, *The Position of Women in Hindu Civilisation*, 2016.

she could challenge the powers of the prince of the nether regions and forcibly take her husband out of hell if he happened to be there. A sati proceeding towards the site of the rite was believed to be capable of bestowing eternal bliss on any mortal she cared to look at.

With such exaltation of sati, it is not surprising that innumerable widows voluntarily burnt themselves to death on the funeral pyres of their husbands. There have been cases in which the sincerest persuasion of relatives failed to dissuade women from their determination to commit sati.

In stark contrast were incidents in which unwilling women were forced to commit sati. A widow was considered a curse to herself and her relatives, and many widows committed sati to escape the wretchedness which otherwise would be in store for them. Those who preferred a miserable life over death were, at times, coaxed by their relatives to perish in the flames. Some relatives desiring the widow's wealth would even pressurise her to take this shortcut to heaven. Tales also abound of widows who, while trying to escape from the devouring flames, were held down by long poles by her relatives and thus consigned to the fire.

The attempts of medieval era-Muslim rulers to abolish sati couldn't make any headway. Every district magistrate during the Muslim period had to ensure no woman was coerced to commit sati in places under his jurisdiction, and every widow had to apply to him in person for a permit before committing herself to flames. The granting of permits, however, became more or less formal, and the institution flourished unchecked till 1828 when it was stopped by Governor-General William Bentinck at the instance of Hindu reformers, of whom Raja Ram Mohan Roy deserves special mention, being the pioneer of modernism in India.

However, the abolition of sati did not immediately uplift the position of widows. Rather, the life of a widow became more pitiable. The notion that the death of a man was mysteriously brought about by the sins of his wife became widespread in Hindu society and the widow was more or less considered a murderess and treated likewise. She had to continue living in the house of her deceased husband and his relatives viewed her as the prime cause of their bereavement.

Following the death of the husband, the widow's head was shaved and she was subjected to rigorous persecution. She was expected to live an ascetic life—prohibited from eating nutritive food and wearing fine clothes or ornaments. The drudgery of household chores fell to her lot. She was not permitted to visit a household on festive occasions as her presence forbode evil. Married women shunned her lest seeing her bring them widowhood.

The tragedy was even more pitiable when the widow subjected to this treatment happened to be a girl in her teens or a child. She had probably no love for her husband as marriage was contracted before she came of age, and the sense of blighted youth led to heartbreak and even immoral practices. Seducing young widows was easy and rampant; some were even consigned by seducers to brothels.

From this medieval degradation, Hindu women have risen considerably high as we shall see ahead.

❧❧❧

Chapter 5

From Sati to Selfhood

The advent of modernity in India brought significant shifts in the status and rights of women. The abolition of sati, the push for widow remarriage, and the establishment of schools for women under British rule marked crucial steps toward female emancipation. Legislative acts, like the Sarda Act, sought to reform practices such as child marriage, highlighting the changing view of women's roles in society. This chapter explores how modern India began to break away from ancient practices, moving toward a vision of women as equals in education, family, and society, while grappling with the ongoing tensions between tradition and progress.

The modern phase in Hindu social development may be said to have started with the advent of the British in India. Muslim invasions did not leave Hindu society untouched. Most of these changes were confined to religion and rigidifying of the caste system. As far as Indian women were concerned, the only Muslim influence was their degeneration from a previously held high position in Hindu society. Medieval as well as some contemporary orthodox Muslims are strict observers of the *purdah* (veil); Islam holds women's freedom to be incompatible with its beliefs and morals. Hence, respectable women were seldom permitted to venture outdoors. When necessity demanded their venturing out, elaborate precautions were taken to prevent temptation. Women of the nobility were protected from public gaze by a portable enclosure manned by eunuchs. When the royal harem was on the move, males were chased away for miles around the area where the camp moved. The middle classes could not afford such a costly seclusion, and it is for their benefit that the *burqa* was invented. The burqa covered a lady from the crown of the head to the tip of the toes. No Muslim lady with any claim to modesty could walk about the streets in medieval India without a burqa.

Owing to the Muslims and their political domination, many Hindus—especially in the northern parts of the country where Islam was harsher—adopted the purdah. Hindu royal families, again especially in the north, copied the Muslim custom in its entirety; the *zenana* (women's quarters) of some Rajput rulers exceeded the Mughals in strictness, privacy and membership. Middle-class Hindu ladies did not adopt the burqa when outdoors, but they did cover their heads and faces with their saris, effectively serving the purpose of a veil. In medieval India, women who enjoyed relative freedom were either poor, or courtesans.

Nonetheless, Muslim power could never gain absolute mastery over India. Hindu resistance proved undying—the Rajputs, Marathas, Jats and the Sikhs waged a titanic struggle against Islamic rule, and the Deccan and south of India became the graveyard of Mughal rule. The collapse of Muslim rule coincided with the arrival of the British, complicating India's political landscape, yet opening up vistas of some change for Hindu betterment. The British East India Company snatched power, erasing the Bengal nawabship of Siraj-ud-Daulah. After the failure of the 1857 Mutiny, the last Mughal emperor, a pale tottering shadow of his dynasty, was exiled to Burma, consigning Mughal rule to pages of history. However, East India Company officials were not driven by any religious or humanitarian zeal, and they consciously did nothing to bring about social progress among the Hindus. Their main interest lay in exploiting the country, and their methods were as greedy as those of other foreign intruders. Many of the Company's officials and clerks were adventurers or common thieves and rogues in their native country who found life at home shorn of fortune or meaningful prospects for the future. Indians who came into contact with them and studied their way of life often spoke of these *firangis* (as the early Europeans were called in India) as devils from some remote region. However, there were a few noble Englishmen who came with a missionary zeal and wished to do something for the progress of India. But more than their efforts, the contact the British mercantile fortune seekers opened up between India and Europe brought significant changes in Hindu society. Indians travelled abroad and were struck by the structure of European society, especially the freedom that European women enjoyed.

These enlightened Indians returned to India full of reforming zeal; their number and influence increasing with time. Of these pioneers, mention must be made of Raja Ram Mohan Roy, generally known as the Father of Modern India, and of Pandita Ramabai, a gifted Indian lady who laboured all her life for the emancipation of her sisters. The origin and progress of the movement for women is captured in her interesting book, *The High-Caste Hindu Woman*, published towards the end of the nineteenth century.

The situation of women in India before the British occupation of the country was by no means favourable. Sati was common among the affluent ruling classes. Hindu widows were ill-treated by society; their heads were shaved, and they were shunned as ill-omens and given the drudgery of the house to work out their salvation through hard labour. Child marriage was the rule not only among the three higher castes, but also among the majority of well-to-do Shudras. Those who could afford it, practised polygamy; polyandry was unknown except among some insignificant hill tribes. Respectable women were secluded from all public activities, and a knowledge of letters was denied to them. She was, more or less, a bonded appendage of her husband.

The first significant step towards the liberation of Hindu women in the nineteenth century was taken by enlightened Hindus who agitated for the abolition of sati by law. Raja Ram Mohan Roy's efforts are particularly noteworthy in this regard. The British officials were initially neutral for their fear of disturbing the Indian beehive from which they were extracting honey. But, the enlightened public opinion among Hindus and the voice of some well-meaning Englishmen were too strong for those in power. Hence, in 1829, William Bentinck, the then Governor-General of India, took a bold step and prohibited sati by law. Orthodox Hindus did not keep quiet. They maintained that this legislation was a wanton Christian interference with their 'sacred' right to burn their women alive, and fought their case in the Privy Council. But their petition was dismissed and sati soon became a thing of the past.

However, sati abolition did not bring about an immediate improvement in the condition of the widows. On the contrary, it was thought justifiable to torture the widow as her husband's death was mysteriously traced to her own sins. In fact, it was irreligious to show pity or kindness towards a widow. Her suffering was believed to lead to expiation of sins and bring peace to her soul.

Gradually, the spread of education and modern notions of marriage began to bring change in the medieval attitude toward widows. Progressive public opinion recognised widow marriage legally. However, only a few Hindus leveraged this legislation. With time, Hindu widows who were bold enough to ignore the orthodox sentiments and wealthy enough to be independent of their relatives realised the irrelevance of lifelong mourning for departed husbands whom they married before attaining maturity. The more enlightened community members supported this and even put forward sacred texts in their defence. After all their efforts, only a few Hindu widows remarried as the majority had become mothers. Sentiment against widow remarriage in Hindu society has not been easy to overcome, though contemporary times have perceptibly changed.

Even the Arya Samaj, an avowed organisation of reform in Hinduism, did not approve of widow remarriage, except for virgins whose husbands had died before consummation of marriage. The idea of a woman submitting herself to another man after her husband's death—in or out of wedlock—is anathema to most Hindus. Reform in this direction has been very slow even today. Presently, widow remarriage is confined to those who are socially and economically independent of their orthodox relatives, and are intellectually bold enough to ignore social mores.

The treatment meted out to widows has considerably changed for the better. Although the old ideas of persecution still persist among some village communities, the general tendency at present is to treat the widow as an object of pity. Tonsure, a source of deep humiliation for Hindu women, is no longer imposed on widows, except among some orthodox castes in southern India; even here it is confined to elderly widows, and young widows are allowed to grow their hair. However, no widow, young or old, meets approval if she wears bright-coloured attire or ornaments, and this is still widely followed.

Right from the outset of the British colonisation of the country, there has been a slow but effective process of woman's emancipation through the spread of female education. This has yielded astounding results by removing most of the disabilities of women from the higher classes of the Hindus. While the missionary work of Britain and America is noteworthy, it must be remembered that their efforts were not driven by altruism but by the desire to convert heathens, the Hindus. It is, by and large, the awakening of Hindu society that could enable foreign reformist endeavours to bear meaningful fruits. Else, what explains the zero impact of Western missionaries on reforming the non-Hindu sections, primarily Muslim women, of the subcontinent during the long spell of colonial British rule? The truth is that reform within Hindus was possible because of the nature of Hinduism itself, which has always been adaptive to change. Indeed, *Sanatana Dharma* is the foremost proponent of change in accordance with *desha* (space) and *kala* (time), both of which are characterised by constant change.

While the first schools for women's education were set up under the British, progressive Hindus soon began setting up schools for education of girls. Initially, these schools were exclusively meant for education of girls—the idea of mixed education was considered too bizarre then. It was gradually recognised that such institutions for exclusive education of women would not quench the newly awakened thirst for knowledge among women. Gradually, people began to think that there could not be much harm if women attended the same school as boys provided the seats were set apart for girls. Over the years, mixed education has become common in India. The percentage of girls attending schools, compared to the total Indian women population, still lags behind, but this is more concerned with literacy levels and its state-wise imbalance in the country.

A major impetus to women's education was the Sarda Act of 1929 which prohibited marriage of girls below the age of fourteen. The marriage of girls in childhood meant negligible education. The old taboo of education being improper for a girl from a respectable family persisted. Once this prejudice was overcome, it became easier for parents to send their girls to school, though this was by no means an easy transformation. Many parts of rural India still continue to suffer from lower female literacy due to this age-old mindset. However, literacy and education in today's age is no longer the taboo it once was, and is regarded as an accomplishment. There would hardly be an educated young man willing to marry an illiterate girl. The present upper and middle classes look for brides who are well-educated in their mother tongue and know at least a smattering of English, if not fluency in the language. Among the respectable modern classes, reasonable education—at least, graduation—is a prerequisite for marriageable girls. This has become the norm in Indian cities and towns with villages slowly falling into line. The one difficulty in villages is dearth of educational facilities.

Today, no Hindu worth the name considers education harmful for women. However, higher education for women has to still gain approval from the orthodox who believe that women, by their very nature and physique, are unsuited for strenuous work—physical or intellectual—and that the ultimate objective of a woman's life is motherhood or housekeeping. But modern Hindus have shed these beliefs, and it is no longer a surprise to find highly educated, professionally qualified Hindu women in every sphere of life, including information technology and space engineering.

Women's interest in music and dance has moved in tandem; these arts were condemned as the domain of courtesans in medieval India. But such prejudices have now been overcome, making them popular among girls as seen in the widespread popularity of song and dance competitions on private television channels. Indian families no longer baulk at sending their young daughters to prestigious, or pricey institutes for learning these arts which were confined to certain communities in ancient India. This is undoubtedly a revolution, though debate on its ethical desirability is an ongoing thing. During social functions, young ladies dance or sing without hesitation to show off their skills; some have even taken to dancing as a profession without lowering their social status. Hindu women have also shed their familial and social inhibitions about acting in films, which again was the exclusive preserve of the courtesans or the less respectable communities in the old days.

The change in outlook brought about by this partial emancipation of women has affected the institution of marriage among Hindus. Of the eight forms of marriage prevalent in medieval India, the most common form today is the Brahma or its modified version. The Vedic ceremony, described earlier in chapter 2, is still performed among the orthodox with slight modifications. The ceremony usually takes place in the bride's house, though hiring marriage halls is the norm today, and the bridegroom, his family and wedding party reach her place on the appointed day.

The Sarda Act's increase of the marriageable age and the spread of female education have introduced a hitherto unknown factor in modern Hindu communities—love. Young men and women nowadays have ample opportunities to meet each other; co-education, especially in high schools and colleges, has led to social contact between boys and girls of marriageable age. This modern development, together with the influence of Western notions of love and marriage, has led to many instances of the Gandharva form of marriage, condemned by medieval legislators but praised by Kalidasa, Vatsyayana and other ancient writers. Many parents often accede to the desire of the young people in love, though a girl's parents heave a sigh of relief if her lover is of the same caste and the marriage has no social complications. Unfortunately, love rarely abides by social laws. Instances of Hindu girls falling in love with men of lower caste or even with Christians, Muslims or Parsis do come to light; even today such inter-communal or inter-caste marriages are abhorred by the orthodox who always want their women to marry in their caste and status.

In the case of inter-communal marriages, parents and their daughters often fall out especially when the parents are orthodox, and because of social and religious complications, the marriage is performed in civil registries. For obvious reasons, only independent individuals who can afford to ignore their relatives' sentiments and their parents' financial support take advantage of the Civil Marriage Act. Such marriages are, however, exceptional and confined to the ultra-modern section of society. The vast majority of enlightened Hindus consult their sons and daughters before marriage, and strike a balance between the extreme individuality of love and the hard but worldly-wise realm of conventions. A desirable social convention that has gained ground among the educated class of Hindus is obtaining the consent of the girl and the boy before accepting a marriage proposal. Among the orthodox, especially in the villages, even today it is considered improper for parents to consult their sons or daughters in fixing their marriage or for the young to express their views in marital affairs. It has been mentioned elsewhere that dowry has become an important part of marriage contracts. In ancient India, certain communities gave their girls in marriage on receiving a bride price—a custom that has now fallen into disrepute among the higher Hindu classes although it continues among some lower castes. However, wealthy, middle-aged men practise it secretly to marry pretty young girls from poor families. Among modern upper class Hindus, the general tendency is to buy bridegrooms by paying exorbitant sums of money. Buying of bridegrooms is what is generally known as the dowry system in modern India.

Modern awakening of women throughout the world has significantly contributed towards the emancipation of women in India. Hindu women have discovered that their disabilities are not just limited to social or economic spheres, but are also political in nature. Several enlightened women have striven to achieve political equality with men.

Chapter 6

Divine Yet Dismissed

The Vedas and epics, like the Mahabharata and Ramayana, celebrate the feminine as essential to cosmic order, portraying figures like Draupadi and Sita as embodiments of strength and devotion. Yet, there are texts that present women as volatile, emotional, and sometimes unreliable, reinforcing patriarchal notions of male superiority. This duality reveals how the sacred and the flawed coexist in the Hindu view of womanhood, shaping both spiritual ideals and societal norms throughout history.

Two opposing tendencies are discernible in the Hindu attitude towards women. Shaktas deify the woman believing that the female is greater and nobler than the male. They speak of the fair sex as Devi or goddess. Hindus believe the same, and so do the epics, ancient Hindu law books, and modern Indian literature.

In stark contrast, an ascetic and pessimistic outlook also dominates certain schools of Hindu thought. These have inspired literature not altogether complimentary to the fair sex. The universal male weakness for exaggerating the wiles of a woman has enriched this literature with fantastic tales of her wickedness and her insatiable love for variety in sex. Women's infidelity is a pet theme of many storytellers, holding on to the popular imagination from ancient times. But we must acknowledge the brighter side of the picture before arriving at what many today would dub a misogynistic view of women.

The *Manusmriti*, maligned by self-appointed spokespeople of modernism and feminism as 'anti-feminist', pays some glorious tribute to women. 'Women,' says the Mahabharata, 'Shall be worshipped, served and paid homage to. Offspring, wealth, and the prime joys of this earthly pilgrimage rise from women. They are the goddesses of happiness and beauty and must always be held in honour.'

Murdering a woman is considered a crime more heinous than Brahmanicide, and no penance can expiate it. Even the books that extol human and animal sacrifice prohibit slaughtering female victims. It is said that instead of appeasing the deity, sacrificing a female victim brings divine wrath upon the world. In a discourse on the evil institution of sati, the *Mahanirvana Tantra* observes, 'Every woman is a picture of the great Goddess; if a woman, in her blindness, climbs on to her dead lord's pyre, she then goes to hell.'

Most lawgivers consider a woman as essentially pure and clean of all physical and spiritual impurities. Even an adulteress is believed to be clean after her periods. 'A woman, a child and an old man are never unclean.' Moreover, 'A woman is pure in all her limbs, while the cow is pure only behind.'

The Mahabharata stresses on the tenderness and sweetness of a woman thus:

Our love these sweetly speaking women gain,
When men are all alone, companions bright,
In duty, wise to judge, and guide aright,
Kind, tender mothers in distress and pain.

Wife-beating is prohibited by the Tantras—'If a man utters ill words to his wife,' says the *Mahanirvana Tantra*, 'he shall fast for a day; three days, if he hits her.'

Hindus have always held the mother in great esteem; both their literature and practice emphasise the greatness of the mother. He who ill-treats his aged mother is a miserable person. Respecting this time-honoured sentiment often has a Hindu in a rather unenviable position when his wife and ageing, often old, mother don't get along or fall out, as often happens in domestic matters. In such situations, a man usually sides with his mother, following his sense of duty and social codes, even if it displeases his wife. A man who incurs the curses of his weak and aged father is not considered as lost to decency as one who brings upon himself the curses of his mother.

Those who commit matricide are forsaken among Hindus. There is Parashurama, the Brahmin avatar of Vishnu, who knocked down his mother to satiate his father Jamadagni's anger. This emphasises the absolute authority of the father, which, however, was not a common conception in the ancient world. The status of the wife is almost as great as that of the mother. Hindus consider marriage a religious duty. As his companion for life and as the mother of his sons, a man holds his wife in great esteem in theory even though the ideal is yet to be realised practically. The ancient Hindu literature extols the wife's status and dignity with utmost praise. 'The wife is the home,' says the Rig Veda. 'He who unjustifiably forsakes his wife,' observes a Tantric text, 'shall put on an ass's skin and beg in seven houses with the words "give alms to the one that has left his wife".' A wife so forsaken is even allowed to consort with another man without being considered an adulteress.

Indiscriminate asceticism and celibacy are not glorified in

Hinduism, though both are permitted in exceptional cases. A man has a duty to himself and society. A person's life is divided into four ashramas or stages for the better discharge of this dual responsibility. The first of these stages is the *brahmacharya* or studentship during which a man prepares himself for his later life by intensive study and discipline under a guru. In the second stage called *grihastha,* he marries, sets up house and raises children for the propagation of his line. When his sons reach manhood, he is at liberty to leave his domestic affairs to them and abandon his home to pursue a spiritual life. This stage is *vanaprastha* when he prepares for the final stage of earthly existence, known as *sannyasa* or renunciation, in which he cuts himself off from the world, and leaves for a forest to lead a life of contemplation and asceticism till the end of his life.

Though each of these stages is considered equally important for a fulfilling life, marriage and domestic life have a definite religious value for the Hindus. And the wife, an all-important partner in the second stage of a man's life, is highly spoken of in Hindu sacred literature. Thus, the Mahabharata says:

> The wife is half the man, his priceless friend;
> Of pleasure, virtue, wealth, his constant source;
> A help and stay along his earthly course;
> Through life unchanging, yea, beyond its end.
> When racked by pain, by sickness worn,
> by outrage stung, by anguish torn,
> Disturbed, perplexed, oppressed, forlorn,
> Men find their spouses' love and skill
> The surest cure for every ill.

Similarly, the plight of the unhappy celibate is thus described:

> The luckless wight who lacks a wife

And leads a doleful single life,
Should leave his home, and cheerless dwell
In some secluded forest dell.
And there should spend his days and nights
In fasting, penance, painful rites
For now, without a helpmate dear,
His home is but a desert drear.
Who then would live without a wife
His house's joy and light and life?
With her the poorest hut will please
And want and toil be borne with ease.
Without her spacious gilded halls
Possess no charms—all splendour palls.

The ascetic, however, is not without his answer. For, 'the wife is an all-devouring curse,' he says. The fall of a good man through his wife and children is thus described:

> Through blindness, men fall into desire. Desire gives rise to anger, greed and selfishness. Self-seeking leads to works and works to bonds of love. Love sets in motion the cycle of births and deaths and the misery that is life. Life starts in the womb and is brought about by seed and blood mixed with excrement and water and fouled with the impurities of blood. Led on by the unquenchable thirst for life, miserable man is ever ensnared by woman who is the continuer of the web of life. Women are the ploughed field and men the seed; women are bewitchers who bewilder the foolish and are the embodiment of lust. Therefore, are children born out of lust. Just as lice that come out of our body are deemed unclean and foreign, so let the wise put away the vermin called children though they are born of their loins.

Fortunately, these extreme views are not shared by the vast majority of Hindus who seek fulfilment in married life and believe that children are a source of happiness in this world and in the next. But, there is a general tendency among the Hindus, as among the rest of humankind, which primarily adheres to patriarchy—to speak of women as fickle and unreliable. Though there are tales of female devotion and fidelity, their moral weakness is equally stressed in many books. Manu is particularly blunt on the nature of women. According to this ancient legislator:

> It is in the nature of women to seduce men in this world; for that reason, the wise are never unguarded in the company of females. For, women are able to lead astray in this world not only a fool but even a learned man, and to make him a slave of desire and anger. Women do not care for beauty, nor is their attention fixed on age; thinking 'It is enough that he is a man,' they give themselves to the handsome and to the ugly.

Some other impressions on the nature of women can be sampled:

> 'Through their passion for men, through their mutable temper, through their natural heartlessness, they become disloyal towards their husbands, however carefully they may be guarded in this world.'
>
> 'Knowing their disposition, which the Lord of Creatures laid in them at the creation, to be such, every man should most strenuously exert himself to guard them.'
>
> 'For women, no sacramental rite is performed with sacred texts, thus the law is settled; women who are destitute of strength and destitute of knowledge of Vedic texts, are as impure as falsehood itself, that is the fixed rule.'

The Catholic Church has had no less malicious views on

women, especially in the medieval ages. Some Popes believed that every woman is a rake at heart—a view also shared by some Hindu writers. Mahabharata claims to present an exposition of the true nature of woman. Sage Narada, wishing to know the fundamental nature of woman, decided to get first-hand information on the subject from a woman herself. Hence, he approached the celestial dancer Pachasuda who revealed to him the true nature of woman in these words:

> Of a truth, there is nothing worse than woman in the three worlds—the root of all evils. Even ladies of good family, beautiful and happily married do not observe the moral laws. They are ready to forsake their rich and worthy husbands and bestow their favours on others as soon as they get an opportunity. We, women, know no moral bars and are ever ready to throw ourselves into the arms of evil men. Women are not swayed by considerations of beauty, youth or character. Any man is good enough for a woman. Ladies of rank envy those fair ones who are in glorious youth and wander about free in sex wearing costly ornaments; and women held in esteem often fasten themselves on to hunchbacks, fools, dwarfs, cripples and other detestable men. When women do not get any man, they even fall on one another.... The fire has never too many faggots, the ocean never too many rivers, the all-devouring time never too many beings, and a beautiful woman never too many men. Death, the storm, fire, poison, serpents, the sharpness of the sword, and hell itself—women are all these in one.

Ability to quarrel over petty things and be jealous are said to be peculiar to women. The age-old Hindu institution of polygyny is probably responsible for this view. The much-married kings of ancient India usually had a *kopa bhavan* (chamber of anger) in which an angry wife who had any grievance, fancied or otherwise, could occupy and demand redress. Husbands of many women wasted much of their time in settling quarrels between his wives. A jealous wife often took recourse to spells, charms and witchcraft when her husband failed to accede to her unreasonable demands.

Stories around Krishna, the husband of eight wives, contain many amusing anecdotes about the jealousies and intrigues of his wives. The jealousy of Satyabhama regarding Rukmini, Krishna's eldest wife, is one of the standout episodes in the *Shrimad Bhagwat*. Even highly-placed ladies like Kunti, Draupadi and Kausalya were not above it. Kunti did not like Madri in whose arms her husband Pandu died; Draupadi was stung by jealousy when Subhadra, Arjuna's second wife, entered their lives. Kausalya, Rama's mother, did not approve of the ways of Kaikeyi, the youngest wife of Dasharatha.

Hindu scriptures also record many episodes of jealousy among goddesses, who often appear to be no better than mortal women in this respect. The handsome moon-deity Chandra married the twenty-seven daughters of the celestial patriarch Daksha and had to suffer much at their hands. At the time of the marriage, the foresighted patriarch made Chandra promise that he would treat all his twenty-seven wives alike. But Chandra found it difficult to keep his promise and doted on the beautiful Rohini with whom he spent most of his time. The other twenty-six ladies complained of this partiality to their father, and Daksha admonished his son-in-law to mend his ways and keep his word. The moon made a show of repentance and agreed to abide by this promise. But the attractions of Rohini proved too strong for the niceties of domestic justice and the same complaint reached Daksha again. The angry patriarch then cursed the moon to wane away in fourteen days, and only after a protest from all the gods of the pantheon did Daksha let his son-in-law regain his original shape in as many days. However, it is doubtful if Chandra could have avoided a complaint by treating all his wives alike. Equal treatment does not always bring happiness to the several wives of a man. Thus, the impossibility of pleasing women.

Hindus have given some thought to the question—who out of a man or woman is the better sex. It is generally admitted that she has a stronger sex nature. Man is said to be no match for her. 'Love of scandal and lust of sex did the Creator give women. A man can never keep a woman under control, whether by strong words, blows, bonds by inflicting pain—women are always unbridled in their passion.' Kalyanamalla, author of *Ananga Ranga* says, 'A woman eats twice as much as a man, she is four times as much clever, her determination is six times as strong, and her sexual desire eight times as strong as a man's.' Despite these observations, the general view among Hindus is that man is the superior, though not necessarily better, sex. Woman being bound and subjected; Hindus believe it is a blessing to be born as a man. Intellectually, women are considered inferior to men; it is an insult to call a man a woman as it dubs him as weak and cowardly. The Mahabharata age depicts some instances of men and women who had the rare opportunity of changing their sexes. The experiences of these gifted individuals as narrated in the epic will give the reader some idea of what Hindu society thinks of the relative advantages of the sexes.

We have already seen how princess Amba of Kashi was abducted by the Kuru elder Bhisma and released on his realisation of her love for Shalva, the king of Saubha. However, despite her release from Hastinapura, Amba was rejected by Shalva and had to go into a forest to live the life of an ascetic. Her thirst for vengeance on Bhisma was insatiable and she took to severe penances to propitiate Shiva. Pleased with her strict austerity, Lord Shiva appeared before her and Amba begged of Him to grant her a boon by which she could slay Bhisma. Shiva blessed her before disappearing; she would have her revenge, not in her present life but the next one. She would be born as the son of king Drupada of Panchala. To hasten her rebirth as a man, Amba lit a funeral pyre and ascended it.

Accordingly, Amba was reborn as Drupada's child, but the baby was a girl and not a boy. Drupada himself was desperately praying for a son. His queen who had birthed the infant girl was in consternation. In the Kshatriya world, particularly in monarchical dynasties, the queen who bore her husband the eldest son—and thus the heir to the throne—would be the *rajmahisi* (the reigning queen) and would, by default, become superior to the other consorts of her husband. The newborn girl child's mother was Drupada's first wife who would naturally not want to lose her position as the chief queen. She, therefore, concealed the sex of the child and brought it up as a boy. The secret was well guarded, but strange things began to happen in the queen's life thereafter. She had lied to her husband, Drupada, about their first-born and presented it as a boy, covering up the infant with extra clothing, and keeping the infant away from her father. But, to her utter dismay, the girl child, named Shikhandi, showed no girlish behaviour and was surprisingly masculine in her appearance. Gradually, but alarmingly, it dawned on her that the girl child she had tried to pass off as a boy was in fact a boy in spirit and mind trapped in a girl's body. It was too late for her to do anything; she simply had to continue the deception of Shikhandi being a boy. Clad in more attire than was normal for a male, Shikhandi began growing up more masculine and muscular than a girl, though not as strong as a full-fledged male. Drupada later went to beget other sons, but he would always wonder why his firstborn son rarely spoke to him and did his best to avoid his father's company. He was to know the reason in a few years.

Not wanting to be a girl became the obsession of Shikhandi's life. She was, after all, Amba reborn as Drupada's daughter, carrying the wrong and humiliation of her previous life at Bhisma's hands. She scorned any girl-like pastime of singing, dancing, playing with female companions and the like, but trained hard as a warrior, though her physical frame often failed to support her aggression and anger. When she came of age, Drupada married her off to the daughter of Hiranyavarman, king of Dasarna, an important monarchy in central India. The Panchala ruler had arranged this match for his eldest 'son', but except Shikhandi and her mother, no one knew the truth.

The bride, Hiranyavarman's daughter, discovered the true sex of her 'husband' on her nuptial bed and fled to her father's house and revealed the hoax played upon her. Hiranyavarman blazed with wrath—his Kshatriya honour had been violated most crudely—and he threatened Drupada of marching to Panchala with his army to avenge himself. But the Dasarna king knew that this was but impotent rage. He and his kingdom were militarily no match for Drupada, one of the most formidable warriors of his times. Moreover, Panchala was not a military power to be trifled with, ruled by a king who was a disciple of the rishi Bharadwaja, father of Dronacharya. Drupada's sons or commanders would have made short work of Hiranyavarman and his army. But Drupada held himself guilty; his family had wronged the girl's family, and he was hesitant to use his military superiority to quell a fellow Kshatriya who had been wronged. He summoned his queen and ordered her to lay bare the truth, which she did, begging her husband for forgiveness.

Hearing this, Shikhandi fled 'his' home and kingdom to disappear into a forest and end 'his' life. As 'he' wandered in the forest looking for a convenient spot to commit suicide, 'he' met a *Yaksha* (a semi-celestial being below the celestial Devatas) who wished to know the cause of 'his' distress. On hearing Shikhandi's story, the Yaksha took pity on 'him' and volunteered to exchange his sex with the princess. Shikhandi thankfully accepted the offer and exchanged her sex with the Yaksha. He promised the Yaksha that he would return to the forest after satisfying Hiranyavarman and his family, and give his sex back to the Yaksha. Converted into a handsome young man, Shikhandi returned to his capital Kampilya and called upon his father to inform that he was now a male and not a female.

By then, Drupada had somehow been convinced not to go to war over this matter and thus invite his own destruction, but to come and have a look at his son himself or send reliable persons to examine him. Accordingly, Hiranyavarman had Shikhandi examined through old women who reported to the king that the youth was really a man and his daughter was probably suffering from hallucinations. A chastised Hiranyavarman apologised to Drupada for his rash behaviour and, rebuking his hysterical daughter for all the unpleasantness, returned to Dasarna.

True to his promise, Shikhandi went back to the forest to return his sex to the Yaksha. Meanwhile, things had happened in the forest making this impossible. While the Yaksha was living in the forest as a woman, his King Kubera, the presiding deity of wealth, happened to visit the area. All the Yakshas of the forest appeared before their King to pay homage except the metamorphosed one. Kubera noticed his absence and immediately enquired about him. On being presented, the Yaksha was found to be a woman. Kubera demanded to know the reason and decided that the Yaksha should retain the gender he had voluntarily accepted. When his companions interceded on the Yaksha's behalf, Kubera permitted him to regain his original sex after Shikhandi's death (he perished after the Kurukshetra War, in a vengeful night ambush by Ashwatthama, son of Dronacharya).

The episode illustrates the stronger affection of the mother for her children as compared to a father. The general tendency—and not among Hindus alone—is to treat woman as sexually more virile. Polyandry has, therefore, been outlawed and erased in most parts of the world, while polygamy survives because of the dogmas of other religions.

Chapter 7

Enchantment and Intellect

In Hindu scriptures, like the Ramayana, the Mahabharata and the Vedas, the power of a woman is portrayed as a formidable and often transformative force. Whether through divine enchantment or intellect, women are shown as possessing the ability to shape the world around them. Characters, like Draupadi, Sita, Mohini, or Menaka, illustrate the immense, often unpredictable, power of the feminine. From charm to intellect, the power of women, whether seen in their relationships with men or in their spiritual pursuits, speaks to a deep and lasting influence that transcends societal boundaries.

Hindus might harbour differences of opinion regarding the nature of woman, but there appears a unanimity in their recognition of her power, and its worship. The word, *Shakti* is a synonym for woman, and its etymological meaning is power or energy. The active principle in the universe is described as feminine by the Shaktas, a powerful and widely distributed sect of Hindus which merits a separate discussion.

Some Hindu proverbs say that all strife in the world is caused by gold or women, predominantly women. The

Ramayana, like Homer's *Illiad*, has the abduction of a beautiful woman for its theme. However, the Mahabharata does not attribute the epic struggle and ensuing war between the Kauravas and the Pandavas to its central female character, Draupadi. Yet, common perceptions of Vyasa's itihasa tend to identify the Panchala princess and queen of the Pandavas as the cause of the Kurukshetra War. Duryodhana's jealousy of his dharmic cousins, his greed of dispossessing them anyhow and the internecine feud over inheriting the Kuru legacy were the main factors that started the enmity between the cousins. Yet, it certainly was aggravated by the attempted violation of Draupadi's honour in a fraudulent game of dice meant to dispossess the Pandavas and humiliate them to the maximum extent possible. However, Draupadi's passion for vengeance is not to be discounted—a fallacy born of popular folklore and modern and progressive distortions of the Mahabharata, along with monumental ignorance of the itihasa that Krishna (one of the names of Draupadi) alone was the cause of the holocaust. It was an unavoidable clash of dharma and adharma and of diametrically opposed values.

Numerous episodes can be found in the sacred Hindu literature on a woman's power in creating strife. One such popular tale is the destruction of the demons Sunda and Upasunda. These two *daitya* brothers were so devoted to each other that nothing could cause rift between them. They ate, played, slept and travelled together. Both brothers propitiated Brahma together and obtained a boon from him by which they could be destroyed by no one except themselves. Blessed with this boon, Sunda and Upasunda considered themselves as good as immortals since a quarrel between them was impossible.

Secured from harm inflicted by men or gods, the two daityas started doing what daityas do—tyrannising the three worlds.

They waged war on the devatas and drove them out of heaven. The three worlds and the beings thereon lived in fear of them. The full moon was forced to shine every night without waning, and the sun was ordered to exude just a pleasant, mild heat. Likewise, the gods of wind and rain had to dance attendance on the demon brothers. Many devatas of heaven were forced to become their menials. Reduced to wretchedness, the gods approached Brahma for redressing their grievances. The Creator, though the bestower of the boon, had no power to revoke it. He took counsel with celestial sages and started thinking of ways to destroy the aggressive demons. The obvious method of their destruction was by causing strife between the brothers and making them kill each other. But the affection between the brothers was legendary throughout the worlds, and no plan could be potent enough to cause strife between them.

At last, Narada, the celestial sage and a genius of dissention, told the distressed gods that a woman, and a woman alone, could make the brothers fight among themselves. The gods applauded his wisdom, and Brahma commanded Vishvakarma, the celestial sculptor, to produce a lovely nymph surpassing everything created before. Vishvakarma laboured for days and created Tilottama, the nymph of extraordinary form, gait and beauty. When she was presented in the court of Indra even austere sages were noticed behaving awkwardly. The gods blessed the beauty and sent her on the delicate but crucial mission.

When Sunda and Upasunda were engaged in the pleasures of a chase in a beautiful and wild forest, Tilottama appeared before them. Vayu, the deity of wind, skilfully blew her transparent clothes off her body while Kamadeva, the god of love, shot his sharpest shafts at the brothers. Both of them immediately fell in love with the nymph, and proposed to her. Tilottama, oozing coyness, said she was a strict monogamist and could bestow her favour only on one of them. They were to decide between themselves who should possess her. Each of the brothers pressed his own claim for her hand. The elder brother maintained that being senior in age, he had the right to marry the beauty. The younger daitya expressed astonishment that his brother should so blind himself by selfishness as to overlook the universal rule that youth and love always go together. Polite expression of claims soon degenerated into use of vile language which eventually led to blows. The two daitya brothers, otherwise secured by Brahma's boon, fiercely fell upon each other; the battle ending only with the death of both of them. Tilottama returned to heaven to report the success of her mission.

Similarly, eons ago, when the *asuras* were on the verge of overwhelming their cousins, the *devas*, Vishnu took on the form of an extremely beautiful woman, Mohini, to save the celestials from falling into permanent inferiority. Due to the curse of the powerful sage Durvasa, the devas and their king, Indra had lost their energy and become emaciated. To recoup their lost vigour and restore them to their lost position, Vishnu advised them to churn the milk ocean of heaven and feed on the *amrit* or ambrosia. However, churning the ocean was no mean task. The mountain Mandara had to be used as the churning stick and the emaciated gods could neither uproot the huge mountain nor twirl it in the ocean of milk. Hence, they requisitioned the help of their asura cousins who demanded half the nectar as a reward for their cooperation, a condition the gods had to agree to. The churning began with the celestial serpent Vasuki as the rope, with the devas on one side of Mount Mandara and the asuras on the other. When the nectar finally emerged on the surface of the milk ocean, the asuras made a grab for it. The demon world had no place for promises, and they were not going to part with any portion of the divine amrit. The helpless devas could only argue, but their cousins contemptuously ignored their protests.

Vishnu assumed the form of a dancing girl, Mohini, and appeared before them. The demons were so enamoured by the beauty and rhythmic gait of the dancer that the amrit was almost forgotten. Mohini sweetly smiled on the asuras and they cheered her with thunderous shouts. She gave a minor performance and they were so impressed by her beauty and perfection that they wanted her to mediate between them and the gods. She accepted the offer with a show of reluctance and declared that since she wanted justice to triumph, the nectar should be divided equally between the devas and asuras. Though both the devas and asuras cheered her, the asuras demanded the first share of the amrit. Upon this, Mohini said that as the devas were the younger of the two sets of cousins, they should be served first and asked the devas and asuras to be seated in two separate rows. When all were seated, she gracefully took the vessel containing the nectar and served the devas while keeping the lusting asuras enchanted with her charm and coy gestures. When the last deva was served, Mohini just vanished with the nectar!

The enraged asuras then fell upon the devas, but the latter, invigorated by the nectar they had obtained from Vishnu's intervention, not only defended themselves, but also vanquished the asuras, driving them away to *patala loka* (the nether regions). This was probably the first of the innumerable Devasura wars that were to follow.

Another beautiful episode illustrating the charm and power of women and incidental wondrous passion, new-born love, is told in both the Ramayana and Mahabharata. It is the tale of the youthful penitent Rishyasringa, son of Sage Vibhandaka.

Rishyasringa was mysteriously born of an antelope and was brought up by his father in a forest without his ever having a chance of seeing a woman. Thus, unaffected by the weakening influence of women, the youth enjoyed many occult powers, one of which was that he could bring rain down from the heavens by his mere presence.

The kingdom of Anga once had to endure a long, dreadful drought. Its king, Romapada, consulted all the learned Brahmins of his kingdom to propitiate the rain deity and save his kingdom from a devastating drought that was causing famine and pestilence. The learned men informed the king that the easiest way to bring rain was to get the young ascetic Rishyasringa from the forest to the capital of Anga. It was well known that Rishyasringa was devoted to the forest and his hermitage, and no ordinary offer could bring him to Anga. A wise man then said that a beautiful woman would probably be able to entice him to the city. But, fearing the wrath of the chaste youth and his equally mighty father, Sage Vibhandaka, no nymph in the kingdom would undertake the hazardous mission. After much persuasion, an old bawd agreed to go to the forest leading an army of youthful heart ravishers.

The bawd camped on the forest outskirts with her company, and sent her lovely daughter, who was adept in the game of seduction, to Rishyasringa's hermitage. The young courtesan reached the hermitage at an opportune moment when Rishyasringa was alone, his father having gone out to gather berries for their meal. The charming woman, with her smiles and honeyed words, her gait, poise and figure, offered him fruits and drink. Her touch and caress raised unknown emotions in the man, and when he was thoroughly worked up, she slipped away from the hermitage and returned to her mother.

Shortly after, Vibhandaka returned to the hermitage and noticed a remarkable change in his son. The melancholic youth sat in the hermitage yard gazing vacantly at the sky, unmindful of his sacred duties, and sunk in deep thought. Vibhandaka spoke to his son, 'Why art thou, my beloved son, sunk in melancholy thoughts, and distressed? Tell me who came here today?' Rishyasringa answered:

> Dear father, when you were away, a chaste and lovely youth came here. He was resplendent as a god, of correct stature and build, had long tresses and eyes like lotus blossoms. On his snow-white neck gleamed a runnel-shaped light. And beneath the neck he had two globes—most delightful to touch. He had a slender waist and large round hips and from his garb a gold girdle gleamed forth. On his wrists and ankles, he wore jingling gold, and he moved about with the ease and grace of a swan in a lake.
>
> His face was the embodiment of light and his words were like nectar to my soul. When the gentle breeze fanned him, scents more fragrant than those of forest flowers filled the air. His black shining tresses, parted in two, bound in golden braid and adorned with flowers, hung down in folds, curling on the forehead. His ears were decked with many fair things, in colour as the feathers of the peacock and the *Chakravaka*.
>
> The beautiful youth was playful as a fawn; he took me by the tresses, clasped me in a close embrace and pressed his lips to mine. And O! Father, I shuddered with delight never known before! And then suddenly he disappeared in the woods. Father dear, I cannot live without that delightful young man. Pray, take me to the hermitage in which he lives; I will do the penance he does and live the chaste life he leads. My soul burns to have a sight of the godlike youth.

His son's words disturbed Vibhandaka who feared that some evil spirit in a lovely shape had appeared before his son to lure him from his pious activities. He set out on a vain hunt for the devil and returned baffled to the hermitage and warned his son to be on guard against the wiles of roving fays. However, all this advice was lost on the young penitent. For once again, when Vibhandaka was away from the hermitage, the enchanting courtesan appeared before Rishyasringa. The youth was so impatiently waiting for her that as soon as he saw her, he said, 'Let us depart immediately to thy hermitage before my father returns.'

The courtesan, well pleased with this eagerness of her victim, took him to her mother and the bawd triumphantly proceeded to her city and presented the penitent to Romapada. Rishyasringa, already charmed by the fair women of the city, was further honoured by the king who gave his most beautiful daughter, Shanta, in marriage to the young sage. The penitent forgot all about his father and the hermitage and settled down in Anga. The long-awaited rain came, and plenty ruled the land.

The ire of Vibhandaka had, however, to be counted with. This mighty sage learnt of his chaste son's seduction, and, infuriated, set off to Romapada's capital to reduce it to ashes by his scorching anger. Foreseeing such a contingency, the king had already given strict instructions to all his subjects and state officers to treat the sage with the utmost hospitality and reverence wherever he might appear. On his way to Anga, Vibhandaka was so courteously received and lavishly entertained by the people and, on reaching the capital, by the king himself, that he forgot his hostility to Romapada and reconciled to his son's seduction and marriage. In fact, Vibhandaka went back to his hermitage blessing the king, his daughter, her husband, and the people of Anga.

Ancient stories often delight in the theme of the power of

woman deployed for evil, and have enjoyed popularity over time. The notion is that there is nothing a woman will not stoop to, once she sets her heart to it. The Mahabharata both extols a woman's virtues and bluntly proclaims the power of her wile and guile.

As words of truth she praises lies,
As arrant falsehood truth decries,
And mistress of deceptive sleight,
Treats right as wrong, and wrong as right.
All powers which wizard demons old,
Of whom such wondrous tales are told,
Displayed the gods themselves to cheat,
To blind, elude, and so defeat,
Such fascinating powers we find
In artful women all combined;
So skilfully they men deceive,
So well their viewless nets can weave,
That few whom these syrens clasp
Can soon escape their grasp.

Living amidst such wily charmers, it is no wonder that men often go astray. But, great is the man who successfully resists the degenerating influence of a woman! By denying themselves the pleasures women afford, men are said to have become gods and even displaced Indra. However, Indra is ever on the lookout for such mighty ascetics only to bring about their downfall. His favourite method of degenerating such pure souls is to send one of the beautiful dancing nymphs of his court to display her charms and seduce the ascetic at an opportune moment. This would often work well, for as the sages themselves admit, there are few strong men in the world who can resist the charms of a beautiful woman. The well-known episode of Vishwamitra and

Menaka narrated here is a typical example.

King Vishwamitra, humbled in a battle by Vasishtha, decided to give up his Kshatriya life to become a Brahmin and propitiated Brahma by severe austerities. By the accumulated virtue of his penances, Vishwamitra became powerful enough to challenge Brahma and create a parallel world of his own. While the *rajarshi* (royal ascetic) was thus engaged in the practice of austerities, Indra grew suspicious of his intentions. To safeguard his own throne, he sent the lovely nymph Menaka to tempt Vishwamitra and lead him astray from his severe tapasya. Menaka appeared by the riverside when the sage was having his ablutions and started playing about in the sand bed of the river. A gentle breeze waved apart her scanty clothes showing a most symmetrical body. The sage, a good connoisseur of figure and poise in his Kshatriya days, slipped from his resolve in a moment of weakness. He fell for the charms of the celestial courtesan, gave up his austerities and enjoyed conjugal bliss with Menaka.

However, after living with Menaka for some years, Vishwamitra awoke to a sense of his duties, sent the nymph away and returned to the forest to continue his austerities. But, the union was not without fruit, for Menaka was pregnant with his child when she was driven away. Of her was born Shakuntala, later the wife of Dushyanta, one of the emperors of the Bharata race.

Hindus consider celibacy as conducive to the attainment of exceptional physical and occult powers. Bhisma, one of the greatest warriors of the Mahabharata age, was a strict celibate. Hanuman of the Ramayana age is incomparable in physical might, mental astuteness and spiritual endowment; celibacy is a prime reason of his powers. This praise of the celibate and of celibacy, however, has not been carried overboard in Hindu scriptures and literature. Greater than Bhisma was Krishna, a married man. Hanuman's lord and master was Rama, though both Rama and Hanuman are worshipped.

With their love of exaggeration, some writers—and not Hindu or Indian alone—have caricatured the power of woman for evil. On the contrary, Hindus generally have sound respect for woman as man's indispensable partner in life, and have recognised her power in all fields of human activities. Sex as a mysterious, all-pervading force has its supporters as well as opponents in Hindu society.

While asceticism is held as a man's way to obtain occult powers, a woman is generally considered incapable of attaining spiritual heights by the practice of austerities because of her supposed weakness of mind and intellect. Though a part of popular belief and folklore, this is far from reality. There have been quite a few instances of women achieving greatness through asceticism. Uma (Goddess Parvati), won Shiva's grace and married him by the severity of her penance. Amba of the Mahabharata age made Shiva appear before her with her tapasya (austerities) and obtained a boon from Him by which she brought about the destruction of Bhisma, albeit in her next birth as Shikhandi. However, these are exceptions rather than the rule. The power of a woman is primarily of a worldly nature. Yet, there is one method by which a woman can attain occult powers denied even to man. This is by her *pativratya*—absolute devotion to her husband.

In the well-known episode of Satyavan and Savitri, the virtuous lady reclaimed the soul of her dead husband from Yama, the deity of death, and revived him. Damayanti, wife of Nala, used the scorching power of her pativratya to burn to ashes a hunter who approached her with evil intent. Sita lived in the fortress of Lanka protected by the occult powers obtained through her devotion to her husband Rama. Most striking of all is the story of Anasuya, wife of sage Atri and the model of domestic virtue, who converted Brahma, Vishnu and Shiva into harmless babies when the three great gods went to tempt her.

There is also the episode of a dutiful Brahmin housewife on whom the rage of a most potent learned sage was ineffective. One day, a sage learned in the Vedas was meditating under a tree when a crane on a branch above soiled his head. The sage looked upwards in rage, and scorched by his anger, the bird fell down dead from the tree. Though this cooled the hermit's rage, he repented his unreasonable anger, realising that it is the nature of cranes to relieve themselves from the branches of trees. To expiate his sinful anger which destroyed a life, the sage went on begging for alms in the village. In the first house he approached, he addressed himself to the busy housewife asking for food. The lady was engaged in her domestic duties; her husband was expected home, so everything had to be ready before his arrival. She naturally told the sage to wait till the arrival of her husband. The quick-tempered sage could not understand the attitude of a woman who asked an ascetic like him to wait for an ordinary individual like her husband. He uttered a mighty curse to destroy her but was surprised to find that the curse, always so potent, had no effect on the lady. The housewife smiled and informed the hungry sage that she was no crane to be withered away by his anger. Further edifying him, she told him that for a married woman her husband was greater than all the sages of the fourteen worlds and the thirty-three gods. Thus instructed in the prime duties of women, the learned sage had his pride humbled. His rage cooled, and he went away blessing the lady.

Sex is not the only power of a woman. The power of matrons over their irretractable sons has been narrated in many books. Kunti, mother of the five Pandava princes, brought up her sons with matriarchal authority. Gandhari, mother of the Kauravas, was also a woman of extraordinary ability, and her independent son Duryodhana submitted to her wishes at times, though not to his father's.

In medieval times, matriarchal power had declined considerably, but mothers in Hindu society have always been women of exceptional courage and ability who have ruled not only their sons, but husbands, too. However, the authority of mothers in modern India is confined mainly to social matters. It is not uncommon to hear of neglected mothers complaining of their ungrateful sons. Such complaints, howsoever modern they might seem today, were also present even in ancient times. The passage below shows that these stories are at least as old as the age of the Mahabharata. Says the wise Vidura:

> These six always despise those who earlier had done them good: disciples despise the teacher when their instruction is ended; the sons, the mother when they are married; the lover, the woman when his love is dead; they whose business has been carried through, him that does it; he that has crossed the waste of the sea, the ship; a healed sick, the leech.

The power of a daughter over her doting father is illustrated in the tale of Devayani. This young lady was the only daughter of Sage Shukracharya, the preceptor of the asuras. Shukracharya was a learned sage who knew the Sanjeevani mantra that could bring the dead back to life. He was so devoted to Devayani that she often behaved like a spoilt child. To please her, he even taught Kacha the art of reviving the dead and brought about ruin upon his own proteges, the asuras. Kacha, son of Brihaspati, the preceptor of the devas (gods), had been secretly sent by the gods to become a disciple of the preceptor of the asuras to learn the mantra of bringing the dead back to life. Until then, only the asuras had this power, thanks to their guru, and their dead could be revived in every battle with the gods while the latter's numbers kept dwindling with every clash.

Devayani had fallen in love with Kacha and proposed to him, but he had refused to marry her. Moreover, he returned to the gods after having learnt the secret from Shukracharya, and used his knowledge against the asuras to help the devas prevail in future Devasura wars.

Later, Devayani had picked up a quarrel with Sharmishtha, daughter of Vrishaparva, the king of the asuras. Sharmishtha called Devayani the daughter of her father's slave. Devayani had gone weeping to her father and demanded to know if he was really the slave of the asura king. Shukracharya told her that he was far from being the slave of the asura king, since he was the king's preceptor and as such, his master. Devayani now told Shukracharya to prove this assertion by bringing over Sharmishtha as a slave to her. The old doting father immediately proceeded to the asura ruler, Vrishaparva and threatened to leave his service if he would not give princess Sharmishtha as a slave to Devayani. The distressed king made enquiries and found out the reason for this extraordinary demand of the Brahmin. He reprimanded his daughter for insulting Devayani and commanded her to serve Devayani as a slave. However, this trouble did not end there. Devayani married King Yayati, and Sharmishtha often waited on Yayati and Devayani. While Devayani undoubtedly had a stronger will, Sharmishtha had better looks. The outcome was what could be expected of such a situation.

A woman is essentially an emotional being and her greatness is believed to be in the direction of her sentiments. However, there have been exceptions to this rule. The Hindu scriptures mention several women distinguished for their vast learning. Sulabha was such a woman. She was a famous philosopher and scholar, said to have instructed King Janaka (Sita's father) of Mithila—no mean intellectual himself—in metaphysics. So vast was Sulabha's learning that no man could be found equal to the task of marrying her, and she had to lead a single life.

The power of women in Hindu texts reveals an enduring and multifaceted force—one that challenges traditional boundaries and shapes both personal and cosmic destinies. Whether through allure, wisdom, or moral strength, women wield their influence with subtlety and depth, often swaying the course of history and fate itself. These texts highlight the significance of female power in Hindu tradition. They show how women have been respected for their strength and complexity, roles that continue to influence their position in society even today.

Chapter 8

The Poetry of Love

Hindu texts—ranging from scriptures to epics and literary works—provide rich, often contrasting portrayals of women: as paragons of virtue, as embodiments of love, or as symbols of devotion. As we explore the poetry and literature that have shaped these representations, we gain insight into the roles women were expected to play in relation to men, love, and society. These poetic depictions—often tender and emotional—offer a glimpse into how ancient culture both revered and constrained women, illustrating their complexities not only as figures of devotion but as powerful agents of love and desire within the confines of societal norms.

Devotion and love have been inspiring poetry in the Hindu literary world. The two emotions meet on a higher plane, and some of the great ancient poets of love were also great devotees. The blending of love and religious fervour in mysticism merits treatment in far greater detail than the scope of this work permits; we shall, therefore, confine ourselves to mundane love.

Hindu writers categorise cardinal emotions into nine; of these, *Shringara* (amorousness) is considered one of the most important. This emotion is given a unique place in the fine arts, and no individual is considered perfect without an adequate experience of shringara. This brings us to the episode of the sage and philosopher Adi Sankara, wherein his claim to *sanyasa* as the highest path for dharmic resuscitation was challenged by Ubhaya Bharati because of his ignorance of the master passion. Ubhaya Bharati was the wife of the renowned *Purva Mimamsa* scholar Mandana Misra (who Sankara had overcome in *shaastrartha* or scholarly debate). Sankara's reputation for erudition was great and his followers and disciples spoke of him as 'all-knowing.' Ubhaya Bharati's husband too had accepted his eminence and was ready to take sanyasa to join Sankara's quest. But Bharati's question was equally potent. How could Sankara, a celibate having no knowledge of shringara, be truly all-knowing? The sage-philosopher was honest enough to admit his ignorance of this branch of human experience, and asked for six months to gain an experience of the same. It is said that Sankara was initiated into the pleasant mysteries through his entering the body of a deceased king, or by deep contemplation and discourse.

Arguably, most Hindu love stories have their origin in the Ramayana and Mahabharata. The former could also be considered a continuous love story with Sita's love for her husband forming an important part of the saga. The delightful love stories of Nala and Damayanti, Satyavan and Savitri, Dushyanta and Shakuntala and numerous others are found in the Mahabharata. Further, Draupadi, the common wife of the five Pandava princes, plays a leading role in this epic.

Later, Sanskrit poets wrote love poems and romances borrowing their themes mainly from the epics. However, no Hindu poet has been able to depict love, especially maiden love, in so exquisite a manner as Kalidasa in his play, *Abhijnana Shakuntala*. Though the original story is found in the Mahabharata, Kalidasa made considerable changes in the plot and setting in his adaptation for *natya* (play), and the play, as it stands today, differs substantially from the original.

The opening scene of the play is set in the forest hermitage of Kanva, Shakuntala's foster father. While hunting in the forest, King Dushyanta strays into the hermitage and sees Shakuntala and her two companions, Priyamvada and Anasuya, watering the flower plants of the hermitage. On beholding Shakuntala, the King exclaims to himself:

In palaces such charms are rarely ours;
The woodland plants outshine the garden flowers.

Not wishing to intrude, Dushyanta hides himself behind a tree and watches the playful maidens. The girls, after watering the plants, rest in the shade of a tree. Shakuntala, reclining on a lawn, asks her friend Anasuya to loosen her bark girdle as Priyamvada had tied it tightly. Priyamvada is in no mood to accept the charge and retorts: 'Why do you lay the blame on me? Blame rather your own youthfulness which imparts fulness to your bosom.' The King tells himself:

A most just observation!
This youthful form, whose swelling charms
By the bark's knotted tissue are concealed
Like some fair bud close folded in its sheath,
Gives not to view the blooming of its beauty.

Priyamvada compares Shakuntala, sitting near a slender Kesara tree, to a blossoming creeper twining around the young tree.

The hiding Dushyanta was delighted with the simile and adds in approval:

Her ruddy lips vie with the opening bud;
Her graceful arms are as the twining stalks;
And her whole form is radiant with the flow
Of youthful beauty as the tree with blossom.

A bee hovers round Shakuntala's face and the maiden in annoyance tries to drive it away. The King already drunk with love of Shakuntala speaks in envy of the circling bee:

Wherever the bee his eager onset plies,
Now here, now there, she darts her kindling eyes,
Ah! Happy bee! How boldly dost thou try
To steal the lustre from her sparkling eye;
And in thy circling movements hover near
To murmur tender secrets in her ear;
Or as she coyly waves her hand, to sip
Voluptuous nectar from her lower lip!
While rising doubts my heart's fond hopes destroy,
Thou dost the fulness of her charms enjoy.

Dushyanta, now, shows himself to the maidens. They are somewhat surprised by his sudden appearance, but he works himself into their confidence with his easy, royal manners. He tries to drag Shakuntala into conversation, but the bashful maiden, much agitated by her own inexplicable interest in the intruder, dares not speak. The King notices her embarrassment with some measure of satisfaction. For,

Although she mingles not her words with mine,
Yet do her listening ear drink in my speech
Although her eye shrinks from my ardent gaze,
No form but mine attracts its timid glances.

After a brief conversation, the King leaves. While parting, Shakuntala pretends that a blade of grass has pricked her foot, and she turns apparently to pick the blade but actually to steal a glance at her departing lover. As he departs, Dushyanta mutters to himself:

My limbs drawn onward leave my heart behind,
Like silken pennon borne against the wind.

On his return to his hunting camp in the forest, the King describes Shakuntala to his friend Madhavya in these words:

Man's all-wise Maker, wishing to create
A faultless form, whose matchless symmetry
Should far transcend Creation's choicest works,
Did call together by his mighty will,
And garner up in his eternal mind,
A bright assemblage of all lovely things
And then, as in a picture, fashion them
Into one perfect and ideal form
Such the divine, the wondrous prototype,
When her fair shape was moulded into being again,
This peerless maid is like a fragrant flower,
Whose perfumed breath has never been diffused;
A tender bud, that no profaning hand
Has dared to sever from its parent stalk;
A gem of priceless water, just released
Pure and unblemished from its glittering bed.
Or may the maiden haply be compared
To sweetest honey, that no mortal lip
Has sipped; or rather, to the mellowed fruit
Of virtuous actions in some former birth,
Now brought to full perfection? Lives the man
Whom bounteous heaven has destined to espouse her?

The comically inclined Madhavya does not understand the King's passion for a hermit's daughter in preference to the accomplished women of the palace. However, he admits that a King satiated by the pleasures of his harem may take a passing fancy for a rustic maiden, just as a city-dweller overfed on dainties may taste a jungle berry for a change. Nonetheless, Madhavya is curious to know if Shakuntala was responsive to the advances of Dushyanta. The lovelorn prince is doubtful, but had discerned some hopeful signs; for,

> She did look towards me, though she quick withdrew
> Her stealthy glance when she met my gaze;
> She smiled upon me sweetly, but disguised
> With maiden grace the secret of her smiles;
> Coy love was half unveiled; then sudden checked
> By modesty, left half to be divined.

Not only that, but more:

> Scarce had the fair one from my presence passed,
> When suddenly without apparent cause,
> She stopped, and counterfeiting pain, exclaimed,
> 'My foot is wounded by this prickly grass.'
> Then glancing at me tenderly, she feigned
> Another charming pretext for delay,
> Pretending that a bush had caught her robe,
> And turned as if to disentangle it.

Dushyanta is too overcome with love of Shakuntala to leave the forest without meeting the maiden again. He finds an excuse to leave his camp and seek the welfare of the hermits in the neighbourhood. Musing to himself and dreaming of the fair maid of the woods, he wanders over the haunts of the maidens hoping to come across Shakuntala. Nor is he disappointed, for he finds Shakuntala in the company of her two maids, reclining on a rock strewn with flowers. She looks distressed, and her garb is in disorder, and the two maids are fanning her. The King, dazed by the beauty of her youthful, lovely limbs and the partly exposed heaving bosom, retains sufficient sense to hide himself. He is anxious to know the cause of Shakuntala's distress. The weather undoubtedly is warm, but Dushyanta cannot believe that a maiden brought up to bear that climate could fall ill because of the sun. He hopefully fears that her troubles are nearer the heart than the skin.

The maiden's spotless bosom is overspread
With cooling balsam; on her slender arm
Her only bracelet, twined with lotus-stalks,
Hangs loose and withered; her recumbent form
Expresses languor. Never could noon day sun
Inflict such fair disorder on a maid,
No, love, and love alone is here to blame.

Unable to restrain his interest and expectation, the King stealthily listens to the conversation between Shakuntala and her companions. Shakuntala looks much confused because she was keeping a secret which she dare not share with even Priyamvada and Anasuya from whom she had never concealed anything. However, her clever companions, noticing her strange behaviour following her meeting with Dushyanta, rightly conclude that he is the cause of her distress. After much coaxing and persuasion, they wrench the guarded secret from Shakuntala. Once the secret is out, the maiden completely surrenders to her companions' mercy: 'You must consent, my dears, to contrive some means by which I may find favour with the King. Else, you will have to, before long, assist in my funeral.' The three fair conspirators then put their heads together and decide to pen a love note to the King; Priyamvada and Anasuya approve of the following lines Shakuntala has composed:

I know not the secret thy bosom conceals,
Thy form is not near me to gladden my sight;
But sad is the tale that my fever reveals
Of the love that consumes me by day and by night.

The King could not bear it any longer. He comes out of his hiding place and boldly advances towards the confused maidens. He tells Shakuntala:

Nay, Love does but warm thee, fair maiden; thy frame
Only droops like the bud in the glare of the noon;
But me he consumes with a pitiless flame,
As the beams of the day-star destroy the pale moon.

The King, thus, openly and unexpectedly proclaims his love for Shakuntala; her clever companions drag her into conversation with the King. Shakuntala, becoming bolder, rebukes her companions for detaining the King with their idle talk while the ladies of the royal harem anxiously wait for the King. Dushyanta notices Shakuntala's concern for the ladies of his palace and tells her:

Sweet maiden, banish from thy mind the thought
That I could love another. Thou dost reign
Supreme without a rival in my heart
And I am thine alone; disown me not,
Else must I die a second deadlier death
Killed by thy words, as erst by Kama's shafts.

The two companions of Shakuntala now come up with an excuse and depart, leaving the lovers together. A confused Shakuntala tries to stop them, but they laughingly go their way, consigning her to the care of her royal lover. Dushyanta, at last, finds the great opportunity he had been looking for, and addresses the maiden with passionate love. Shakuntala, now, faces a conflict between duty and personal inclinations. She is genuinely troubled as the King was infringing the rules of decorum.

However, Dushyanta has a ready answer to support his behaviour:

In Indra's heaven, so at least it's said,
No nuptial rites prevail, nor is the bride
Led to the altar by her future spouse;
But all in secret does the bridegroom plight
His troth and each unto the other vow
Mutual allegiance. Such espousals, too,
Are authorised on earth, and many daughters
Of royal saints thus wedded to their lords
Have still received their fathers' benison.

Before things could go further, Gautami, the venerable matron of the hermitage, comes on the scene, and Dushyanta goes into hiding. The persevering King got his chance later as the resistance of the maiden broke; he was united to her in a Gandharva rite (a secret form of love marriage without witnesses or officiating priest, recognised as valid for kings).

Kalidasa's description of Shakuntala's behaviour on the dawning of love is typical of maidens of the higher orthodox classes of Hindus even today. Girls among the orthodox class are brought up under strict parental authority and from time immemorial, it has been considered immodest for a girl to express her love for a man by word of mouth. A girl's approval or disapproval of a man is usually understood by her general behaviour. Only when hard pressed by her mother or cornered by her lady companions will a maiden let her secret out. Discerning parents and elderly ladies usually discover a girl's inclinations by watching her behaviour in the presence of her suitor and in his absence, that is, when they wish to ascertain her opinion in the matter. However, in most of the arranged matches, the girls have little or no say. When a marriage proposal is finally accepted, the shy bride-to-be becomes a constant object of teasing by her girl friends and relatives who unnecessarily drag the bridegroom's name into the conversation. Upon this, the modest maiden often leaves them in ostentatious disgust.

Another scene typical of present-day customs in Kalidasa's play is Shakuntala's departure from the hermitage to her husband's palace. Dushyanta, as the reader is probably aware, never returned to the hermitage once he took leave of Shakuntala. Shakuntala began to show signs of pregnancy and her foster father Kanva decided to send her to her husband's palace with two hermits and a matron. The departing of a newly-married girl to the house of her husband is a matter of much lament among the Hindus. The girl herself is greatly distressed by the fact that she is leaving the home of her childhood for a distant place to live among strangers. The parents who had pampered the child all along are also much affected by her departure. The mother usually bursts into sobs while the father, as a man, bears the bereavement with a show of fortitude, although his eyes shed tears. The pathos of the scene is much heightened if the girl is their only daughter.

Shakuntala, though the foster child of Kanva, was the pet of the hermits, and even the animals of the hermitage loved her. She had grown up with the plants, trees and animals of the hermitage and was greatly attached to them, and to the hermits and her two young companions.

Finally, Shakuntala bids farewell to the home of her childhood. Kanva, though a hermit, and as such, detached from domestic sentiments, is much distressed. When Shakuntala appears before him dressed for her journey to the big city, the old sage could hardly speak. All that gushed forth was:

This day my loved one leaves me, and my heart
Is heavy with its grief: the stream of sorrow
Choked at the source, repress my faltering voice.
I have no words to speak; mine eyes are dimmed
By the dark shadow of the thoughts that rise
Within my soul. If such the force of grief
In an old hermit parted from his nurseling,
What anguish must the stricken parent feel
Bereft forever of an only daughter!

Kanva blesses Shakuntala and addresses the trees and plants of the hermitage that stood still, as if stunned by the impending bereavement:

Hear me, ye trees that surround our hermitage!
Shakuntala ne'er moistened in the stream
Her own parched lips, till she had fondly poured
Its purest water on your thirsty roots;
And oft, when she would fain have decked her hair
With your thick-clustering blossom, in her love
She robbed you not even of a single flower.
Her highest joy was ever to behold
The early glory of your opening buds
Oh, then, dismiss her with a kind farewell!
This very day she quits her father's home,
To seek the palace of her wedded lord.

(The note of the *koyal* is heard)
Hark! Heard'st thou not the answer of the trees,
Our sylvan sisters, warbled in the note
Of the melodious *koyal*? They dismiss
Their dear Shakuntala with loving wishes.

Shakuntala takes farewell of the trees and lovingly lingers in a jasmine bower which she used to water daily with great care. The animals and birds of the hermitage sense tragedy and they watch Shakuntala. Priyamvada speaks:

In sorrow for thy loss, the herd of deer
Forget to browse; the peacock on the lawn
Ceases its dance; the very trees around us
Shed their pale leaves, like tears upon the ground.

With great effort, Shakuntala bids every one farewell. She consigns her jasmine bower to the care and protection of her two friends Priyamvada and Anasuya. Both the maidens burst into tears and ask their beloved Shakuntala: 'And to whose charge do you leave us, dearest? Who will care for us when you are gone?'

Old Kanva, himself in tears, makes a brave attempt to pacify the girls and asks them to rejoice on the occasion of the bride's departure for her husband's house. While leaving, Shakuntala feels herself drawn by her clothes and looks around to find her pet fawn endearingly clinging to her, as if imploring to follow her. She desperately tells the fawn:

> My poor little fawn, do you ask to follow an unhappy wretch who hesitates not to desert her companions? When your mother died, soon after your birth, I took her place, and reared you with my own hand; and now that your second mother is about to leave you, who will care for you? My father, do

become a mother to her. My child, go back, and be a daughter
to my father.

Kanva replies:

Weep not, my daughter, check the gathering tear
That lurks beneath thine eyelid, ere it flow
And weaken thy resolve; be firm and true-
True to yourself and me; the path of life
Will lead over hill and plain, over rough and smooth
And all must feel the steepness of the way;
Though rugged be thy course, press boldly on.

The party now leaves the hermitage. Kanva and Shakuntala's friends accompany her to the nearest stream on the way, where, after much expression of grief, they embrace Shakuntala and take final farewell of her. Kanva gives his daughter this parting advice:

Honour your betters; ever be respectful
To those above you; and should others share
Your husband's love, never yield yourself a prey
To jealousy; but ever be a friend,
A loving friend, to those who rival you
In his affections. Should your wedded lord
Treat you with harshness, you must never be
Harsh in return, but patient and submissive.
Be to your menials courteous, and to all
Placed under you, considerate and kind.
Be never self-indulgent, but avoid
Excess in pleasure; and when fortune smiles
Be not puffed up. Thus, to your husband's house
Will you a blessing prove, and not a curse.

Kanva at last tears himself apart from his daughter and walks homeward. His sorrow is not unmixed with a sense of relief. While walking back, he muses:

A daughter is a loan—a precious jewel
Lent to a parent till her husband claims her.
And now to her rightful lord and master
I have delivered her, my burdened soul
Is lightened, and I seem to breathe more freely.

This scene is enacted, though not with the same poignancy, in every orthodox Hindu household even today when after marriage the bride is taken away to her husband's home. Evidently, the mental state of a Hindu bride leaving her parent's house after marriage is quite different from that of the merry European or American girl going out on her honeymoon.

Second in renown to Kalidasa was Bhavabhuti, a great poet in his time. Though he wrote plays like Kalidasa, he is not widely known as a love poet; he is a master in describing the weird and the terrible. But, Bhavabhuti can be tender and lyrical, too. The description of Madhava meeting Malati in *Malatimadhava* is worth quoting:

One day by curiosity impelled
I sought the temple of the god of love.
There I roved to and fro, glancing around,
Till weary with my wandering, I stood
Close to a pool that laved a Vakul tree,
In the courtyard and precincts of the temple.
The tree's sweet blossoms wooed a swarm of bees
To cull their nectar; and in idleness
To while away the time, I laid me down
And gathered round me all the fallen flowers

To weave a garland, when there issued forth
From the interior fane, a lovely maid.
Stately her gait, yet graceful as the banner
Waved by victorious Love over prostrate men
Her garb with fitting ornaments embellished
Bespoke a youthful princess, her attendants
Moved proudly as became their noble rank;
She seemed a treasury of all graces,
Or beauty's storehouse, where collected shone
A bright assemblage of all fairest things
To frame a perfect form; or rather she
The very guardian Goddess of Love's shrine;
Or did the great creator mould her charms
From some of Nature's loveliest materials
The moon, the lotus-stalk, and sweetest nectar?
I looked and in an instant both my eyes
Seemed bathed with rapture and inmost soul
Was drawn towards her unresistingly,
Like iron by the iron loving magnet.

In his romance, *Kadambari*, Banabhatta, the poet, describes women interestingly. Though his wild exaggeration and farfetched similes may sound strange to English readers, Banabhatta's style was exceedingly popular in his time and is imitated by Indian writers even now as an orthodox form. Besides, what may appear strained and even fantastic in the English translation, will sound almost natural in Sanskrit because of the peculiarities and associations of the language. The following description of a Chandala (keepers of cremation grounds) maiden who appeared before a king in his court will be of interest as typical of Banabhatta's style:

She seemed by the darkness of her hue to imitate Krishna when he guilefully assumed a woman's attire to take away the *Amrita* (nectar) seized by the asuras. She was, as it were, a doll of sapphire walking alone; and over the blue garment which reached to her ankle, there fell a veil of red silk, like evening sunshine falling on a blue lotus. The circle of her cheek was whitened by the ear-ring that hung from one ear, like the face of night inlaid with the rays of the rising moon; she had a tawny *tilaka* of *gorochana,* as if it were a third eye like Parvati in a mountaineer's attire, after the fashion of the garb of Shiva.

She was like Shri (the goddess of beauty and wealth), darkened by the sapphire glory of Narayana reflected on the robe of her breasts; or like Rati, stained by smoke which rose as Madana was burnt by the fire of a wrathful Shiva; or like Yamuna, fleeing in fear of being drawn along by the ploughshare of wild Balarama; or from the rich lac that turned her lotus feet into budding shoots, like Durga, with her feet crimsoned by the blood of the asura Mahisha she had just trampled upon.

Her nails were rosy from the pink glow of her fingers; the mosaic pavement seemed too hard for her touch, and she came forward placing her feet like tender twigs upon the ground. Like autumn, she opened her lotus eyes; like the rainy season, she had cloudy tresses; like the circle of the Malaya hills she was wreathed with sandal; like the zodiac, she was decked with starry gems; like Shri, she had the fairness of a lotus in her hand; like the moon she entranced the heart; like a forest she was endowed with living beauty; like the child of a goddess she was claimed by no tribe; like sleep she charmed the eyes; as a lotus pool in a wood is troubled by elephants, so was she dimmed by her Matanga birth; like a spirit, she might not

> be touched; like a letter she gladdened the eyes alone; like the blossoms of spring, she lacked the *jati* flower; her slender waist, like the line of Love's bow, could be spanned by the hands; with her curly hair, she was like the Lakshmi of the Yaksha King of Alakapuri.

Another classical romance which has much literary merit and is popular among the Hindus is *Dasa Kumara Charita* or the *Story of Ten Princes* by Dandi. Here is a description of the belle of Avanti, one of Dandi's heroines:

> She shone, a creation of Love. Yes, Love had fashioned a paragon of a woman, as if he wished, in wistful memory of charm, to image forth this duplicate. He formed her feet from the sweetness of two autumn lilies in his own pleasure pool; the languid grace of her gait from the course of a wanton swan down a long lake in a planted garden; her calves from a quiver curve; her comely thighs from the shapeliness of two plantain stems by the door of a summer house; her generous hips from the sweep of conquering chariots; her navel (which seemed an eddy in the Ganges' stream) from the semblance of an early flowering ornamental lotus bud; her three plicatures from the ordered rise of a palace stairway; her capillation from the lovely sheen of bees that cling from Love's bowstring; her breasts from the beauty of two full golden bowls; arms from the delicacy of vines in a bower; her neck from the symmetry of a conch of victory; her lip, like the *bimba* fruit, from the redness of mango flowers that maidens fondly wear above the ear; her sweet smile from the splendour of Love's flower-arrows; her every word from the witchery of the soft song of Love's first messenger, the cuckoo; the breath of her sigh from the gentleness of the southern breeze, leader of all Love's soldiers;

> her eyes from the pride of two fishes figured on his conquering banner; her brows from the curve of his bow; her face from the spotless enchantment of Love's first friend, the moon; her hair from the similitude of a pet peacock's fan. Then he bathed the image in sandal paste, mingled with essence of honey and musk, and polished it with camphor dust.

This is a typical descriptions of heroines by some Sanskrit writers. For their love of exaggerating their heroines' charms, the writers use fantastic similes and metaphors. Few descriptions of a presentable girl are considered complete without dragging in the lotus, the lily, the *bimba* fruit, the moon, Love's bows and arrows and the better looking of the goddesses of the pantheon. This style is often imitated by present-day writers and there is a large number of readers who appreciate it.

The amorously inclined Hindu poets followed a literary fad of composing eight stanzas or verses to honour a beautiful lady or describe love impersonally, and these stanzas or verses are called *Shringara Ashtaka* (the eight chapters or episodes of love). We shall quote a few verses from the *Ashtaka* of Mayura. This *Ashtaka* is said to have brought upon the poet the curse of leprosy. The poet, so goes the story, was so overcome by the beauty of his own daughter that he described her in a lascivious manner in the *Ashtaka*. Enraged at the incestuous leaning of her father, the young lady cursed him to become a leper. Mayura repented his unholy passion and to expiate the sinful *Ashtaka*, he composed a *Shataka* (a composition of one hundred verses) in praise of Surya (the sun deity) who, pleased with the hundred verses, cured the poet.

Some of the verses of the *Mayurashtaka* are as follows:

> Who is this timid gazelle? Why has this gazelle with a burden of firm, swelling breasts,

> With roving glance, and slender waist, gone forth from the frightened herd?
> Drunk with love, unsteady of steps, she totters as if fallen from the temple of a rutting lord of elephants.
> Beholding this divine form, adorned with beautiful, well-shaped limbs, even an old man becomes youthful as Kama.
> Who is this beauty, her face shining like the full moon, advancing along the path, in the full bloom of youth,
> Drunk with love and sleep, her eyes rolling, her lips full and red like the ripe *bimba* fruits,
> Her locks in bewildering disorder, wounded by her lover's nails, and torn to pieces by his teeth?
> Has this fair maiden been loved by a demon, and has he, imitating tiger sport, enjoyed her?
> Has this maiden been ravished, and then let go? With wandering glance, and garments clinging to her perspiring limbs,
> She flits, at dawn, like a fawn, timid and frightened. What bee has sipped the nectar of her blooming lips?
> By whom has Paradise been enjoyed today? Whom has Kama, once slain by Shiva's eye, blessed today?
> With her hand holding her heavy hair adorned with flowers crushed in the game of love,
> Her upper garment and loose girdle gathered in her right, her hair dishevelled and face swollen and languid, her passion sated,
> Here she comes from the private chamber, having yielded to the power of love, longing for the breeze.

Ancient Hindus were ardent admirers of wild forest scenery and their poetry is full of charming descriptions of the beauty and grandeur of the great forests of India. In ancient India, there were regular ashramas of sages who lived in the forests, and the better class of poets lived much of their life in these natural colonies in close contact with nature. Nothing in the world attracted these bards so forcefully as the wild charm of nature, especially during spring, with the trees in full blossom, lakes sparkling with lilies and lotuses, the birds and animals seeking their mates and the whole forest resounding with humming bees and singing birds. Hindus have always considered this atmosphere as the inspiring source of love; hence, their great love stories have forest scenery as the background. The wild, primeval forest, free from the pettiness of mortal men, was thought as the ideal place where the hero or the heroine of the bard could do daring acts of love which would otherwise be censured in a man-made village or city.

While hunting, men who strayed into wild woods teeming with flower-choked trees and resounding with humming bees are said to have fallen into paroxysms of passion and done violence to their own persons. Kuru King Pandu, father of the five Pandava princes, died in the arms of his wife Madri in a forest into which he had retired to pursue his austerities, with his two wives Kunti and Madri. The five Pandavas were born in those Himalayan forests. Pandu was under the curse of a sage who had condemned him to die in the arms of a woman, and the King had assiduously kept himself aloof from women, including his wives, Kunti and Madri. The ladies were also aware of the curse and were careful not to tempt the King or be alone with him. However, none of this was of any avail on the fated day.

In the spring that maddens all creatures with love, Pandu and Madri roamed in the woods teeming with blossoming trees and plants. His eyes were delighted to behold the Palashas, mangoes, Champakas, Paripardakas and the Karnikaras. He saw the Parijat tree with the Koels sitting atop and pouring forth their melodies from within thick foliage—the echoes of their sweet music filling the forest. The branches of the trees were drooping with the weight of flowers and fruits. The trees stood by lakes full of lotuses and lilies.

Seeing all this, King Pandu, unmindful of the fatal curse, fell an easy prey to the shafts of the god of love. Supremely joyous, blissfully ignorant of the impending doom, the King roamed the delightful forest like a celestial with his youthful, beautiful wife beside him, lightly clad in a thin robe. Seeing the lovely Madri thus attired, the King's passion flamed up like a forest fire. Alone with her in the wild, the King was overpowered by a desire to embrace the lotus-eyed Madri. Before she could stop him, the unrestrained King, impelled by fate, forcibly sought the embrace of his wife as if to put an end to himself. His reason clouded by the Destroyer, the King, intoxicated by love of his wife, shed his life in her arms. Thus, the virtuous king succumbed to the inevitable influence of all-devouring Time while embracing his wife.

Madri burst into violent sobs, and Kunti ran towards them with her children. As they came near, Madri cried piteously to Kunti, 'Pray, come alone; let the children stay back. See what a terrible thing has happened.'

Kunti saw her husband lying dead on the ground with Madri beside him. She addressed Madri moved by an affliction mixed with jealousy:

> This self-disciplined hero was constantly watched by me with care. He was well aware of the curse of the sage; then how did this thing come to pass? O Madri, this great King, our beloved husband ought to have been protected and guided by you, but you enticed him into solitude and into ruin. My lord was always melancholy, burdened with the ill-effects of the curse of the sage; then how was he roused to joy and merriment by

> you? But O princess, you are greatly favoured on this day, for you have seen the face of our lord in gladness and in joy which I have never witnessed all my life.

Similar instances of forest scenery inciting men and women to madness in love can be cited from Sanskrit literature. Most of the Ramayana and Mahabharata deal with the life of hermits and wandering heroes in the forests, and the Hindu poet is quite at home when dealing with forest life. The Ramayana is particularly rich in beautiful descriptions of the forests of South India, and a most pleasing picture of lake Pampa, considered a classic, is to be found in the *Kishkindha Kanda* of this epic.

♣♣♣

Chapter 9

Literature on Love

In Hindu thought, love is not only a spiritual and emotional bond, but also a science—an art of erotics that intertwines desire, intimacy, and societal norms. The ancient texts approached love and sensuality as part of human experience, treating it as both a divine and worldly pursuit. From the structured teachings of the *Kama Sutra* to the more nuanced understandings found in texts like the *Ananga Ranga*, these writings illuminate the cultural significance of love, desire, and eroticism, reflecting the complexities of women's roles and relationships in ancient Hindu society.

Hinduism categorises life into four stages: *dharma* (virtue, righteousness and duty, both religious and social), *artha* (acquisition of wealth, material prosperity and well-being), *kama* (gratification of material desires, or pursuit of pleasure, especially sex) and *moksha* (liberation from the cycle of birth and death and total attainment of the Supreme One or Ultimate Reality).

Kama, in its broader sense, includes all pleasures a person is capable of experiencing through the senses. A good meal, thus, comes under the category of kama. Hindu hedonists insist that there is no pleasure equal to that of love, no bliss greater than the ecstatic all-powerful physical union between a man and a woman. Hindu writers have studied the phenomenon with a thoroughness only they are capable of. In their detachment, they are not plagued by the notions of decency that often disturb the equanimity of Western sexologists.

In the Hindu world, literature on love is believed to be of divine origin. Brahma, the Creator, wrote a work of 100,000 chapters dealing with the three prime objects of life—dharma, artha and kama. The chapters on dharma were summarised by Manu, ancient India's lawgiver—also believed to be the first ever lawgiver of humanity—and handed down to mankind as the eponymous code of conduct. Brihaspati, the preceptor of the gods well-versed in the material and the spiritual, condensed the chapters on artha into a handy volume. Nandi, Shiva's mount as well as faithful companion, abridged Brahma's treatise on kama and wrote a book of 1,000 chapters. Finding Nandi's work too voluminous for mortals, Sage Shvetaketu Uddalaka summarised it into a book of 500 chapters. Even this was unreasonably lengthy; a pundit of the Panchala kingdom (in present northwestern Uttar Pradesh) named Babhravya rewrote the entire work, grouping the subject into seven sections:

- General
- Sexual union
- Courtship
- Married love
- Love out of wedlock
- Venal love
- Secret instructions

Each of these seven sections was worthy of special attention.

Charayana (an ancient grammarian referred to by Patanjali in the *Mahabhashya* as a scholar who had a line of pupils named after him) wrote a book on the first section, Suvarnanabha on the second, Ghotamukha on the third, Gorandeya on the fourth, Gonikaputra on the fifth, Dattakacharya on the sixth and Kuchumara on the seventh. While little is known of the other six authors, we are told that Dattakacharya had immense knowledge of the subject and lived among the courtesans of Pataliputra who commissioned him to write a text on the profession for the use of novices.

None of these books have come down to us. The earliest and authoritative work that remains extant is the *Kama Sutra* of Vatsyayana who wrote a treatise dealing with the seven sections of Babhravya's work.

His work depicts Hindu society as a highly developed one. It had a luxurious aristocracy that exploited all fields of pleasure, and Vatsyayana's works were mainly for ease-loving, pleasure-seeking aristocrats. For the development of a refined class, such as the one that *Kama Sutra* portrays, internal peace, economic security and freedom from fear of foreign aggression must have been a necessary prelude. India rose to unprecedented heights of material prosperity, geopolitical power and cultural refinement under the Gupta Empire. Vatsyayana probably lived in this era. Other works which mention the *Kama Sutra* also affirm this assumption. It might, therefore, be safe to surmise that sage Vatsyayana penned his famous work in the third or fourth century CE. There are possible interpolations in his original work; later authors might have been a tad too free in using Vatsyayana's name and adding considerably to the original.

The *Kama Sutra* in its present form is a comprehensive work that treats sex and love from a purely mundane point of view.

Vatsyayana's magnum opus is an exhaustive study of woman (and man, too, though incidentally) with the purpose of obtaining the maximum pleasure out of her. Vatsyayana's central character is the wealthy man, an urban dweller, with no serious commitments in life but plenty of leisure to pursue pleasure. The then fashionable men of the great cities were patrons of arts and literature and of courtesans who virtually ruled high society. The *Kama Sutra* was exceedingly popular among this gentry significantly because of its intrinsic merit and its value as a scientific work. Knowledge of Vatsyayana was considered essential for artists, poets, sculptors, kings, noblemen, royal ladies and women of fashion and taste. Courtesans who aspired to fame and position would assiduously study the *Kama Sutra*. As is everywhere, the ruling classes, nobility and the learned would set the trend(s) and the classes below followed suit. Over a period, *Kama Sutra* and Vatsyayana became synonymous with anything to do with the erotic.

Vatsyayana, though, is no mere erotic writer; Hindus consider him a *rishi* (sage) and his work is regarded as a revelation. His *Kama Sutra* is often mentioned along with other Hindu *Dharmashastras* (scriptures that lay down the code of dharma) and the *darshanas* (the various systems of Hindu philosophy). Myths and legends about Vatsyayana abound as well. One legend says that Vatsyayana was an ascetic and celibate, and his *Kama Sutra* was a work of pure inspiration. However, a careful study of the book reveals that it has been written with scientific detachment. Vatsyayana himself states that his interest in the subject is objective. Even while dealing with pervert practices, he makes effort to explain that he does not recommend it, but treats it as a medic who may 'describe in detail the taste, appearance and qualities of the flesh of a dog with no intention of prescribing it as an item of diet.'

Rati Rahasya by Koka Pandit is another work of importance on the topic of love and sex, though it occupies second place after Vatsyayana's *Kama Sutra*. Koka Pandit was a learned man who lived in the eleventh century AD. While the *Rati Rahasya* is based on the *Kama Sutra*, Pandit's personal experience considerably added to his own study of the erotic. Vatsyayana was a sage, but Koka Pandit was very much a man of the world and engaged with it intensely. He is reputed to have been an exceptionally virile man. An amusing story of Koka's virility is much prevalent. The learned pandit was also a courtier; one day, a naked *Yakshini* (a female Yaksha) burning with passion presented herself in the open court before the king. The king demanded to know the reason for her shameless behaviour, upon which she explained that she had been wandering in the fourteen worlds in search of a male who could satisfy her in sexual congress. Many men, gods and even Rakshasas had tried, but failed. She had now come to the royal assembly to see if she could meet a male equal to the task. The king, himself a master of many women, shrank from her challenge; many of his courtiers hung their heads in shame. Not Koka Pandit, though, who rose from his seat and took her by the hand. He led her to the antechamber and, before the court had dispersed for the day, brought her back to the king well clothed, a picture of modesty. The Yakshini was now sighing with fatigue by repeated congress with the master of the art and science of love!

Koka Pandit's work was as popular with Muslims as it was among Hindus. Its translations and adaptations found their way into various languages used by the Muslims and paved the way for Kalyanmalla's famous work *Ananga Ranga*. Kalyanmalla was a Hindu who lived in the fifteenth century under the patronage of a Muslim nobleman of the Lodi dynasty—Lad Khan, and he wrote the *Ananga Ranga* mainly for the benefit of his master. The work benefited from wide circulation because of Muslim patronage in those times. It is based on *Rati Rahasya* and *Kama Sutra*, though free translations in Urdu, Persian and Arabic by Muslims pass for original works.

Apart from these three important works, there are numerous other erotic treatises that gained popularity. The *Kama Sutra* has five commentaries—*Jayamangala* of Yashodhara, commentary by Bhaskara, commentary by Malla Deva, *Kandarpachudamani* by King Virabhadra, and commentary by an anonymous writer. Further, Kshemendra, the well-known Kashmiri writer on erotics summarised the *Kama Sutra* in his *Vatsyayana Sutra Sara*.

The *Rati Rahasya* has four commentaries—by Kanchi Natha, Avancha Rama Chandra, Kavi Prabhu, and Harihara. Some ancient Hindu writers seemed to have been in a favourable position to study the science of erotics. For one, polygamy was permissible; kings, nobles and wealthy merchants had multiple wives and well-endowed inner chambers. Sex was considered neither indecent nor irreligious. Moreover, from the ancient till medieval times, society was ruled by courtesans who were considered adornments of cities.

The author of *Ananga Ranga* observed that in this world of passing shadows, there was but one reality, and that was the pleasure of the company of women. It was equal, he wrote, if not superior to the pleasure of union with the Infinite, the bliss of the ascetic and the mystic.

Vatsyayana is more restrained in his praise of sexual pleasure. According to him, kama is subordinate to dharma and artha, but he observes that it is for each individual to decide the prime object of their life. No two men are alike; one may be born with a preponderantly religious bent of mind and another with strong leaning towards the acquisition of wealth or the pursuit of pleasure. Besides, the circumstances of birth and social status make men devote themselves to different objects and pursuits in life. An heir to a throne or a courtesan's daughter cannot be expected to prefer dharma to artha or kama. Age also plays an important part in one's prime objective in life. Naturally a ninety-year-old cannot pursue the pleasures of life with the same vigour as a young man of twenty-five.

Vatsyayana has not pulled any punches in expressing his contempt for lean ascetics who condemn women as sinful, and for the incorrigibly isolated and unthinking who propagate that woman is a cause of misery. Then there are self-appointed moralists who believe that Sita proved fatal to Ravana, eventually bringing about his ruin, and dish out other anecdotes in the same vein. These too are the targets of Vatsyayana's ire; he says that because of the gluttony of certain misguided individuals, no sane person should reject food. Gratification of the sexual urge is as essential for the happiness and well-being of men as food. Over indulgence is fraught with dangers and is to be avoided; it is no argument in favour of celibacy or asceticism.

Chapter 10

Love as Fine Art

Vatsyayana's *Kama Sutra* stands as one of the most prominent texts on love, offering profound insights into the art of erotics. While often reduced to mere sensuality, it is a guide to the intricate codes of courtship, marriage, and intimacy, deeply rooted in the cultural norms and gender roles of its time. Understanding this text helps us unravel how love was viewed not just as an emotion but as a refined practice, intricately connected to societal expectations. In today's context, it holds modern-day significance by challenging traditional ideas of desire, consent, and relationships, while also shedding light on the cultural frameworks that shaped women's roles and their agency in love and marriage.

For a full appreciation of the joys of love, Vatsyayana considers a sound knowledge of sixty-four auxiliary arts, known as the *chausath kala*, a prelude, if not a necessity.

These sixty-four arts are: 1) vocal music, 2) instrumental music, 3) dancing, 4) painting, 5) art of decorating one's forehead, 6) floor decoration with white powder, 7) floor decoration with flowers, 8) colouring the teeth and painting lips and cheeks, 9) art of setting coloured stones on floor, 10) making bed for sleeping, II) water sports, 12) bewitching by charms and spells, 13) making flower garlands, 14) arranging flowers as hair decoration, 15) selection of costumes for theatricals, 16) making earrings out of ivory, 17) preparation of scents and cosmetics, 18) renovating old garments by setting precious stones, 19) minor magic for amusement, 20) art of preparing mixtures for beautifying the skin and stimulating sexual desire, 21) sleight of hand, 22) preparation of beverages, 23) art of cooking, 24) needle work, 25) doll making, 26) mimicking the notes of the Veena and other musical instruments, *27*) inventing and solving riddles, 28) verse competition, 29) recitation of verses difficult of pronunciation and meaning, 30) melodious recitation of verses from the epics, 31) acting, 32) skill in filling up blanks in a stanza from a given line, 33) making furniture from canes and reeds, 34) wood carving, 35) carpentry, 36) architecture, 37) evaluation of articles made of gold and precious stones, 38) alchemy, 39) tinting crystals, 40) horticulture, 41) training of fighting animals and birds, 42) training parrots to talk and using them for conveying secret messages, 43) massage of the body and limbs, 44) the art of gestures, 45) use of code languages, 46) study of languages, 47) floral decoration of vehicles, horses and elephants, 48) knowledge of omens, 49) making of toy carts and images of animals from flowers, 50) memory training, 51) composing verses for particular occasions or in praise of certain dignitaries, 52) composing poems in general, 53) lexicography, 54) filling up blanks in verse, 55) figures of speech, 56) ventriloquism, 57) the art of disguise, 58) gambling, 59) chess, 60) the art of dressing 61) ball games, 62) training of pets, 63) the art of war, and 64) physical culture.

In addition to a working knowledge of these sixty-four arts, the lover is recommended to acquire proficiency in the language of signs. In India, free social intercourse between the sexes has been a taboo from early times. Hence, on meeting in public or in the houses of relatives and friends during social functions, lovers had to exchange greetings and convey messages by means of gestures and signs. Hindu society has evolved an elaborate language of gestures, mainly used in classical dances. However, lovers do not use this language as it is known to most of the educated gentry. For the lovers, there is a special secret code insignificant to others but indispensable to the vigilant lover. A flower dropped by a lady, seemingly by accident, may be pregnant with meaning. A red flower dropped from the hair may convey one thing, while a white flower may suggest another. Touching the earlobe, as if to scratch, may convey a definite message to the watching lover.

The classical language of signs falls under six categories:

- **Language of flowers and fruits**: The use of flowers and fruits to denote certain ideas, places and time falls under this category. The usual method is to pluck particular flowers or fruits, and eat or play with them in a manner as to convey a message to the lover on a pre-arranged plan.
- **Body language**: Touching, scratching or exposing certain parts of the body can convey messages to a lover. Touching the chest usually denotes deep-seated love, while touching the hair signifies passion. Each finger, except the little one, denotes a particular direction. The thumb stands for east, the index finger south, the middle finger west and the fourth finger north. Fifteen lines of the palm represent the fifteen days of the lunar cycle, including the full moon or the new moon day. Thus, if a man meets his love in public and shows his thumb and a particular palm line, the lady will come to know the date and place of a possible appointment—the eastern direction suggested by the thumb denoting some

place where they have already met. Now they only need to play with a flower or a fruit to fix the time of the appointment.

- **Language of spices**: Spices represent the intensity of one's passion. Aromatic substances stand for mild love; bitter spices denote urgent desire. A girl watching her lover eating can understand the nature and extent of his love by his preferred spices.
- **Language of clothes**: Touching or displaying coloured garments convey certain ideas. A red robe, for instance, indicates a desire for immediate union, a yellow garment separation or rejection of a suit.
- **Language of betel leaves**: The offering of a betel with a slit in the middle denotes rejection or breaking off; on the other hand, a betel leaf with an arrow cut in the middle indicates burning love.
- **Language of flower garlands**: A garland with predominant red flowers indicates an overwhelming yearning for immediate union; brown denotes a passing fancy; yellow shows indifference and black, disgust.

A person mastering the sixty-four auxiliary arts and sciences and the language of signs is considered qualified for the more serious pursuit of love. Such a person should now try to know his or her sexual type. Women are broadly classified into four types:

- ***Padmini* or Lotus Woman**: She is the most desirable type of woman. She has eyes as beautiful as those of the fawn—with reddish corners. Her face is charming like the full moon, neck smooth and graceful, and bosom, full and elevated. She has a well-shaped delicate nose. Three exquisite folds encircle her navel. Her voice is sweet and musical. Her skin is soft as the petals of a *sirisha* blossom, and her complexion as golden as a Champaka flower. Her gait is like that of a swan. Her secretions have the perfume of the lotus.

The Padmini's mental traits are as agreeable as her appearance. She is bashful, generous, loyal, religious, and dignified. Her favourite colour is white.

- ***Chitrini* or Art Woman**: Of medium stature but slim, the Chitrini has dark, black hair and restless eyes. Her lips are full as the *bimba* fruits. Her conch-shaped neck is round and graceful; she has a slender waist, large hips, plump and heavy breasts and supple body. Her voice is like the cooing of the peacock. She has the majestic swing of an elephant while walking. Her love secretions smell of honey.

  Less spiritual than the Padmini, the Chitrini is refined and cultured, with a taste for music, painting and literature. She is fond of beautiful clothes and ornaments, and is flattered by the attention of admiring men. She delights in courtship and love play, but dislikes violence or even force in love. She has too refined a sense of aesthetics to be much enamoured of the actual sex act. The Chitrini is sociable and amiable. She is a good conversationalist, liberal in her views and skilful in the management of domestic affairs.
- ***Shankhini* or Conch Woman**: She is not much to look at, being thin, tall or stout. Her blood is warm, and her blue veins are visible through her tawny skin. She has long legs and arms, a thick waist, small breasts, and a long, tilted face to match. Her voice is harsh and her gait, precipitate. Her favourite colour is red. Though selfish and cunning, she is capable of making a show of generosity. She has polite manners and is ever on the lookout for chances to enhance her own interests. Hard-hearted, malicious and vicious by

nature, the Shankhini is clever enough to hide her real nature and appear pleasant and obliging. When roused, she is violent and delights in inflicting nail marks on her lover during the act. She eats and talks a lot.

- ***Hastini*** **or Elephant Woman**: She is the lowest sexual type and men of refined tastes and habits avoid her. She is short, fat and ugly. Her lips are thick, neck short or bent, if long, and mouth broad. Her eyes are red and small. If of light complexion, the Hastini appears rather anaemic and lustreless. She is slow of foot and walks ungainly on crooked feet and toes. She is shameless and cruel, and has an insatiable capacity for love.

But Brahma has created a mate for every woman. There are four kinds of men to go with these four types of women. The classification of the male is mainly based on the length of the membrum virile. The smaller and thinner the member, the better the man. The four types of men are:

- ***Shasha*** **or Hare Man**: This type is gracefully built, though strong. Shasha has large eyes, a full, manly face with a prominent nose. His hair is silky. He is loyal, kindly disposed, god-fearing and virtuous. His actions are motivated by altruism. He is the correct mate for a Padmini.
- ***Mriga*** **or Buck Man**: The Buck is something of a he-man. Tall, broad-shouldered and handsome, he has a commanding personality. He is scrupulous, clean, brave and chivalrous. A warrior by nature, he respects the gods and elders. He is a patron of arts and letters, and is fond of music. He has a royal appetite. He is selfless, hospitable, generous, public-spirited and honest. The Buck is the man for a Chitrini.
- ***Vrishabha*** **or Bull Man**: The Bull is a rough and ready man with a quick temper and overbearing disposition. His limbs

are sinewy, forehead high, and eyes red and large. He loves music, but of the vulgar sort. He has little inclination for the delights of the soul or even of the intellect, but is fond of the pleasures of the flesh. Not particularly loyal, he delights in the company of several women and can satisfy the desires of all of them. He is the male counterpart of a Shankhini.

- ***Ashva* or Stallion Man**: This is an ugly man with long limbs, coarse hair, uneven teeth and a broad, scaly chest. He is rough, but of strong build. He has a large, wide mouth and neck and ears that do not seem to fit in with the general layout of the head. His legs are bent and he walks clumsily. He stares at people and is incapable of mild speech. Blessed with a phallus nine inches long, he has only contempt for the frail Padmini, but loves to mate with large women of the Hastini type.

These four types, more or less, correspond to the four castes of Hindus. The Hare corresponds to the Brahmin, the Buck to the Kshatriya, the Bull to the Vaishya and the Stallion to the Shudra.

Having understood his type, the studious man of pleasure will do well to learn the nature of the shifting erogenous zones in women. Kalyanmalla describes in detail a mysterious connection between the varying digits of the moon and the changing erogenous zones in women. Hence, each day of the lunar month is supposed to have a definite bearing on the exact position of the erogenous zone in a woman.

Generally, from the full moon day, the *Chandrakala* (as the erogenous zone is termed) descends by the left side of the woman from the forehead through the eyes, cheeks, lips, chin, neck, shoulder, armpit, breast, side, hip, pubic region, genitals, knee, ankle and the foot. On the new moon day, it starts its similar course upward by the right side and reaches the forehead on the full moon day.

However, the extent of amorous urges centring around Chandrakala is not equal for all women on a particular day. A Padmini is the most excitable on the first five days (excepting the third) of the lunar fortnight (both bright and dark), a Chitrini on four even dates commencing from the sixth, a Shankhini on the third, seventh, eleventh and thirteenth, and a Hastini on the remaining two days of the fortnight and on the full moon and new moon days.

It is not enough to catch the shifting zone at the correct spot on the correct day; it must be caught at the correct time. Love-making is an exact science; the persevering voluptuary should consider the time of sexual congress and the woman's sexual type before hoping to derive full pleasure out of the act. A Padmini, we are told, is most amenable to the pleasures of sex from 3 am till sunset, and a Hastini from midday till sunrise. Chitrini and Shankhini have brief spells of excitability; the former may be tackled between 6 and 9 pm and the latter from 12 to 3 pm. However, it is difficult to confirm the veracity of these pedantic assertions.

More interesting and helpful are the hints on courtship. Though marriages in India are usually arranged by parents, even the strictest sect have lovers who have courted and married mates of their own choice. Certain men cannot have matches arranged for them because of their position. A man of good family, for instance, at times finds himself without a friend to arrange a match for him, and has to find a bride for himself. Wealthy men of quarrelsome nature, the newly rich of low birth wishing to marry above their social position, and independent men who do not wish to be dictated to by relatives, are likely to court and marry women of their choice. For such people, Vatsyayana gives some useful hints on courtship.

A young man unlikely to be suspected of having designs, may manage to engage himself in play with a girl he loves. He is advised to be pleasant not only to the girl but also to her companions and nurse as a girl is often swayed by their opinions. Maintaining a good relation with nurses and companions may, Vatsyayana tells us, make them a willing accomplice in arranging secret meetings. If the girl's nurse takes a liking for a young man, she may even act against the wishes of the girl's parents and arrange the marriage of the lovers without the parents' knowledge.

There are very few places and occasions in India for young men and women to mix together without raising elders' suspicion. Most men who wish to approach young ladies have to seek the services of an intermediary in the initial stages of courtship. Vatsyayana suggests the young daughter of the girl's nurse as a desirable intermediary. The lover must win over this girl, a friend of his love, and tutor her to recite his qualifications for the hand of her friend. If bought over with gold, the nurse herself will serve as an excellent intermediary. If neither of these two persons can be won over, the man must procure the services of:

- A common friend or relative, preferably an elderly woman
- An elderly widow
- The washerwoman or barber common to both the families
- A hawker of perfumes
- A mendicant
- The milkman or milkmaid who visits both the houses
- A florist or gardener
- A dancing girl
- A palmist or fortune teller
- A professional jester
- A reliable menial
- The family tailor

- Any clever woman
- A cowherd
- A bawd

For the successful termination of courtship, it is necessary to please the intermediary by every means. Those who are not above accepting bribes must be paid in cash; relatives and friends who cannot be thus bought must be kept in good humour with desirable presents. It is even said that if a woman-intermediary, smitten with the good looks of the man, requests for the satisfaction of her sexual desires as payment, her request must be granted without demur.

After establishing contact with the girl he loves, the lover must improve their good relations by sending her presents and seeing her as often as possible. For the latter, he must visit the places she frequents. On such occasions, he must dress elegantly and give her a favourable impression of his personality and qualifications as a lover. In all probability, he would meet her on these occasions in company of other relatives; hence, he should watch for signs that may indicate her interest in him. Some signs that betray dawning love in a maiden are:

- Not looking at the lover directly
- Blushing
- Laughing when the lover speaks even if his conversation is not particularly humorous
- A tendency to linger near the lover longer than necessary
- Kissing or embracing a child when the lover is nearby
- Talking loudly to companions on irrelevant subjects or teasing them within the lover's sight
- Casting side glances at the departing lover
- Adjusting robes to expose parts of the body or limbs

After the lover has noticed these signs indicating dawning love in a maiden, he may arrange for a secret meeting. The time and place of the meeting should not raise any suspicion among her guardians. The most convenient time is said to be when the guardians have gone away to visit friends or the shrine of the village gods, leaving the girl with the nurse or some elderly woman servant already won over by the lover. On meeting the girl, the lover is exhorted to engage her in pleasant conversation and regale her with love stories from the epics and the classics. Tickling, kissing and even embracing are permitted on such occasions, but further liberties are prohibited before marriage. So much for premarital courtship.

Hindu litterateurs emphasise the need for courting, coaxing and generally working up a newly married girl before she is initiated into the deeper mysteries of love. Forcing oneself sexually on brides is absolutely forbidden. There are detailed instructions on how to gain the young wife's confidence. If the girl has been courted before marriage, the task becomes easier since some confidence has already been gained before the amorous moment in the nuptial chamber. But, working up a girl in an arranged match is a complicated affair. The husband is probably meeting her privately for the first time, and the memories of their nuptial night strongly influence their subsequent relationship. A husband unfamiliar with the ways of young girls may antagonise his wife for life through his clumsy or impatient behaviour. Hence, a newly married man must ingratiate himself with his wife, disarming all resistance and making her yield herself with pleasure and delight.

On the bride being conducted to the nuptial chamber, the husband awaiting her should welcome her with a pleasant smile. The initial pleasantries may be followed by an agreeable conversation. Vatsyayana tells us that a young bride is extremely shy; she guards the centre of her charms most jealously and is even suspicious of conversation. Noticing the bride's reticence, the clever husband engages her in conversation by enquiring solicitously about the welfare of her parents and relatives. If she is responsive, as she is bound to be, he invites her to sit, gently leads her by the hand to the couch or the bed and sits by her side. He may proceed to tell her clever stories about lovers and their ways, inserting appropriate comments on the art forbidden in respectable society. Next, he can coax her to play chess or dice as this will give him plenty of opportunities for teasing, tickling and generally dragging her into the net he is cunningly weaving. If she accedes, the lover must make her win the game. If she does not know how to play chess or dice, he can teach her and make her an expert on the spot.

After playing with her for a sufficient time, the husband may take the liberty of embracing her. At this stage, it is advisable to conduct further proceedings in the dark. For maidens, like cats, are bolder in the dark.

After the embrace, comes the kiss. Experienced sages tell us that a maiden may submit herself to an embrace, but may revolt at a kiss. They assure us that once the bride is won over, further progress is bound to be satisfactory. The one infallible method of winning over the shy bride to the first kiss may seem strange to Westerners unfamiliar with the Eastern art of love. The lover holds a spiced betel leaf between his lips and offers it to the girl requesting her to receive it directly into her mouth. When the enamoured bride takes the bait with a wide-open mouth, things become pretty easy for the lover. However, if the girl shows reluctance or hesitation, the husband must supplicate her in passionate words praising her beauty and confessing to a mad, hopeless love. This may not work in some cases; the husband may then threaten to commit suicide and leave the young bride a widow. If the bride is still equanimous, the husband should fall at her feet and beg for her favour. This masterstroke is bound to succeed, for, as the sages say, no woman has ever kicked a sincere lover fallen at her feet.

Once the bride has thus been won over, she may be taken to bed with ease. Through proper management of her person, she can then be worked up, step by step, to the mental condition in which she will delightfully seek the satisfaction of her aroused desires.

The sages warn us that a man should not indulge in secret pleasure in the presence of fire, near a pious or respectable individual, in a temple or a holy place, in the cremation ground, on the king's highway or in a friend's house without his knowledge. Sacred days and inauspicious times should be avoided. The last day of the month and the new moon are considered inauspicious. Congress with women should be avoided at sunrise and sunset. It is undesirable to make love during a religious fast or vow of abstinence, during illness and after labour.

There are six auxiliary pleasures that complete the union. These are:

- *Alinganam* or embrace
- *Chumbanam* or kiss
- *Nakhakshata* or scratching
- *Dantakarma* or biting
- *Sitkrata* or making inarticulate sounds
- *Panighata* or stroking with the hand

Vatsyayana and, following him, Kalyanmalla classify embrace into twelve categories:

- ***Spripaca* or mild contact**: This can be indulged in public without raising any suspicion. When in a crowd or a social gathering, a man expresses his love brushing his body against hers. The loved one feels the pleasure of the contact but others do not notice it.

- ***Viddhaka* or breast pressure embrace**: This, like the first, is a secret physical contact but here the woman takes the initiative. She passes her lover, either in front or behind, brushing her bosom against him, unnoticed by others.
- ***Udgrishtaka* or rubbing**: This type of embrace is recommended in a crowd, in the dark, when the lovers may frequently rub their bodies against each other for a considerably long time, with darkness preventing detection.
- ***Piditika* or pressure embrace**: This is an advance form of Udgrishtaka. In the darkness, one of the lovers manages to stand against a wall or a pillar and so the other can apply greater pressure.
- ***Lataveshtitaka* or the creeper embrace**: In this form, always indulged in private, the woman twines her arms around her lover, like a creeper entwining a tree, and lovingly looks at his face as he bends down to kiss her. The woman takes the lead here and inflames the lover's passion.
- ***Vrikshadhirudhaka* or tree-climbing embrace**: Standing on one leg, the woman raises her right leg and twines it around the man's right thigh and lifts herself up for a kiss, like a man climbing a tree. Her one arm holds the lover by the shoulder and with the other pressed at his waist, she heaves herself upward. This difficult embrace is resorted to by women who wish to work up dull lovers.
- ***Tilatandulaka* or rice-sesame embrace**: Balls of unboiled rice coated with sesame seeds are offered to manes in Hindu funeral rites. The lover's intimate physical contact in this type of embrace suggested the name.

- ***Kshiraniraka* or milk and water embrace**: Just as water gets mixed with milk, a complete fusion of man and woman is attempted in this violent embrace. Under the urge of passion, the lovers clasp each other sitting or lying down, as if to unite themselves into one. This violent embrace usually precedes coitus.
- ***Urupaguhana* or the pincer embrace**: Lying on their sides, face-to-face, the lovers embrace each other, their thighs interlocking.
- ***Jaghanupaghuhana* or hip-thigh embrace**: The man lies on his back, while his partner clasps him violently, with their torsos in close contact.
- ***Sthanalingana* or bosom embrace**: With the lovers either sitting or lying down facing each other, the woman clasps the man applying the maximum pressure by her breasts.
- ***Lalatika* or forehead embrace**: This is a mild embrace in which eyes, nose and lips of the lovers are in close contact as their foreheads touch.

Like embraces, kisses are of several kinds; a few of them are mentioned below:

- ***Nimitika* or restrained kiss**: This is the kiss of the bashful maiden, almost forced from her lips. It is a gentle quick kiss, the coyness or nervousness of the maiden preventing it from being prolonged or passionate.
- ***Supritika* or trembling kiss**: The man, bent upon impressing with a passionate kiss, takes the lower lip of the maiden between his lips, holding it against her will, while the girl, out of shyness or fear, makes repeated efforts to withdraw her trembling lips from his vicious lock.
- ***Ghattitika* or the probing kiss**: After much coaxing, the shy

girl takes the lead. She covers the eyes of her lover with her palm, closes her eyes, takes the lover's lower lip between both her lips and caresses it with her probing tongue.

- ***Sama* or straight kiss**: This is an honest kiss by the man given straight on the lips of his beloved.
- ***Vakra* or round-about kiss**: In this form, the face of the lover is turned sideways and the lips are pressed in the shape of a circle or an egg.
- ***Udbhranta* or revolving kiss**: The man kisses the woman on her lips, drawing her face towards his.
- ***Avapitika* or pressure kiss**: An improvement on Udbhranta, this kiss applies greater pressure.
- ***Akrishta* or high-pressure kiss**: The lower lip of one of the partners is held by the other between the thumb and the forefinger and is pressed to the lips exquisitely.
- ***Samputaka* or cupping kiss**: Both the lips of the lover are caught and retained in a kiss as long as he or she wishes.
- ***Jihvajudha* or tongue-tilting kiss**: While the lovers imprint passionate kisses, the tongues too kiss and caress each other.

Vatsyayana describes several other forms of kisses and observes that the objective of the kiss is to heighten the pleasure of love. He also mentions the places where a kiss may awaken desire. Apart from the lips, the forehead, cheeks, eyes, chin and bosom are also mentioned as desirable places for kissing. The kissing of a woman's hand is permissible, but not her toes. However, a woman may kiss the toes, feet, legs and thighs of the man she loves. Vatsyayana asks every lover to thoroughly master the art of kissing, and recommends a kissing combat between lovers as a pleasant form of diversion that heightens the delights of love. So much for the kiss.

Before going into the details of scratching and biting, it is necessary to mention that in India, lovemaking has always been recognised as a peculiar form of pleasure wherein some pain, physical or mental, is conducive to enhancement. The surrender of a woman to order is repugnant to all, except the moralist who views love as an unpleasant duty imposed on man by the need for progeny. Writers on erotics necessarily give great importance to the play aspect of love and maintain that teasing, inflicting minor injuries and even reconciling followed by quarrelling realistically add zest to the pleasures of sex. Petty pain always aids love. Inflicting exquisite wounds on a woman by nails or teeth by a lover has been studied as an art in India. In fact, great lovers grow long nails and trim them carefully to scratch their beloveds in love warfare.

The standard nail marks are eight:

- ***Achchuritaka* or mild scratch**: The nails of all the five fingers are mildly applied on a sensitive part, preferably on the woman's breasts, with sufficient pressure to cause slight pain but not to leave a mark. All women, including shy and bashful maidens inexperienced in the game of love, are said to love it.
- ***Ardhachandrika* or crescent**: The nails apply sufficient pressure to cause a crescent-shaped mark on the region below the navel, about the sacral dimples or hip joint.
- ***Mandala* or circle**: Nail marks in the shape of two crescents that make a circle.
- ***Rekha* or the line scratch**: Here, the nail marks form a vertical line. The head, the thighs and the chest are the appropriate places for the *rekha*. Nails of the middle finger, the index and the third fingers should be used.
- ***Vyaghranakha* or the tiger's claw**: These are straight marks converging towards the navel, deep and long, like a tiger's claw.

- ***Mayurapada* or peacock's foot**: This is a nail mark made around the beloved's nipples and is shaped like a peacock's foot.
- ***Shashaplutaka* or leaping rabbit**: This is an advance on Mayurapada and is suggestive, in its vigorous application, of a leaping rabbit.
- ***Utpalapatraka* or the lotus leaf**: This nail mark, shaped like the lotus leaf, is made on the breasts or waist of a woman.

Vatsyayana mentions a supplementary scratch called *Smaraniyaka* (the token of remembrance) that a lover uses before going on a long journey. It is formed of two lines suggesting an angle if the separation is of short duration, of three lines in a triangle for longer periods, and of four lines making a rectangle or parallelogram if parting for good.

Biting, like scratching, falls into eight main categories:

- ***Gadhaka* or secret bite**: This is a mild bite leaving a reddish mark scarcely visible to the naked eye, made with one of the more prominent front teeth.
- ***Uchchunaka* or canine bite**: When the teeth are applied with sufficient pressure to cause a swelling, the bite is called canine.
- ***Pravalamani* or the coral bite**: When any part of the body is bitten with sufficient violence to cause a red contusion on the skin, it is called a coral bite.
- ***Manimala* or chain of corals**: A number of coral bites forming a lengthy chain make a *Manimala*.
- ***Bindu* or the dot**: This is a quick, vigorous bite leaving a prick mark not bigger than a dot on the skin.
- ***Bindumala* or dot chain**: A series of *bindus* make a *Bindumala*.
- ***Khandabhraka* or the broken cloud**: This oblique mark on a woman's breasts, results from biting with uneven teeth.
- ***Varahacharvitaka* or the boar's bite**: A vigorous chewing

of the shoulder down to the breasts causing a long unbroken chain of scarlet veals is known by this name. This is indulged in only by men who are excessively passionate; the women who appreciate it have similar temperament.

Though these are the standard types of scratching and biting, Vatsyayana agrees that it is difficult to strictly adhere to these types always, and a man, under the urge of passion, is likely to indulge in scratching or biting that has no name.
Stroking also enhances pleasure. It can be of four kinds:

- ***Apahastaka* or back palm strike**: As the name indicates, this is administered by the back of the palm on the hollow between the woman's breasts.
- ***Kilataka* or close fist stroke**: While the lovers are in a close embrace, the man strikes the woman on the back with his closed fists. The woman is recommended to hit back, adding abusive language.
- ***Prasritaka* or hollow palm stroke**: This stroke is administered on the head of the woman with the hollow of the lover's palm. It is an alternative or corrective to *Apahastaka* when the woman is not quite pleased with it and expresses her protest by word of mouth or, if she is too excited for words, by gestures.
- ***Samatalaka* or flat palm stroke**: This is a blow with an open palm in the chest or buttocks of the man if the woman finds him not playing the game.

Vatsyayana observes that people of different provinces have different ways of stroking. The men from the Deccan are said to be specialists in this form of love play, their strokes causing broad marks of contusion on the skin. The stroking peculiar to the Deccan has a classification of its own.

With stroking goes *Shitkrida* or erotic articulations. These are inarticulate sounds made during the excitement of sexual congress—either involuntary groans expressing complete abandonment to the violence of passion, or voluntary cooing for stimulating desire. Shitkrida has been studied in detail and classified. A long list has been drawn, out of which a few are given below:

- The nasal sound 'Hind'
- The rumbling sound 'Hrong'
- The moan
- Cooing
- Hissing
- Clucking

In addition to these classified noises, phrases such as 'I am dying,' 'spare me,' 'kill me,' and 'for pity's sake, stop,' among others are also recommended during sexual congress.

Hindu writers on love and the science of amorousness often speak of 'love's warfare' and the soldiers wounded in this battlefield exhibit their wounds with pride. The nail marks, scratches and other minor wounds caused in the battle of love form a perennial theme for teasing, joking and sham quarrelling among lovers and friends. For obvious reasons, any form of violence that leaves marks on the skin are avoided in clandestine love.

From the auxiliary or preliminary pleasures hitherto mentioned, we now come to the 'real thing'. The same details that characterise the precepts regarding the preliminary and auxiliary pleasure is available in the matter of coitus too. Coital postures fall into three main divisions:

- The normal attitude in which the man plays the leading role

- The reversed attitude in which the woman takes the lead
- Fellatio

Basing his arguments on these three fundamentals, Vatsyayana describes eighty-four coital postures. Yashodhara, his commentator, maintains that there are 729 possible coital postures from which the lovers can select those they consider best for themselves. Some of the postures have a scientific base, while the others are the offspring of a fertile imagination.

Readers' attention must be drawn to Vatsyayana's shrewd remark that a study of all the postures may prove of no avail to a man who, in the grip of the anarchic passion, may invent his own postures defeating the imagination of the most erudite scholar on erotica. He also observes that marital unhappiness is often due to unequal sexual combinations. Of such combinations, the following are a few:

- Union between a sexually weak male and a moderately virile female
- Between a weak man and a strong woman
- Between a moderately virile man and a weak woman
- Between a moderately virile man and a strong woman
- Between a virile man and a weak woman
- Between a virile man and a moderately virile woman

In other words, the strong must mate with the strong, and the weak with the weak. Similarly, a middling must look for the same type.

In true scientific spirit, Vatsyayana describes certain perverted practices but forbids men and women from indulging in them. However, he is careful to add that one should not be unduly harsh in judging others as there is no universally accepted standard in sexual morality conditioned by local customs and usages.

In perverted practices, eunuchs and courtesans in Vatsyayana's time played the leading role. A king or noble with many wives and mistresses indulged in communal sexual congress, while the women in the harem who, for obvious reasons, could not completely satisfy their sexual urges through their husbands, were not considered particularly sinful if they smuggled men into the harem or indulged in perverted practices among themselves or with the eunuchs guarding the palace. The women of Strirajya (women's country), Vatsyayana says, married many young men, and the queen and the matriarchs entertained themselves in the company of a multitude of young husbands. The impotent took recourse to charms and medicines for rejuvenation. Those who could not regain their lost vitality through medicines, magic and prayers used artificial methods for pleasing their partners. As seen in the *Kama Sutra*, a profitable trade in artificial phalli was secretly carried on in Vatsyayana's time. These phalli were made of gold, silver, brass, lead or wood according to the status of the possessor. Royalty went for gold, while the poor opted for base metals or wood.

The general belief of male sexual virility being proportionate to the size of the membrum virile was prevalent in Vatsyayana's time, too. The seer of love describes several methods for increasing the length and thickness of the male member. He mentions a method much favoured by his conetemporaries who used to increase the thickness of their phalli by rubbing some hairy insects on them which caused a permanent swelling of the skin. Some also bored holes at the base of the phalli for wearing metallic devices for enhancing pleasure.

Hindu writers on erotica have made an exhaustive study of the psychology of women and have found that men who are generally successful with women are:

- A master of *Kama Sutra*
- A clever storyteller
- A handsome youth
- A childhood companion or playmate separated because of social restraint or any other cause
- A wealthy man under whom a close relative of the woman he courts, works
- A man of free and easy manners
- A man who can keep a woman's secrets
- One who is obliging and willing to perform small, pleasant jobs for women
- A man known to be a successful intermediary between lovers
- A secret friend or paramour of a well-known lady's companion
- A man well thought of by ladies of fashion
- A libidinous, but popular, neighbour
- A bridegroom new to the family and surroundings
- An attendant on a lady who is passionately fond of her
- A lover of theatrical performances
- A good dancer or actor
- A famous musician
- A comedian
- A magician
- A man known to be liberal with his money
- A strong man with an established reputation for virility
- A man of exceptional courage and daring
- A lover of picnics and garden parties
- A superior of a lady's husband in intellect, beauty or wealth
- A man of taste and culture who dresses fashionably and lives luxuriously
- A lucky man

Women who fall easy prey to men are:

- One who is fond of standing on balconies or in front of doors for sightseeing in general and watching men in particular
- A society lady showing eagerness to freely mix with young men
- An officious woman
- One who watches strangers slyly through the corners of her eyes
- One who often looks around
- A neglected wife
- A superseded wife, if not neglected
- A wife who hates her husband for some reason
- An accomplished woman with a taste for fine arts
- A barren woman
- A woman whose children die frequently
- A woman who breaks the laws of her society
- A poor woman fascinated by the way of life of the rich
- A wife separated from her husband and living in her father's house
- The wife of an actor or dancer
- A vain, bragging woman
- A finery loving woman married to a miser
- A young widow
- A woman whose husband has several unmarried brothers living with him
- A pretentious woman anxious to be known as a friend of men of letters and culture
- The wife of an impotent man
- A woman married against her will
- The large wife of a small man
- A vivacious young lady married to a pot-bellied man
- The wife of an ugly, deformed or slovenly man
- An insulted wife seeking revenge

- A woman whose husband works abroad and frequently lives away from her
- The wife of a jealous man
- A restless woman
- The wife of a man whose body stinks
- The young wife of an old man
- A village girl newly come to the city and fascinated by the marvels of the city
- A drunken woman
- A woman who dresses herself in a tight-fitting jacket so as to display the shapeliness of her breasts

Women have their varying moods or states of mind. Numerous factors cause these varying moods in women—disappointment, age, frustration, expectation, anxiety, coyness, and natural reserve being a few of them. Most writers on erotics have noticed these. The sixteenth century writer Kesava Das has classified them in his *Rasikapriya*; artists of the Rajput, Kangra and Pahari schools have personified them in *Nayikas* or heroines.

Some of the Nayikas are:

- ***Nabodha:*** The shy girl frightened to meet her lover alone.
- ***Mughdha:*** A woman conscious of her charms.
- ***Sambhoga Nayika:*** One who looks forward to a union with her lover.
- ***Swadhinapatika:*** One conscious of having her lover in subjection.
- ***Rupagarita:*** A woman given to affected resentment.
- ***Smarandha:*** A woman in blind love.
- ***Vipralabdha Nayika:*** A woman frustrated in love.
- ***Abhisarika:*** A lovesick woman going out to meet her lover.
- ***Vasakasayya Nayika:*** The expectant heroine who waits for

her lover at the doorway of her bedchamber.

- ***Prositapatika:*** A woman who suffers separation from her husband.
- ***Agata Bhartrika:*** A woman meeting her husband after a long separation.

It is, however, difficult to judge a woman by her apparent disposition. Women are clever at dissembling and can easily affect a mood quite different from the actual. Hence, the wise man is asked to study certain physical conditions in women which can indicate their true nature and destiny. Having great faith in palmistry and auspicious marks on the body, Hindus have developed an elaborate literature on the subject called *Samudrika Shastra*. It is believed that a student of this science can judge a person by his appearance and foretell his destiny. Kings in exile have been recognised by the mystic mark of the discus every royal person is supposed to have on the palm. In erotic literature too, auspicious signs and marks play an important role, and the lucky, the suitable and the desirable are often judged by these signs or marks.

In the Ramayana, on hearing the false news of her husband's death, Sita observes:

> I do not see on my body the inauspicious marks that indicate widowhood. My hair is fine, glossy, and dark. My temples are well proportioned and eyes, auspicious. My teeth are even. My thighs, legs, ankles and hands are well formed. My brows do not run together. My breasts are full, elevated and swell up leaving no gap between, and the nipples are deep set. My skin is smooth and transparent, and I stand firm on my ten toes and soles. So am I known as a woman with auspicious marks.

Though brows that run together are considered inauspicious in women, they are a good sign in a man—'The peculiar makeup of the hero is that he is tall, has a nose like a parrot's beak, straight looking eyes over-shadowed by brows that run together, and a disposition that is easily aroused and inclined to anger and strife.' A prominent nose and long arms are greatly prized in men. Most heroes of Hindu legend had hook noses and long arms that reached below the knees *(ajanubahu).* In men, a big organ of smell is a great distinction. In the Mahabharata, Yudhisthira is known for his huge, long, hanging, handsome nose. Charudatta, the ideal man in the *Mrichchakatika*, has a very high arched nose. In *Harshacharita*, Bana says in praise of Skandagupta's nose that it is as long as his pedigree. A big nose with the tip turned down is the mark of a hero and a king. The Aryan nobility of India was especially distinguished by this characteristic. A flat nose, on the other hand, is a mark of ugliness.

In arranged matches, parents of the bridegroom get only one or two chances to see the girl before accepting the proposal. In such cases, the girl's eligibility should be decided in keeping with the following points:

- A girl likely to make a good bride should be neither too tall nor too short; she must have a fair complexion and shapely body.
- Her gait must be like that of an elephant or swan, neither too brisk nor too slow. She must have tender feet and palms, and rosy-tinted fingers.
- She must have large eyes, and a delicate, straight-cut, high-bridged nose.
- She must have a full set of even teeth of pearl colour, a neck shapely like the conch shell and thighs as smooth and round as the stem of the banana tree.
- Her hair must be black and smooth, moderate in volume. Her voice must be sweet like the cuckoo's.

The undesirable types are:

- A girl who is too thin or too short
- A girl of black complexion
- A girl with a face like a horse
- A girl with low shoulders, ugly thighs or a protuberant brow
- A girl with rough and scaly skin
- A girl with a large mouth
- A girl with obvious defects like cock-eye or lame leg
- A girl who has a deficient or redundant finger or toe
- One who has triangular ears, or a blunt and flat third toe, or whose little toe is raised
- One who has perspiring hands and feet
- One with an inauspicious name. The name of a star, river or tree is considered inauspicious, and a name ending in the letter L or R.

Besides the physical appearance of the girl, the bridegroom's side is also exhorted to look for omens and the behaviour of the girl. If they find the girl sleeping on their arrival, they must immediately break off negotiations and seek a girl elsewhere. If the girl weeps, leaves the house or hides when the bridegroom's people call her, it is obvious that she is not much in favour of the match.

The female relatives of the bridegroom will be able to study the girl closely, and may look for mystic marks on the girl which would indicate her future. A girl with the mystic mark of the discus or lotus on the left sole is born to be a queen. A line extending from the little toe to the base of the big toe on the left sole indicates a happy married life. The mark of a circle or garland on a girl's left palm indicates the birth of heroes as sons. A girl with three lines around her neck will be fortunate.

A long neck in a maiden signifies ill-health and a cruel

disposition, while a short neck denotes misery and selfishness. Girls whose toes are long or out of proportion compared to the rest of the foot are capable of fornication. A little toe that does not touch the ground indicates early widowhood. A maiden whose thighs and legs taper like an elephant's trunk is fortunate. The mark of the *ankusha* (a spiked hook) on a girl's palm is indicative of royalty and noble motherhood.

A mole on the lip, whether in a man or woman, means luck in love. One on the tip of the nose indicates a successful career and an adventurous life. A black mole on any of the cheeks shows mediocrity and a red mole on the right temple denotes happiness after the age of thirty.

A bright-eyed man is fortunate; white, shining teeth ensure a supply of wholesome food; a big head indicates kingship; a wide waist brings many wives and children. A man with soft, smooth skin will get beautiful beds to sleep on; one with soft feet will get good vehicles to ride in.

A man with a long organ is destined to be poor, and one with a thick member is headed for unhappiness, while 'the man who is called to high things and good fortune has a thin, short member, a smooth gland and hanging testicles.'

Some local peculiarities find mention here, which Vatsyayana, followed by several other Hindu writers, have noted. They studied the variations in sexual practices among different people in India and elsewhere, mainly with the objective of instructing travellers and merchants who had to visit various lands and live among unfamiliar women. A few of their observations are reproduced randomly.

Women of Madhyadesa were moderate in expressing their desires. They loved flirting, courting and a straight union, but abhorred all perverted and abnormal practices. They did not care for kissing, scratching and stroking, but delighted in embraces.

Women of Avantipura also disliked kissing, scratching and stroking, but loved sexual congress in unusual postures.

Women of Malwa and Abhira were fond of being kissed, caressed and embraced and could stand a good deal of biting and scratching, provided these did not cause bruises or hurt.

Women of the Lata country had a passionate temperament and were fond of strokes. A daughter of this land had an artistic and beautiful body; she would dance with joy at the prospect of meeting her lover.

Women of Andhra and Karnataka were delicate and beautiful in appearance. Adept in the art of love, they could be quite bold when excited.

Women of Strirajya were voluptuous. They delighted in hard blows and loved mating with extraordinarily virile men. In the absence of such bulls, they resorted to artificial methods for satisfying their powerful passion.

Women of Magadha and of Maharashtra were smiling beauties, well-versed in the sixty-four arts. However, they had a strong sex nature and used strong language during congress. Experts in the art of love, they delighted in petty quarrels. They dressed with taste and behaved boldly when roused.

Women of Nagara, like those of Maharashtra, were fond of using strong language at the time of mating, although they were gentle by nature.

Women of Vanga were delicate and sweet smelling as flowers. They loved to be kissed and embraced but did not take kindly to scratching and biting. Gentle of speech, they were religious and fond of pilgrimages. They abhorred obscene language even during sexual congress and hated those who used them.

Dravida women responded to men's advances quickly; an

embrace was enough to melt them.

Being bold, women of Utkala were fond of being scratched and hurt, and engaging in love play with the male in sexual congress.

Women of the Gurjara (Gujarat) region were fond of finery. They delighted in the pleasures of love but were satisfied with the lighter, milder forms of love play. They had beautiful eyes, curly hair, slender bodies, heaving breasts and sweet voices.

Women of Kamarupa were sweet of speech. They were extremely sensitive, melting at the mere touch of men. Though fond of caresses, they disliked kissing, scratching and biting, and detested all forms of abnormal practices.

Women of Tirabhukhi had lotus-like eyes and were skilled in the art of love. The very sight of these beautiful women was enough to raise the most violent passion in men. These women were very loyal, and libertines often got into trouble with them.

Women of Malayala were well-proportioned in build, sweet in speech and enthusiastic in love. Though they were bold during sexual congress, they disliked perverted practices.

Chapter 11

The Dangers of Seduction

In examining the position of women in ancient Hindu society, the concept of seduction plays a complex role, tied to the preservation of virtue, social order, and gender norms. Women were both protected and constrained to maintain their honour, often burdened with domestic duties to deter infidelity. Vatsyayana's study of the art of seduction uncovers how deeply women's virtue was tied to social stability and personal honour. In this context, the mechanisms to control women's desires and actions reflect the wider societal preoccupation with the roles women were expected to play in love, marriage, and power.

Hindu lawgivers and moralists constantly remind men of the need for guarding their wives against the designs of evil men, for 'as the birds of prey sweep down on meat thrown on the ground, so do men swoop on an unprotected woman.' However, merely restricting women is no guarantee against seduction. Evil men have many subtle ways of tempting women; a woman so tempted might elude the vigilance of the most jealous husband. Hence, the best method of keeping a wife virtuous is to give her too many domestic responsibilities to allow her time for intrigue.

Wives must be assigned the management of household affairs and kept constantly busy. Attention to cooking and keeping the house clean form the main responsibilities of women in middle class homes, and the scriptures promise eternal bliss to good housewives. Women who cook well are the favourites of gods. Shrutavati, the daughter of the learned Brahmin Bharadwaja, won a deity for a husband because of her devotion to the culinary art. Good housekeeping is as dear to the gods as good cooking.

> Where earthenware is strewn about or there are broken utensils or seats, in such a house, ruined by sinful dirt, women perish. The gods and forefathers go back again hopeless on festivals and holy days from the house of sinful dirt. Broken utensils and bedsteads, cock and dog, and a tree growing by the house, these are all things bringing misfortune. It is said that in broken vessels dwells strife, in the bedstead decay of wealth; the gods do not partake of sacrificial food in the presence of the cock and a dog; in the foot of the tree dwells assuredly a goblin; therefore, the tree shall not be planted.

The need for a woman's devotion to domestic duty is emphasised in the epics:

> Be it her duty to preserve with care
> Her husband's substance; let her be trusted
> With the expenditure, with management
> Of household property and furniture,
> Of cooking and purviewing daily food,
> Let her be ever cheerful, skilled in all domestic work
> and not to be free in spending.

Again, a good woman must know what to avoid:

> Drink, bad companions, absence from her lord,

Rambling about, unseasonable sleep,
Dwelling in other's houses, let her shun,
These are six things that tarnish woman's fame.

A dutiful wife must find interest in gardening—growing various kinds of vegetables for the kitchen and cultivating fruit trees and flower plants. The decoration of the house and family deity's altar should be her special delight.

A woman must always appear cheerful in the presence of her husband. Harsh words and sulky looks are unbecoming in a good wife. If her husband goes astray, he should be reclaimed to the path of virtue by sweet, persuasive methods but never by open antagonism. A slight annoyance is all that a lady is permitted as a protest against the most objectionable behaviour of her husband. She must take care to avoid the company of vagrants, fortune tellers, magicians and necromancers.

When a husband comes home after work, a dutiful wife receives him with a sweet smile, asking him if she could be of any service to him. She then proceeds to bathe his feet and wipe them—never leaving this service to a menial. The faults of one's husband should never be discussed in the presence of others; if he is a drunkard or libertine, she must speak to him in private and try to reclaim him by persuasion and never by threat or antagonism.

A wife must always take pains to understand her husband's taste in food and dress, and please him by all possible means. She must know that perspiration, unclean teeth and body odour are impediments to successful lovemaking. In the bedchamber, a sensible wife must appear beautifully attired, adorned with flowers and jewels. A dutiful wife goes to bed after her husband, and gets up before him. When he is asleep, he should not be awakened.

When her husband is away or on a long journey, a dutiful wife must lead an austere life, strictly keeping religious vows so that he may be saved from all possible harm and return home quickly and safely. She should do away with all ornaments and personal adornments. She must take charge of his business, if he has any, and conduct it skilfully, taking advice from reliable employees and close relatives. While religious duties should receive her attention, she should not leave her house for attending weddings and/or temple processions.

The sages summarise the qualities of the ideal wife as follows:

> The ideal wife is a nurse in illness, a drudge in housekeeping, a wise counsellor in calamity tenderness, the earth Herself in patience (Hindus consider Earth as the symbol of patience. The earth is said to bear the aggregate sins of humankind. The surface of the earth is wet by the blood of carnage, disfigured by the ravages of the ploughman, her bowels are ripped open by miners; she not only suffers all these injuries patiently, but even rewards the ravishers), and a harlot in bed.

The punishments prescribed in Hindu law books for adultery were most severe. This was particularly so where women of the three higher castes were concerned. An adulteress was considered more fallen than a person guilty of Brahmanicide, the most abandoned criminal in the Hindu Penal Code of the time. However, all cases of adultery were not equally heinous; the punishment varied from death penalty to mere fines. A man tempting a woman of a higher caste was considered particularly heinous. Besides the punishments meted out to him in this world, he was threatened with chastisements in the life to come—'He that touches another man's wife is born as a wolf, as a dog, is born as a vulture, a snake, a heron and as a hen crane.' He who seduced his preceptor's wife was considered more fallen than other adulterers and was 'born five lives as a swine, ten as a porcupine, then as a cock, an ant and a worm.'

Adultery itself had many gradations. Speaking with another man's wife in an unseemly manner, winking or smiling at her, touching her garment or any part of her body, sitting with her on the same seat, and caressing her hair among other similar actions constituted adultery, though not of the same objectionable nature as coitus. Sending her gifts or messages were also considered punishable. Even thinking of another man's wife was considered adultery of sorts, though it could not be punished by the state for obvious reasons.

The charm of women has always prevailed over the laws of the pious. In fact, the greatest of the sermons only show how deep seated is human leaning to sin. Not only romantic literature and fiction, but even the scriptures narrate stories of men and women who have succumbed to the weakness of the flesh.

Even the pure and upright Agni (the deity of fire) once fell a victim to the attractions of the wives of the Seven Sages. Chandra, the handsome moon god, once developed an unholy passion for Tara, wife of Brihaspati, preceptor of the gods, and abducted her. More heinous than this was the crime of Indra, king of the gods, who seduced Ahilya, wife of Sage Gautama. When such was the leaning of the celestials to sin, the plight of mortals could very well be imagined.

Vatsyayana had made a separate study of the ways of the seducer. Conditions that led men to seek others' wives were thus enumerated:

- An unprincipled man without any means of livelihood tried to make some money by approaching a wealthy lady prone to temptation.
- A man robbed of his wealth by an enemy tried to seduce the latter's wife with the intention of regaining his wealth through her.

- An unscrupulous man bent upon assassinating an enemy worked on the latter's wife with the intention of making her a willing or innocent accomplice.
- A man whose wife was seduced by another tried to seduce the latter's wife.
- An ambitious politician or adventurer tried to seduce the wife of a rival out of political considerations.
- State spies who wished to obtain secrets from important personages often corrupted their wives to gain their ends.
- Good men were at times tempted to approach beautiful married women known to be free with their charms.

Sometimes, a decent man with no inclination to wickedness fell a victim to lovesickness and tried to seduce a married woman of exceptional charm. According to Kalyanmalla, there were ten stages of lovesickness, the last of which marked the imminence of the lover's death through despair. In this dangerous stage, a man at times contrived the seduction of the woman he loved. The stages of lovesickness which could ultimately prove fatal were:

- The kindling of love at first sight discernible from the tenderness in the eyes of the lover.
- Hallucinations and a delusive feeling that the absent lady was nearabout.
- Restlessness of mind caused from planning schemes to get access to the lady.
- Sleepless nights.
- Loss of appetite and consequent undernourishment and ill health.
- Raving and breaking all laws of decency and decorum.
- Occasional expression, by word of mouth of suicidal tendencies.
- Mental unbalance and signs of insanity.
- Fainting fits, the result of ill health and mental exhaustion.

- Collapse, indicating approaching death.

In the last stage, the lover stopped at nothing.

Women who would not be easily seduced were described as:

- A woman of low sexual ardour.
- Wife of a vigilant husband.
- A lady mourning the death of a near relative.
- A woman deeply attached to her children.
- A lady who values the good name of her family.
- A lady who wishes to avoid scandal.
- A dutiful wife in genuine love with her husband.
- A religious woman.
- Wife of an able and powerful man, stern towards all sinners.
- A lady with natural reserve.

Young wives of old men or men of low sexual vigour, wives of corpulent, impotent, miserly or mean men, hunchbacks, dwarfs and drunkards were easily led astray. Neglected, ill-treated, or superseded wives also fell easy prey to scheming men.

Even virtuous women at times developed a dislike for their husbands for the following reasons:

- Vanity in a husband who is inclined to treat his wife condescendingly or contemptuously.
- Constant ill health of the husband.
- Separation from the husband for long periods.
- A husband's ignorance of the ways of women and the art of love.
- Harsh words and ill-treatment.
- Unfounded suspicion
- Poverty
- Want of refinements in a husband.

An unscrupulous seducer always studied the causes that make women unhappy and fanned the fire of revenge in an ill-treated or suspected wife for furthering his designs. A seducer too, like a lover wooing a bride, employed intermediaries. These intermediaries, always women, were of eight types:

- ***Nishishtartha* or plenipotentiary**: She was a trusted confidante, upon whose intelligence the seducer had total faith. She had full power to act on his behalf, and was left to herself to find out ways and means to win over the woman.
- ***Parimithartha* or messenger of limited power**: As the name indicates, this dignitary's power was limited. After the victim had expressed her desire to meet the seducer, the intermediary's use was to carry the matter, i.e., the intrigue, to a successful end. She arranged the meeting place for the lovers and acted as the woman's companion if the latter had to leave her house to meet her paramour at a distant place.
- ***Patrahari* or letter-bearer**: She took love letters or verbal messages from the seducer to his victim. She was employed only after the secret lovers had made their wishes known to each other.
- ***Swayamduti* or self-messenger**: This person worked for the seducer out of sheer altruism. Usually, she was his intimate lady friend.
- ***Mudhaduti* or foolish messenger**: This simpleton was the innocent wife of a designing man who used her to get access to another woman without her suspecting it, and was a friend or acquaintance of her. She was most skilfully used after the husband had established contact with the woman. By clever instruction, the designing woman taught the 'foolish messenger' what to tell her husband during sexual congress and these verses or epigrams conveyed definite messages to

the husband. While pretending intimacy, she imprinted nail marks and teeth marks on the 'foolish messenger', the import of which was plain to the husband. Similarly, the rogue responded with appropriate words or nail marks, and the 'fool' was thus used as an effective messenger between the two, till the time came when her services could be dispensed with.

- ***Bharyaduti* or wife messenger**: She was not as stupid as the Mudhaduti, but the secret lovers were sufficiently clever to hide their intentions and use her. She was, of necessity, friendly with the lady on whom her husband had designs, and the latter taught her how to behave in the presence of her friend. This behaviour was pregnant with meaning for the lady, and she responded with appropriate actions.
- ***Mukduti* or deaf-mute messenger**: This was a young girl, as innocent as a deaf-mute, so long as love was concerned. She brought seemingly innocent presents, such as toys or books, from the paramour to his lady, in which were concealed love letters or valuable articles which women prized. The girl was incapable of suspecting anything.
- ***Vataduti* or wind-messenger**: She came and went like the wind. She was not a permanent messenger, but one picked up for sending an urgent message.

In matters of temptation, all women were not alike; they had different natures. Women with different dispositions required different techniques. The fair ones, according to their dispositions, were classified into nine by Kalyanmalla:

- **The goddess**: She had a divine disposition, always cheerful, contented and sweet in speech.
- **The Yakshi**: She was fair like the Champaka flower but possessed the disposition of unprincipled Yakshas and

voluptuous Yakshinis, the semi-celestial clan of Kubera, the deity of wealth. She had fleshy breasts, was fond of heady drinks and looked for sexual pleasures with eagerness.

- **The Gandharva**: She was musical like the Gandharvas, the celestial musicians. She was fond of dancing and acting and dressed with taste. In sexual matters, she was inclined to free love.
- **The humane woman**: Kind, hospitable and religious, she was an amiable type. Though disliking sinful adventures, she was incapable of resistance if properly approached.
- **The devil**: This was a woman with a short, dark body and an ugly face. Of unclean habits, she was cruel, but cheerful. She was vindictive and was to be approached with caution.
- **The snake**: Of slimy habits, she was fond of wandering, though always in a hurry. Fond of sleep, she yawned frequently.
- **The crow**: A woman who fretted over nothing, had rolling eyes and was gluttonous, besides having the disposition of a crow.
- **The ass**: A woman who was wicked and voluptuous, and whose voice was as unpleasant and annoying as the braying of an ass; she was known to possess an ass-like disposition. She hated water and washing.

During certain occasions, women fell an easy prey to designing men. During the lassitude that followed strenuous exercise in sports or in dancing, a woman was easily led to the embrace of a designing man. A woman's libido was believed to be at the highest in the middle stages of pregnancy, after a long period of abstinence, a month after childbirth, and just after the purificatory bath following the monthly ailment. The beginning of a mild illness was also a favourable occasion for corrupting women as their resistance was then at the lowest and they craved for masculine sympathy and support. The spring and rainy seasons were exceptionally suited for courting or seducing women.

We have already noticed elsewhere some of the reasons that made married women unhappy, and intelligent men were warned to give their wives no cause for disaffection. But no matter how careful a man would be, some women were likely to develop an interest in other men. Hence, men were warned to watch their wives' behaviour constantly and carefully. A woman losing interest in her husband was likely to act in the following manner:

- Showing no pleasure in sexual congress with him.
- Wiping her lips when kissed by him.
- Showing reluctance to look him straight in the face.
- Shaking her limbs when fondled or caressed by him.
- Replying harshly or evasively to his queries.
- Going to bed before he is ready to sleep.
- Sleeping with her back towards him.
- Getting up early in the morning before her husband.
- Yawning when he tells her interesting stories.
- Delighting at his discomfiture.
- Showing pleasure at his departure from the house, or displeasure at his return.
- Talking indifferently to his friends.
- Praising his enemies.
- Showing no jealousy if he talks of his peccadillos with other women.
- Interrupting him in his conversation.
- Speaking of his shortcomings to her friends.
- Scratching her head when he speaks.

When his wife shows any of these signs of unrest or indifference, the wise man makes efforts to find out the cause of the trouble and proceeds to remedy it. A woman might never confess to hating her husband, but her behaviour can be as eloquent as words, and to the intelligent man this should give all the information he wants in this regard.

The dangers of seduction so far described applied mainly to the ordinary citizen who coveted the wife of his equal. Kings and nobles, too distinguished to contact women outside their harems without raising public scandal, resorted to special methods of seduction.

It was humanly impossible for a king or noble with over a hundred wives to satisfy the sexual cravings of all of them, and Vatsyayana advised the use of artificial methods of coitus for the benefit of the women of the harem. He also gave fair warning to kings about women smuggling men into the harem with or without the knowledge of the palace guards. The occasion usually used for getting men into the harem was when the guards changed duty. When the palace had to be decorated for festivals and ceremonial occasions, artisans and workmen came in and went out of the palace, and the ladies of the harem took advantage of these opportunities to smuggle men into their apartments in the guise of workmen. When the court moved from one place to another for pleasure or pilgrimage, the women's camp was often left without protecting walls, giving men easy access to the harem. Further, the departure of the king on a military expedition or for the hunt necessitated leaving many women of the harem behind. During his absence, vigilance was less strict and intrigues were carried on by the women without much inconvenience or fear of detection.

In spite of all the pleasures, the many women of the palace afforded, a king too, at times, developed an interest in a commoner's wife. But, he could not visit the lady in public or even in her own house for obvious reasons. Vatsyayana tells us that in such cases, kings got the lady into the palace. A daring king sent messengers to her house who, as if not knowing the king in person, asked the lady to form an acquaintance with some influential woman of the harem to promote her husband's welfare. The messengers helpfully suggested the name of a lady in the palace, and introduced the victim to this person. Once she started visiting the harem, the king saw to it that she was shown the most magnificent halls and pleasure gardens of the palace. She was cunningly led to solitary parks or pleasure pools, and the king, as if by accident, came across the party. The messengers then quietly withdrew leaving His Majesty to deal with the situation in person.

Festivals in ancient and medieval India were celebrated royally, and the palaces looked attractive on these occasions. Ladies of the nobility usually visited the palace during the festivities for fun and for forming social connections. Many of the arranged matches of the aristocracy started off from here, as the matrons often came with their young daughters and old women had many opportunities to meet eligible female candidates for marriage. At times, an unprincipled king, who had an eye on a noble's wife or daughter, used this occasion for seducing her through skilful accomplices.

Chapter 12

The Courtesans

Merry Women of the City

Courtesans in ancient Hindu society occupied a unique and often contradictory position—celebrated for their beauty, charm, and wit, yet seen as dangerous figures skilled in the arts of seduction and manipulation. Texts, like *Kama Sutra*, explore their high status and the intricate strategies they employed to captivate and control their lovers. Depicted as masters of affection and wealth extraction, courtesans used a variety of psychological and emotional tactics to navigate relationships. Their roles reflect broader societal views on desire, power, and gender, revealing the complex ways in which women could wield influence while still being bound by societal expectations and moral judgements.

Ancient Hindu society recognised and developed two classes of women—the housewife devoted to her husband and domestic duties, and the woman of the city. The first was known as the *kulavadhu*, daughter-in-law of the family, while the other was called by the rather unflattering term of *nagarvadhu*, daughter-in-law of the entire city, meaning 'belonging' to everyone.

The daughter-in-law was confined to the home and the main objective of her life was childbearing. She had a certain status as a wife, but hardly any individuality. The courtesan, on the other hand, was free and merry, living to please men. She could earn wealth and gain influence of a degree the housewife couldn't even dream of, but a nagarvadhu was a nagarvadhu, and remained one. Social interaction between the sexes was prohibited, and courtship generally denied to the respectable classes during certain phases of Hindu social development. Hence, the male could only display his spirit of emulation in sexual matters concerning the courtesan. Consequently, during these phases, the courtesan occupied an important position in society, the same as the hetaera in ancient Greece.

In stark contrast, prostitution is abhorred in modern India. It continues to flourish in many pockets and is seen as a necessary social evil, but active efforts are being made to abolish it.

In the Mahabharata, we read of courtesans as forming part of a king's retinue or camp. In ancient times, when a king wished to honour distinguished visitors on special occasions, the courtesans of the capital were ordered to go out and receive them at the city gates. Similarly, a hero returning to the city after conquest of foes was received by the city's fair charmers.

In medieval India, accomplishments that men prize as desirable were generally denied to women; respectable women were not allowed to learn music or dancing. Literacy, too, was not easily accessible to them; the most respectable women were those who never stirred out of their homes. Under these conditions, the wife degenerated into a household article and a man of taste and culture could not find intellectual or cultural companionship in his wife. The courtesans, on the other hand, cultivated all the arts that attracted men. They were accomplished singers and dancers; their establishments were tastefully furnished and decorated with a view to lull the senses and capture the heart. A good courtesan also had considerable literary taste, and often competed with poets and authors in the art of composing verses extempore. She patronised men of letters, painters and sculptors who often visited her for the pleasures of the intellect and the senses. She was free to go about as she pleased, and during public festivities, she would ride through the city streets with a retinue of young courtesans and pages. Proprietors of theatres and other places of public amusement looked up to her for patronage. It was a pleasure and a privilege for a man to be seen in her company. Merchants and noblemen often paid her huge sums to get her special attention in public, not to mention the fabulous sums she demanded for the real pleasures in private. In one of the *Jatakas*, we read of a courtesan who charged a lover 5,000 gold pieces as her fee for a single hour!

In Vatsyayana's time, the courtesan was the ruler of high society. Gentlemen of fashion were visited by courtesans who were lavishly entertained in the front halls from where the wives were excluded. Men who wished to impress their friends and the public took beautiful courtesans with them on hunting expeditions or paid social calls. To be known as possessing an accomplished courtesan as mistress was a coveted honour for a wealthy man, and he often made a public exhibition of his mistress and himself.

The establishment of a prince in ancient India consisted of a regiment of courtesans who danced and sang in the court for his pleasure and for the entertainment of distinguished visitors. Kautilya, author of the *Arthashastra*, one of the world's most authoritative works on ancient statecraft, has an interesting chapter on courtesans. All the women of pleasure at the court were under a chief courtesan, who was selected for this honour primarily because of her beauty and accomplishments. She was paid almost the same wage as a minister.

Under the chief courtesan was a rival courtesan, who received half her salary. The main outdoor duty of the courtesans of the palace was to add to the splendour of the court by holding the royal umbrella, golden pitcher and fan, attending upon the king seated on his royal litter, throne or chariot. From the age of eight, a girl was expected to join the daily musical performances held in the palace before the king.

It is futile to talk of any universal standard of moral conduct, as this was nowhere to be found in the ancient world. There was no such universal standard of morality in ancient Greece, Rome, Egypt, Babylon or China. The Hindu world maintained that sexual morality, like dharma or religious duty, depended primarily on birth, environment and caste. What was good for the Brahmin was not always good for the non-Brahmin, and the standards of Shudras were not applicable to the three higher castes. Again, what was permissible for a man was not always permissible for a woman. For women of the three higher castes—Brahmin, Kshatriya and Vaishya—to take up prostitution was a crime for which there was no penance. The women of these castes were bound by strict rules embodied in the *Dharmashastras,* and any deviation was treated harshly.

Courtesans in medieval India were mostly Shudras; certain sub-castes had prostitution as their traditional occupation. Caste had always been considered a divinely ordained institution regulating not only one's social and moral conduct, but also one's occupation. Hence, it was more or less the duty of women of these castes to practise the trade; engaging themselves in any other occupation was considered a deviation from duty. From early childhood, the women of these castes were trained in dancing, singing and other arts that please men. Exceptionally beautiful women with necessary accomplishments rose to the position of *ganikas* (arch-courtesans) and were sought after by nobles, wealthy merchants and even kings.

In the *Dasa Kumara Charita*, a Sanskrit classic by the well-known writer Dandi, there is an interesting moral situation in which a courtesan finds it difficult to distinguish right from wrong. One day, Kamamanjari, the most accomplished courtesan in the city of Champa, capital of the kingdom of Anga, came to the sage Marichi and begged him to take her as his disciple. She told the sage that she found her life of pleasure improper and that she wished to lead a life of renunciation. While she was still imploring the sage to accept her, her relatives, headed by her mother, came to the sage and recounted to him the misery the silly girl had brought upon them by deviating from the path of her dharma or duty. The mother complained that the girl even got angry for bringing her up to follow the traditional occupation of the caste, the pursuit of which was her highest dharma. She lamented thus:

> Obvious duty is as follows for the mother of a *fille de joie*: Care of her daughter's person from the hour of birth; nourishment by a diet so regulated as to develop stateliness, vigour, complexion, intelligence, while harmonising the humours of gastric calefaction, and secretions; not permitting her to see too much even of her father after the fifth year; festive ritual on birthdays and holy days; instruction in the art of flirtation, both major and minor; thorough training in dance, song, instrumental music, acting, painting; also judgement of foods, perfumes, flowers, not forgetting writing and graceful speech; a conversational acquaintance with grammar, with logical inference and conclusion; profound skill in money-making, sport, and betting on cockfights and chess; assiduous use of go-

betweens in the passages of coquetry; display of numerous well-dressed attendants at religious or secular celebrations; careful selection of teachers to ensure success at unpremeditated vocal and other exhibitions; advertising on a national scale by a staff of trained specialists; publicity for beauty-marks through astrologers and the like; eulogistic mention in gatherings of men about town of her beauty, character, accomplishments, charm, and sweetness by hangers-on, gay dogs, buffoons, female religionists and others; raising her price considerably when she has become an object of desire to young gentlemen; surrender to a lover of independent fortune, a phylogynist or one intoxicated by seeing her charms, a gentleman eminent for rank, figure, youth, money, vigour, purity, generosity, cleverness, gallantry, art, character and sweetness of disposition; delivery, with gracious exaggeration of value received, to one less affluent, but highly virtuous and cultivated (the alternative is levying on his natural guardians, after informal union with such a gentleman); collection of bad debts by vamping judge and jury; mothering her lover's daughter; abstraction, by ingenious tricks, of money left in an admirer's possession after payment for periodical pleasures; steady quarrelling with a defaulter or miser; stimulation of the spirit of generosity in an over-thrifty adorer by the incentive of jealousy; repulse of the impecunious by biting speeches, by public taunts, by cutting his daughters, and by other embarrassing habits, as well as by simple contempt; continued clinging to the openhanded, the chivalrous, the blameless, the wealthy with full consideration of the inter-related chances of money and misery.

Besides, a courtesan should show readiness indeed, but no devotion to a lover; and even if fond of him, she should not disobey mother or grandmother. In spite of all this, the

> girl disregards her God-given vocation and has spent an entire month of amusement—at her own expense!—with a Brahmin youth, a fellow from nowhere whose face is his fortune. Her snippiness has offended several perfectly solvent admirers and has pauperised her own family. And when I scolded her, "This is no kind of a scheme. This isn't pretty," she was angry and took to the woods. And if she is obstinate, this whole family will stay right here and starve to death. There is nothing else to do.

In her distress, the mother fell at the sage's feet and wept. The sage concurred with her view that the best means of salvation for each caste was to perform the prescribed duties and follow the traditional occupation. Since a courtesan's duty was to trade in pleasure, the holy man admonished Kamamanjari to give up all ambitions of short cuts to salvation through renunciation, and asked her to go with her mother and religiously practice her trade. However, Kamamanjari could not be persuaded; Marichi reluctantly accepted her as a disciple, asking her mother to go home and call after a few days.

It is interesting to know that this episode is also alleged to be a hoax. There are those who assert that the quarrel between the mother and the daughter was fake. In becoming Marichi's disciple, Kamamanjari's real intention was to seduce him in order to win a wager. In an argument between Kamamanjari and a rival courtesan, the latter taunted her that she was 'talking as if she had seduced Marichi.' Kamamanjari retorted that seducing the ascetic Marichi was not such an impossible task for her as her rival imagined. With tempers rising high, the courtesans laid a wager based on which Kamamanjari, if successful in seducing Marichi, was to have her rival as a slave; failure to seduce the sage would result in Kamamanjari being enslaved!

Ancient Hindu writers were well acquainted with the ways of the courtesan. Says Bhartrihari:

A heart morose; a face lit up with pride,
A nature intricate as mountain pass;
A mind as fickle as dew on tumbling grass;
A vanity the peacock never vied;
A succubus that mimes the gentle bride;
That loves not what man is but what he has;
That dessicates, yet will not be denied.
Such is the ageless, changeless courtesan,
The woman glancing through her half-closed eyes,
Who wisps men's veins with passion like a flail.
I know her now, and yet—how weak is man!
She still allures me to her paradise
That leads to hell—but will she there avail?

While Vatsyayana's *Kama Sutra* deals with the subject in a purely scientific spirit, there are two well-known works on the courtesan's trade which are of literary character. One is *Kuttinimatham* (*Lessons of a Bawd*) by Damodaragupta and the other *Samaya Matrika* (*Harlot's Breviary*) by Kshemendra. The *Kuttinimatham* contains instructions for the probationer and is in the form of professional advice from an elder member to a novice. It is based on the *Kama Sutra*. The *Samaya Matrika* is the biography of a courtesan, embodying her varied experience and adventures. Kshemendra was a versatile genius who wrote on several subjects and his style in *Samaya Matrika* is marked by cruel wit.

It is interesting to note that one of the most popular plays of ancient India, the *Mrichchakatika* (*Clay Cart*) had a courtesan for its heroine. Written by the royal playwright Shudraka, it depicts Indian life in the early centuries of the period after the beginning of what may be termed the Christian era. Unlike other Sanskrit works which mainly deal with the gods, demons and kings, the *Mrichchakatika* deals with the life of ordinary citizens. The fact that a king who had no illusions about royalty wrote the play was probably responsible for this interesting deviation from convention.

The following two well-known stanzas about the courtesan are found in the *Mrichchakatika*:

> In the same tank do bathe the learned as the fool,
> The crow does bend a branch as does the peafowl,
> All men do cross a stream in the selfsame boat;
> A courtesan, like the tank, the branch, the boat must serve all.
> Ever the courtesan is the young man's companion,
> Common to all as the wayside creeper;
> Your body a merchandise saleable for gold;
> Serve then the dear as well as the loathed.

Dattaka, and following him, Vatsyayana had made a thorough and scientific study of the ways of the courtesans.

Vatsyayana classified the courtesans of his time into nine:

- ***Kumbhadasi* or common slave**: Common harlots, cheap as *Kumbhas* or spittoons, came under this category. They gave themselves up to all and sundry for a small fee and had neither beauty nor accomplishments.
- ***Paricharika* or attendant**: She was the virgin daughter or ward of an elderly courtesan 'married' to a man in accordance with a special form of marriage prevalent in brothels. The Paricharika, after deflowering by her husband, was allowed to practice as a freelancer till the expiry of a stipulated period

mentioned in the marriage contract, but was bound to 'attend' on her 'husband' when called.

- ***Kulata* or secret prostitute**: She was a married woman who secretly practised the trade for profit.
- ***Swairini* or free woman**: Like Kulata, she was a married woman but practised the trade openly with her husband's approval and freedom to do so.
- ***Nati* or actress**: Dancers and actresses constituted the better class of common courtesans in medieval India. Their ostensible means of livelihood was acting or dancing, but they never refused a good offer for their favours.
- ***Silpakarika* or the artisan's wife**: Wives of artisans, usually from the Shudra castes, worked in the households of higher castes. If not engaged on a full-time basis, they often visited these households for casual work, for collecting their husband's wages or for receiving gifts on festive occasions, and were easily led astray by designing male members of the household. In fact, women of the lower classes were always attracted towards men of the higher classes. Apart from the obvious pecuniary motive, a woman was usually flattered by the thought of getting a son by a man of a higher caste. Hence, a man found it easy to seduce a woman below his social status, but extremely difficult to seduce a woman of a caste higher than his.
- ***Prakashavinasta* or run-away wife**: She was the wife of a respectably married man, who had eloped with a paramour and lived with him as his concubine.
- ***Rupajivi* or lovely body-seller**: This courtesan was noted for her flawless bodily proportions and physical beauty.
- ***Ganika* or super-courtesan**: This was the highest category of heart ravisher. Besides having a body as desirable as that

of the Rupajivi, she possessed several accomplishments which made her the gem of her class. She was well-versed in the sixty-four arts. Wise as a king's minister, she was sought after by monarchs not only for pleasure, but also for instruction. The fashionable competed among themselves for winning her favours, and poets wrote panegyrics about her accomplishments.

In the Mahabharata, there is yet another classification of courtesans. According to this epic, courtesans were of five kinds:

- ***Rajaveshya,*** or royal courtesan, who catered to the needs of kings.
- ***Nagari,*** or city harlot, who had her establishment in the city and was much sought after by fashionable citizens for pleasure.
- ***Guptaveshya,*** or secret harlot, who came of a good family and practised the trade secretly to avoid scandal.
- ***Devaveshya,*** or girlfriend of the celestials, who was attached to some temple.
- ***Brahmaveshya (Thirthaga),*** or harlot of the bathing places, who sought pilgrims who flocked at the sacred streams during seasons of pilgrimages.

Vatsyayana has allotted several chapters of the *Kama Sutra* to the art and wiles of the courtesan. His treatise is exhaustive and some portions are summarised below to warn men against the snares of the courtesan.

The courtesans of his time were clever dissemblers. While selling pleasure for profit, a courtesan pretended to be in genuine love with her victim. She knew that the knowledge that a woman was yielding her person for mere money was likely to rob the lover of his pleasure. Hence, she cleverly pretended passionate attachment to him. She left money transactions to her mother; if she had no mother, she engaged an elderly bawd to act as her mother.

A successful courtesan employed agents and dependents who could access fashionable society and contact the leisured rich. Some of the types of men whom a courtesan counted as possible victims were:

- A wealthy man not loyal to his wife.
- A boastful dandy.
- A handsome man vain of his good looks.
- An impotent nobleman who wished to be known as exceptionally virile.
- A wealthy spendthrift.
- A childless man whose death was expectantly awaited by near relatives.
- The only son of a wealthy man.
- The head of a religious institution who was publicly celibate and secretly lascivious.
- A youth contemptuous of his superiors.
- An independent young man possessing a large income.

These men were sought after only for the sake of wealth. But, the acquisition and keeping of wealth needed the help of other men whose friendship a courtesan had to cultivate with no thought of receiving cash payment. Because of her profession, a courtesan made many enemies, the most potent of whom were rivals in the profession and jealous lovers. Hence, the careless and unwary courtesan not only ruined herself financially but also put her life in danger. Hence, she required the friendship of reliable and powerful men. Men of this category, to whom a courtesan doled out her charms, were well-placed state officials, and strong men of daring, like distinguished soldiers or wrestlers.

As pimps, procurers, and spies, a courtesan employed a

number of paid servants who were clever but needy; however, these servants were not entertained as lovers. Suitable persons of this type, who were employed on a part-time or full-time basis were:

- Petty police officers
- Clerks in law courts
- Astrologers
- Jesters
- Florists
- Perfumers
- Barmen
- Mendicants
- Barbers
- Paupers who came from a good family and had, as such, contact with the higher classes
- Professors and teachers of fine arts to whom young men of the aristocracy went for instruction.

The duty of these agents was to procure suitable lovers for their mistress. It was bad business for a courtesan to openly offer herself for sale; the buyer was always made to seek her. It was here that agents helped. By enumerating her accomplishments with necessary exaggerations, but without giving the impression that they were advertising their mistress, her agents ensured the courtesan got countrywide publicity. They were always on the lookout for desirable customers, and as soon as one showed interest in her, they faithfully reported his qualifications, tastes, and, above all, financial position to her.

Apart from professional activities, a courtesan had her own life to live. Being a woman, it was in her nature to love a man for the sake of love. In response to this emotional side of hers, she, at times, entertained a lover without any pecuniary motive.

However, blind love in this matter was avoided. The candidate selected for the favour was a cultured man of her own position. A handsome young man of noble birth was usually preferred; he had a thorough knowledge of literature and fine arts, and was able to discuss the comparative merits of works of art and poetry. He was courteous, had easy manners, was a good conversationalist, a student of comparative religion, and fond of social gatherings, picnics, drinking parties, festivities, sports and theatricals. While he showed no objection to drinking and even took pleasure in it, he was not a habitual drunkard. He was never argumentative, for arguments lead to blows. He was a good mixer and was free, for obvious reasons, from jealousy and suspicion. In spite of all these accomplishments, if the favourite gave any trouble, he was thrown out without the least hesitation. The main objective of a courtesan's life was acquiring wealth and fame, and her own personal predilections were not allowed to stand in the way of this all-important duty.

Apart from these desirable lovers, a courtesan would sometimes yield herself to an undesirable one under exceptional circumstances. She would give in to the advances of a desperate man to save her life or avoid injury; to take revenge, sometimes a courtesan would yield to a man if doing so could induce him to injure her enemy. A courtesan usually trained herself, and, as an exercise, consorted with virile men whom she probably did not like. If a pious, but impecunious, man begged for her favours, a courtesan aspiring for religious merit acceded to his request as an act of charity. Compassion for a poor man who was hopelessly in love with her also moved a kind-hearted courtesan to bestow her favours upon him. Sometimes, to oblige a friend, a courtesan slept with another man at his request. Lastly, if a courtesan was taken by the bearing of a virile-looking man, or had heard of the extraordinary virility of a reputedly libidinous man, she gave herself up to him out of curiosity to find out the truth about him.

Having found a client on whom she could depend for a semi-permanent attachment, a courtesan usually ascertained his tastes and financial position through her spies. If he was a man worth taking troubles, she received him with the greatest deference and entertained him. To please him, she selected the amusements he loved the most. Quail fights, cock fights and ram fights were held if he was interested in these; theatricals or musical concerts were organised if he was fond of such performances. Young maidservants attended upon him, and he was regaled with sweet, intoxicating beverages. The courtesan sat by his side and worked him up with her blandishments to an erotic pitch, while playing the shy maiden, lest by officious or bold conduct, she should give herself away. She knew well that men in love did not appreciate what was easily obtained. The courtesan's attendant made suggestive hints while she behaved like a revolted maiden.

When the lover's demand became urgent, the courtesan decided to yield to him; with due coyness, she conducted him to her well-decorated private chamber. Here, she was at liberty to fall onto his chest in a paroxysm of passion and tell him, weeping, that she had never loved a man so worthy, that his conversation was enchanting, and his humour unparalleled. This was easily believed if presented with caresses, kisses and a show of abandon, imitating young maiden deeply in love, alone with her lover in a secluded spot. For most men, she knew, have a high opinion of themselves, and every fool is apt to imagine that there is something peculiarly attractive in him which makes women fall for him.

After the initial protests of passion, the courtesan took her lover to bed and showed him her mastery of the art of love. A woman well-versed in the eighty-four postures gave her lover pleasures hitherto unknown. The wily courtesan was careful not to boast of her knowledge of the art of love. Rather, she took care to tell him that she had learnt more in that one hour with him than in all her life, that she had never met so great a master of the art of love. During sexual congress, she took care to note what pleased him the most and confided to him what she desired the most. When, after coitus, lassitude overtook him, she gazed lovingly into his eyes. When he was half-asleep, she kissed and embraced him passionately, as if expressing her deep-seated love, and ensured that he was wakeful enough to notice her activities.

After such a night, the lover was likely to be a regular visitor to her establishment. If he was wealthy enough to keep her in affluence, she took care not to entertain other lovers in his presence. However, minor lovers who recognised their relationship with her were entertained secretly and dismissed when he was expected.

After establishing initial relations with a desirable lover, the next step was to charm him. With this objective in view, the courtesan showed him a devotion as staunch as a wedded wife's. She would appear cheerful and confiding in his presence. When he was expected, she would stand at the doorway and anxiously wait for his arrival, and when he came, welcomed him with the sweetest of smiles. If he showed absentmindedness during conversation, she expressed concern for his worries and requested him to share his sorrows and troubles. She applauded his tastes, abhorred what he disliked, appeared cheerful when he looked pleased and worried when he was unhappy. She would feign displeasure and pretend to be jealous on noticing any tooth or nail marks on his body inflicted by his wife or any other lady. In his company, she would pay the utmost attention to what he said. While readily agreeing to all his views, his very mention of his wife or any other woman with anything near affection would evince her displeasure, as if she was unable to bear it. When the lover sighed, sneezed or coughed loudly, she would pray for his longevity.

In the presence of her lover, no one else was praised, nor was any physical defect mentioned that could apply to him. While sleeping with him, she expressed her love for him, as if talking in sleep. If the lover was unhappy due to bereavement, she too would go into mourning. If he fell ill, she fasted for his recovery and gave generously to Brahmins and deities, praying for his quick recovery. In case of financial loss and consequential worry for the lover, the courtesan expressed deep concern for his loss and even made a pretext of offering her own wealth to save him the worry. When the lover left her house, she came out up to the gate and stood there mournfully looking at the retreating figure. If he happened to look back and see her, she feigned shyness and confusion, as if surprised in the act of secretly expressing her longing to gaze at him for as long as she could. If, before going on a long journey, he came to take leave of her, she told him that life was not worth living without him and expressed extreme unhappiness. She would even mention how she longed to have a son by him so that she could derive some comfort by seeing the boy when the father was away. In short, a courtesan who desired to have a thorough hold on her lover surpassed the most devoted wife in her show of fidelity.

So much for winning and holding a lover! However, this was not the end of a courtesan's profession, but the means to the end goal, which was profit. It was handling this branch of the trade that called for the greatest cunning. An open demand for cash as the price of her favours was not at all conducive to cultivating a good relationship, but she was liable to give herself away in spite of the most careful plans to play the devoted wife. Herein came the crucial role of the courtesan's mother.

The mother was placed in an ideal position to demand money from the lover. She could openly tell her daughter in his presence that she was a fool, giving herself away to the man out of sheer infatuation when a dozen wealthier men sought her, each offering ten times the price this particular gentleman was able to pay. The courtesan played her part well; on hearing this, she appeared torn between her own predilections and duty towards the other. Such behaviour was likely to make the lover pay the mother generously to save his beloved from distress. The mother always, and invariably, showed displeasure at her daughter's deep attachment to the lover and, in his presence, dissuaded her from going out with him; the daughter would defend the lover with equal obstinacy and go out with him. During these arguments, she even threatened to commit suicide and cursed her fate for being under such a greedy woman and in a profession which compelled her to seek filthy lucre over personal attachments. Nevertheless, she always acted in strict conformity with the secret instructions she had received from her mother, and sometimes even refused to go out with him under the pretext of obeying the mother's imperative orders, thereby making him pay far more when he visited next.

Sometimes, the courtesan would get a good deal of money directly from the lover without appearing to compel payment. Jewellery dealers were secretly instructed to arrive at her establishment with their wares when the lover was in the house. Thus, while looking at the jewels, she would express a desire to possess them while pretending that she was short of cash. She would ask the jeweller for credit, which, of course, would be refused; and only a mean lover would let such a golden opportunity to show generosity slip. At times, fake debtors presented fictitious bills to the courtesan, and, upon her expressing inability to pay at the moment, were permitted to assume an aggressive attitude in the presence of the lover. Moreover, they threw in a word or two to suggest that the debts were contracted because of her arranging lavish entertainments for her lover.

In addition to these subtle external methods of compulsion, at times, the courtesan herself threw in some hints that the lover could not ignore out of decency. For instance, she would tell him that she could not attend an important function at a friend's house as she didn't have enough money to buy a suitable present. She would fake up a theft in her house and express distress at the misfortune which compelled her to appear before him without any jewellery. She would also complain of her mother's extravagance and mismanagement, the high cost of living and the low income, and the impatience of creditors. On hearing these sad stories, the infatuated voluptuary was bound to relieve her of her distress. If he was miser and unmoved, she would plainly tell him that she was on the verge of ruin and he alone could save her.

There was another subtle way by which a courtesan extracted money out of a lover. At times, she acted as a propagandist for physicians, artists, sculptors and architects, convincing her lover to engage them for important work, while secretly levying a commission on the profits without his knowledge. A courtesan constantly dinned into her lover's ears the position of her rivals and of their lovers, who kept them in luxury. If all these methods failed, there was a last resort which ensured extortion from the most parsimonious lover. The courtesan would arrange for someone to bring a fictitious attachment order and seize her possessions, including the lover's jewellery. A lover who lost his ornaments in this way never dared to go to law, out of shame.

A courtesan used these methods to secure a semi-permanent attachment to a wealthy man of fashion, which was likely to yield her more profit than freelance work. However, in certain places and seasons, freelance work was more profitable; hence, she did not attach herself to a particular individual. For instance, in great cities, where foreign merchants and diplomats resided, the better class of courtesans were in high demand and often auctioned their charms. Lower-ranked courtesans also followed the same line of action when the demand was greater than the supply. After a singing or dancing performance at the courtesan's establishment, where her performance was well applauded by the audience, it was a good business for the courtesan's mother to auction off the dancer, accepting the highest bidder as the guest of the night. The courtesan knew that a well-fostered competitive spirit among the guests, especially after they were drunk, was likely to bring in fabulous sums for a single night.

It is interesting to observe that the writers on the profession maintained that in no other trade did the time factor count for so much as it did in this business. A time invariably came when the most desirable lover had to be driven out—maybe all that could be got had been squeezed out of him; maybe he had grown aggressively jealous and overbearing, or was useless for the courtesan, having been financially ruined. It was, then, time to break off relations with him and strike up a new friendship.

In certain cases, loss of fortune or long familiarity has its effect on the lover; a growing indifference probably led to a lover's final departure without any unpleasantness. But not all men are sensible in love; some fools disregarded the fact that without a continuous income even the most beautiful courtesan could be reduced to the position of a beggar woman. They would continue to cling on to her like leeches even after losing everything and becoming paupers. It was then necessary for a courtesan to get rid of them.

Lovers were not antagonised by rude behaviour if subtle methods could be effective. A courtesan's coldness or indifference could give the necessary hint to a sensitive man to break off. If the lover took no notice of such behaviour, more obvious methods were employed. For instance, in his presence, the courtesan would talk at length with others on subjects of which he had no knowledge, and when he blurted out something out of tune, it only exposed his ignorance. When she wished to seek advice, she consulted others in his presence and followed their advice, even if he suggested a different course of action. She openly praised his enemies and spoke ill of his friends. If he sought her in private, she refused to oblige him; if invited to his house, she would send a messenger to openly demand, in the presence of his guests, an exorbitant sum which he possibly could not produce. When he was expected in her house, she would go out, leaving word that she had gone to visit a lover, preferably an enemy of his. In the company of other men, she would laugh in derision on his serious observations and assume a serious expression on his clever jokes.

When by any mischance she had to go to bed with him, she would close her lips when he tried to kiss her. Any attempt to make nail or teeth marks on her body were rudely objected to. If he tried to force her, she would lock her arms to prevent an embrace. When he was exhausted, she would invite him for sexual congress, and if he was unable to satisfy her, question his claim to manhood.

If even these open methods failed to evict the unwanted lover, a courtesan would summon the help of servants. Pretending to be angry at his words or behavior, she would strike her servants in his presence, which, according to the accepted conventions of insolent behaviour, was as good as a slap on his face. She would instruct the servants to be rude to him. If even these did not avail, she plainly told him that he was unwanted and should stay out of the house. If the infatuated voluptuary still persisted, the servants were asked to remove him forcefully.

In her studied misbehaviour designed to eject a lover, the courtesan often relied on the chance that, in future, he would likely be entertained again. He might improve his financial position and be again in a position to keep her in affluence. A clever man might find favour with the king who might pay off his debts and bestow upon him endowments, making him the wealthiest man in the city. An heir to a desirable fortune, thrown out of his house for extravagance or association with bad characters might, upon the death of his father or a near relative, inherit vast wealth. It is because of these possible turns of fortune that a courtesan tried to avoid, if possible, irreparable and rash methods of getting rid of an impoverished lover.

Vatsyayana has a chapter in the *Kama Sutra* devoted to the art of repairing broken relations with a lover. In the case of a lover who had, of his own accord, broken off relations, the courtesan waited for the initiative to come from him. If he had left her after getting attached to another courtesan, only to return and seek his former love as a whim, he was made to pay excessively before being taken back into favour. However, if he had not actually left the second courtesan but was trying to contact his former love seeking reconciliation, she first ascertained the true nature of his intentions. If she was convinced of his sincerity, he was taken back. But, rival courtesans were always treated with suspicion, and men under their influence with the greatest caution. At times, courtesans used their lovers to make fools of their rivals; if this was found to be the lover's intention, then he was not only rejected but humiliated as well.

Rejected lovers often turned malicious and spiteful, and a courtesan exercised great caution in dealing with them. While some men nursed grievances and constantly sought opportunities for revenge, there were others of a softer nature, who readily forgot the past in the joy of the present. In all cases, a wary courtesan left the initiative to come from the lover himself. If a courtesan kept up her fame and was known as the most fashionable in the city, or even as one of the most desirable, men of fashion had to seek her out of necessity as association with her was likely to enhance their reputation. So, when a rejected lover regained his wealth, he returned to the old flame with an added zest and a sense of having regained some precious possession lost through folly or misfortune. Such men were accepted if they were able to pay their way up.

There were certain conditions under which a courtesan took the initiative to repair broken relations. A courtesan would contact a rejected lover who had risen to fame and wealth, or to an extraordinarily exalted position in the state by the king's favour. Again, if a courtesan was convinced that a rival was responsible for his parsimony and consequent strained relations, she went out of her way to avenge herself, take the initiative and humiliate the rival.

In making advances to a rejected lover, the courtesan's mother was often a convenient scapegoat. The courtesan would send word to her lover that the crafty, greedy, old woman was responsible for her foolish conduct towards him. She would tell him that if he would be so kind as to forget the past and take her under his patronage again, she would kick the old woman out of the house, by arrangement with the woman herself. Worries due to financial troubles were also advanced as excuses for past misconduct, and she even repented, putting forward an unconditional apology. Stories of secret sciences employed by a rival courtesan or a jealous admirer were also used to convince a superstitious lover, and secret agents were paid to drop hints to others in his presence, corroborating these statements.

When, by such methods, the courtesan's innocence was forced upon the lover, he was likely to come back to her; if, and when, he did, he was received with happiness, and the occasion was celebrated befittingly.

All things, however, must end, and the beauty of a courtesan, alas, is no exception to this rule. A time would come when the most skilful art would fail to bring any lovers to the ageing courtesan. Time, that cruel destroyer of youth and beauty, would eventually lay low the proudest Ganika, and happy would be the courtesan who had earned enough in her youth and saved something for this rainy day. An old courtesan was not, however, entirely without any source of income. If she had young and attractive daughters, hers or adopted ones, she managed the establishment for them, instructing them in the art and craft of love. A courtesan who had squandered away her money in youth usually made a living by working as a bawd or 'mother' to the earning members of the profession.

Chapter 13

Sex in Religion and as Religion

In exploring the intersection of sex and spirituality, Hindu scriptures offer a nuanced and often symbolic view of desire, union, and divinity. This chapter delves into how Hinduism and Christianity approach the sacredness of sex, particularly within the context of worship. Through Hindu scriptures, like the *Brihadaranyaka Upanishad* and the Mahabharata, we see the dual nature of existence. Shiva's supremacy and his union with Parvati symbolise the cosmic balance of creation, where sexuality becomes an embodiment of divine unity. These scriptures reveal how sex is seen not only as a physical act but as a spiritual practice, where the sacred and the sensual converge, shedding light on the complex relationship between religion, desire, and societal norms.

To Westerners steeped in Christianty, sex and religion are not only opposites, but also opposing. Religion is regarded in Western religion as other-worldly, focused on the hereafter, while sex is material. Dominated by St Paul's views and the austere tendencies of the medieval Church, Christianity considers sex as something unspeakable. Christians view sex-worship as a

Pagan 'evil' that existed in Babylon, Syria, pre-Christian Rome and Greece. The Christian (Western) world would certainly be shocked to learn of its prevalence in the modern world among civilised people.

While Hindu civilisation does not worship sex, it does not condemn or shun it. Sex is subsumed by the second of the *purusharthas,* kama (gratification of human desires, of which sex is a crucial part). Such outrage is the outcome of ignorance and/or deliberate misinformation, often with none-too-hidden missionary agendas. To dispel them, it is imperative that readers take pains to understand Hinduism and view its ideals and practices in their correct perspective.

Hinduism is not a religion like Christianity or Islam, with set dogmas. It is a civilisation that is the outcome of a very ancient, almost timeless, culture. The European civilisation has grown out of the teachings of the philosophers and thinkers of ancient Rome and Greece, and later Christianity—the Church, Luther, Calvin, Voltaire and Rousseau, Francis Bacon, Carlyle, Herbert Spencer, Hume, Fichte, Kant, Nietzsche, Freud, Bernard Shaw, H G Wells, and Bertrand Russell among others. Similarly, Hinduism is a growth of ideas, philosophies and beliefs which, while differing widely, have sufficient fundamental unity to be known as a single culture. Even among orthodox Hindus, one may find people who are poles apart in beliefs and practices—people who hold the view that God is one or gods are many, that there is no God or that there is nothing but God, that there is an afterlife or that there is none, that caste is divinely ordained or that caste is manmade. It would be difficult to locate beliefs in Hinduism that aren't contradicted by Hindus themselves.

But Hinduism is not a mere mishmash of beliefs and local dogmas with no underpinning. The higher Hindu conception of

God is monistic. Western writers and propagandists have criticised what they believe to be a 'lack of ethics' in Hinduism. This again stems from the inadequacy of the Western/Christian mind in understanding dharma, the Western translations of which have been unable to transcend the concept of 'religion'. Formal and structured religions have neatly divided the human realm into good and evil. The latter is categorised not on the basis of lack of universal virtue and its violation—adharma in Hinduism—but on the basis of believers in the doctrine and non-believers, with those who do not accept the supremacy of the Abrahamic doctrine thrown into the category of evil denizens. The fate of non-Western civilisations and cultures that have encountered the ideologies spawned by the Abrahamic faiths is a traumatic one, though that lies outside the scope of this work. Ethics clearly, is different when viewed through different lenses.

Coming to sex, the Hindu thought maintains that all phenomena are emanations of the Supreme Being and, as such, worthy of worship. If the terrors of Nature, such as storms, lightning, thunder, earthquakes, epidemics and cataclysms, fascinate a man, he is free to worship them, just as another man is at liberty to worship the sun or the moon for the benevolent light they emit. Courtesans, as we have seen, are not excluded from the realm of religion in India; in Kama, they have a deity after their own heart. The religious instinct being universal, the Hindu maintains that to fully express his emotional life, every person must have a deity or principle to worship. For all its 'peaceful' portrayal by well-meaning, but ignorant and often deluded, Hindus fed on a diet of debilitating pacificism (also planted and successfully propagated by the very ideologies that are inimical to Hinduism and Hindus), the Hindu divine pantheon has a god of war, Kartikeya (older son of Shiva), and supreme commander of the Devas as well.

It is not surprising then that sex-worship has a place in the comprehensive synthesis of Hinduism. It does not take mystic insight to realise the importance of sex in life. Anyone can see that sex sustains and maintains the continuity of life. The sexual impulse in man is considered by sex-worshippers to be the perceptible expression of the vast, invisible primal power to which is attributed the universe. Certain sectarians conceive this power to be dual, while others maintain that it is one which embodies in itself both the male and female principles.

According to the *Brihadaranyaka Upanishad*, the Supreme Being, desirous of creating man, split himself into two, thus becoming male and female. And, out of the union of the two was produced man. In the Mahabharata, the dual nature of all existence is emphasised:

> He who asserts any other cause than *Ishwara* (the Supreme One, used for Vishnu and Shiva) or affirms that there is any female not marked by Devi (the Goddess) in the three worlds, including all things movable and immovable, let that fool be thrust out. Know everything which is male to be *Ishwara* and all that is female to be *Vema* (a name of the Devi), for this whole world movable and immovable is pervaded by these two bodies.

This dual conception of the universe, though not so popular as the monistic conception, has a sound hold on Hindu religious thought. Even the monistic theory, when well-examined, is inclined to split Godhead into Brahma and its ever-present complement Maya. One of the forms God is worshipped in India is as *Ardhanarishwara*—Shiva in the form of half-man, half-woman. The figure that represents this conception of Godhead is masculine on the right side and feminine on the left.

The most ancient philosophy that explains the dual conception of the universe is *Sankhya*. Sankhya does not support a belief in a Supreme Being or God. It teaches the existence of numerous *Purushas* (the male entities), which are pure and quiescent in themselves, and of *Prakriti* (the female principle), the vast mainstay of the universe. Independent of Prakriti, the Purushas are passive, but they come into constant contact with Prakriti and give rise to the phenomenal world. Prakriti, the female, is essentially active, and since all activity is conditioned by Time, Space and Causation, the Purusha that comes into contact with Prakriti necessarily becomes bound. Every living being is thus a combination of Purusha and Prakriti, and the object of life is the liberation of Purusha from Prakriti.

Early Vedic literature generally contains the worship of male deities, but goddesses like Usha, Saraswati and Aranyani, are mentioned and worshipped as subordinate to the great gods, like Indra, Varuna and the Marutas. Sex-worship did not form part of Rig Vedic worship. Hymns in the *Rig Veda* show that a tribe inimical to the followers of Sanatana Dharma had for their worship the *Shishna* (membrum virile). The post-Vedic period saw Sanatana Hinduism assimilating cultures and beliefs outside the scope of Arya dharma and culture, and the worship of the virile element was probably recognised as desirable.

The prominence of Brahma, Vishnu and Shiva, the supreme of the Hindu triad, was manifested in the immediate post-Vedic period of Hinduism. Brahma is the creator, Vishnu the preserver and Shiva the destroyer (cosmic dissolution before the next phase of creation) of the universe. Worshipping Brahma does not appear to have been widespread in the history of the Hindus. On the other hand, Vishnu as the Sustainer is powerful and commands the allegiance and devotion of millions in the Hindu world and has wealthy shrines all over India. But, the most widespread of the pantheon is Shiva.

Worshipping Shiva is connected with the heyday of Hindu glory. Throughout the long period of cultural, political and religious greatness of the community, Shiva has held the position of the Supreme Deity. The great emperors of Hindu legend, Vikramaditya and Bhoja, for instance, were Shaivas. The well-known literary works of the Hindus, like the plays of Kalidasa or the *Katha Sarit Sagara* of Somadeva, were dedicated to Shiva. The temples of fabulous wealth, which attracted Islamic jihadi invaders and plunderers from Mahmud of Ghazni onwards to India, were of Shiva. In the present too, the noblest Hindu edifices in India are Shaivite shrines. Compared to Shaivism, Vaishnavism is almost modern, rising to its present eminence only after the Rajput period.

Although known as the god of destruction, Shiva's universality transcends such commonplace categorisations. The three-eyed Mahadeva is representative of the cosmos along with Vishnu and, to a lesser extent, Brahma. The worship of Shiva is Hinduism embracing in its wide scope all forms of beliefs—from highest philosophic conceptions to the most mundane forms of worship and devotion. One aspect of devotion to Shiva is related to the phenomenon of sex and procreation as well.

Destruction is not essentially different from regeneration. Destruction is, in fact, a prelude to construction, or better still, an essential part of construction. For nothing can be made out of nothing, and creation is but rebuilding. Hence, Shiva, say the Shaivites in particular, embodies in himself the function of Brahma as well; the god of destruction is also the god of regeneration.

The Shaivas attribute the origin of the *Lingam* to the

primary day of creation when Brahma and Vishnu sprang forth into being out of non-being. Both gods, bewildered by their own birth, started questioning each other about their origin to establish precedence and superiority. They then found a resplendent Lingam of huge dimensions shining beside them, the base or top of which they could not see. Stupefied by the magnificence of the phenomenon, they stopped their argument and asked each other what the appearance of the luminous Lingam meant. Before proceeding further into the enquiry, they decided to first find out the actual dimensions of the Lingam. Vishnu assumed the form of a boar and dived downwards into the primal ocean, which generated the Lingam, to reach its base. Brahma converted himself into a swift-winged swan with a desire to perch on the top of the Lingam and flew upwards. After years of diving, Vishnu found no base to the Lingam and, considering further attempts futile, returned to the surface of the waters to find Brahma waiting for him with news of success of his mission. The Lingam was indeed very high, said Brahma, but with strong wings, he flew and perched on its top. Vishnu confessed he failed to reach the base of the Lingam, upon which Brahma asked him to accept him as his superior. At this, Shiva, the mighty owner of the Lingam, appeared on the scene and asked Brahma to provide proof of his having reached the top of the Lingam. Brahma's inability to present any proof, on the contrary, proved him a liar; Shiva, as a punishment, nipped off one of Brahma's five heads. Shiva approved of Vishnu's humble honesty. The Vaishnavas believe, because of his supreme adherence to truth, Vishnu was recognised by Shiva as his superior, a claim Shaivas stoutly reject.

Unfavourable accounts of Shiva's activities were probably inspired not only by the sectarianism that crept into Hinduism but also likely because it has been given a boost by missionary activity. As we have seen, these activities were always carried out, overtly or covertly, with the agenda to bring Hinduism itself into disrepute. However, admittedly, some descriptions of the Lingam by the Shaivas, themselves, might not conform to 'modern' yardsticks of decorum.

The cult of the Lingam is not to be confused with certain sensuous practices. Lingam worship is not accompanied by promiscuity or sexual activity whatsoever. In fact, Shiva is an enemy of Kama, the deity of love and sex. One of the well-known episodes tells us that in his wrath, Shiva opened his third eye to reduce Kama to ashes. Madanari (the destroyer of Kama) is one of the numerous epithets of Nilakantha (the Blue-Throated one, one of the many names of Shiva).

It may be interesting to learn that the most puritanic Hindu sect, judging from certain standards, are the Lingayats, who worship the Lingam to the exclusion of all other deities. They wear small Lingams, and no Lingayat worth his name would allow this symbol of God to be removed from his body even for a short while. The sect recognises no other god, and maintains that the Lingam is a perfect representation of God. The Lingayats originated in the twelfth century AD under their founder Basava. They are strict vegetarians who abjure liquor and even tobacco. They hold sorcery and magic, essential to some Hindu cults, in abhorrence and maintain that widow marriages are permissible and child marriages are not. The souls of the Lingayats are believed to find union with God on death, and no rites and prayers for the dead are allowed among them. The Lingayats recognise no caste and hold that all men are equal in the eyes of God. Some are priests by vocation and are known as *Jangamas.* Though Lingayat priests are allowed to marry, most of them remain celibate of their own accord and devote their lives to the propagation of their views and serving others. The ascetics usually wander all over the country visiting the five great Lingayat centres called *Simhasanas.* These centres are situated at Kadur, Ujjain, Banaras (Varanasi), Srisailam and Kedarnath. In every Lingayat village, there is a monastery affiliated to one of these five establishments.

The Lingayats are about three crores in population at present and are found mostly in South India, with a few lakh in Maharashtra and Madhya Pradesh. They make no secret of their religion, but take a legitimate pride in it and exhibit the Lingam they carry for public view. The Lingam (usually made of grey soapstone) is worn round the neck enclosed in a red scarf or in a silver locket.

Lingams are mainly of two kinds—*Anadi* (without beginning) or *Swayambhu* (self-generated). Lingams of the Swayambhu type are rocks or stones of a peculiar shape and considered by tradition and legend as self-generated and sanctified on that account. While the greatness and majesty of such Lingams are said to be indescribable, the *Mahanirvana Tantra* maintains that the magnificence of Lingams fashioned by human hands can be described, albeit with difficulty. Brahma, Vishnu, Indra and the other devas reside where Mahadeva is in his *Linga* form.

> Thirty-five million known and unknown places of pilgrimages and all the holy places abide near Shiva. The land within a radius of a hundred cubits of the Linga is declared to be Shiva-Kshetra. This land of Shiva is very sacred. It is more excellent than the most excellent of holy places, because always, the immortals abide by these holy areas and are found there.
>
> There is no doubt that by the installation of a Shivalinga, a man acquires ten million times the merit which is acquired by giving up the world and all its gold, by the performance of ten thousand *Ashwamedhas* (horse-sacrifices), by the digging of a

> tank in a waterless country, or by making happy the poor and such as are enfeebled by disease.

The greatness of the Lingam is by no means limited to the above description. Shiva also has a more pleasing function as an affectionate husband and father. The holy family of the Hindus consists of Shiva, his wife Parvati and two sons Ganesha and Kartikeya. Puranic accounts of Shiva's marriage and family life are interesting. Shiva married Sati against the wishes of her father Daksha, a celestial patriarch. When Sati came of age to be married, Daksha sent out invitations to all the gods of heaven except Shiva, to attend her swayamvara. He thought that Shiva, with his matted locks, serpents dangling around neck and smeared with holy ash all over along with *rudraksha* beads as a necklace, was least worthy of being a suitable husband for his daughter brought up in luxury. But, Sati was a worshipper and admirer of the wandering celestial mendicant. So, on not finding Shiva in the swayamvara hall, thinking of him, she threw the marriage garland she held in her hand upwards. Shiva immediately manifested himself on the spot and received the garland. Daksha was then forced to give Sati in marriage to Shiva with whatever grace he could command under the circumstances.

However, the strained relations were not mended during the wedding feast. Both sides were bitter toward each other and waited for an opportunity to settle scores. Shiva soon got the chance to show his contempt for Daksha. The scene of trouble, this time, was Brahma's palace. The Creator held a feast and invited all the gods and sages to attend it. Shiva, the Destroyer, was one of the guests who came early and took his seat beside Brahma. Daksha came a little later, with most of the gods and sages rising from their seat out of respect for the aged patriarch. Shiva, however, did not. The patriarch noticed the slight and immediately launched a verbal attack on his ill-mannered son-in-law, asking for his expulsion from the hall. Shiva, on the other hand, maintained that, being a member of the Trinity, he was superior to Daksha and was not bound to get up when Daksha entered. Brahma's offer of mediation in the quarrel was not accepted, and an irate Daksha left the hall in disgust.

Daksha now decided to teach his son-in-law a severe lesson. He arranged a great sacrifice and invited all the gods and goddesses, sages and patriarchs for the occasion, deliberately omitting the names of Shiva and Sati from his guest list. The celestial sage Narada, always up to mischief though for the higher purpose of manoeuvring situations to aid the cause of the devatas, went and told Sati all about her father's *yajna* and pointed out the omission. Sati wished to have an explanation from her father and went to the sacrifice uninvited. This led to a scene in Daksha's house, and the patriarch told her openly what he thought of his son-in-law. Sati felt terribly insulted by the affront, and, to vindicate her husband's honour, jumped into the sacrificial fire burning herself to death.

An infuriated Shiva immediately appeared at Daksha's abode with an army of formidable *ganas* (powerful beings devoted to Shiva) and inflicted a terrible punishment on Daksha and his partisans. Virbhadra, one of Shiva's ganas, chopped off Daksha's head and flung it into the same sacrificial fire. Sati, however, was irretrievably lost; in deep grief, Shiva retired to his lonely mountain abode in Kailasa, giving Himself up to cosmic *samadhi* (trance).

But Devaloka (heaven) was not tranquil. Things happened which made the gods contrive for Shiva's remarriage. The asura Taraka obtained a boon by propitiating Brahma that he could be killed by no one except Shiva's son; when he found that Shiva had taken to asceticism, he was assured that Shiva would never beget a son and hence he started terrorising the fourteen worlds. The Devas lived in fear of him. The moon had to shine perpetually without waning. The sun was not permitted to give more heat than Taraka required. The rain deity had to yield his refreshing showers out of season. The wind god had to blow a *zephyr* throughout the year. The earth herself sank in despair because of Taraka's unreasonable demands. In this predicament, the gods made a joint plea to Shiva to give up his ascetic ways, marry and beget a son who would destroy Taraka. But, Shiva turned a deaf ear to the plaints of the gods.

Their pleadings going unheeded, the celestials decided to force a marriage on Shiva. They commissioned Kama to go to Kailasa and arouse desire in Shiva using his love-laden flower shafts. Kama was in trepidation when asked by the Devas to undertake the mission; Shiva was well-known for his cosmic wrath and anyone who disturbed him in his meditation was not likely to get away with it. Anyhow, persuaded by the other gods, Kama went on his perilous mission.

Hiding by the shadows of the trees on Kailasa, Kama crept up the mountain and started looking for a vantage point for shooting his flower shaft. The awe-inspiring atmosphere of the place overwhelmed Kama and his heart sank at the thought of disturbing the divine ascetic. But then he saw a maiden of exceeding loveliness plucking flowers by the bowers near the spot where Shiva sat in meditation.

This lovely maiden was none other than Sati herself, reborn as Parvati, daughter of Himavan (the ruler of the Himalayas). Parvati had knowledge of her former life, and, on coming of age, wished to get married to Shiva once again. To achieve this, she had been worshipping Mahadeva assiduously and was always near Kailasa so that he could fall for her charms and ask for her hand. But neither her charms nor her blandishments proved of any avail, and the great ascetic sat in deep meditation oblivious to the prayers of the lovely Parvati. But now, the sight of Parvati emboldened the god of love. Selecting an opportune moment, when Parvati was in view of Shiva, Kama shot his shaft.

Shiva felt the sting; his mind felt troubled like a calm sea agitated by a sudden gale. He opened his eyes and saw the beautiful Parvati plucking flowers in the bower; he was about to smile amorously on her when he noticed the archer sneaking by the curve of a tree-trunk. Shiva immediately divined the cause of his distraction and opened his blazing third eye, which reduced the god of love to ashes! After this, he closed his eyes again, and continued his meditation.

Parvati found that her beauty was of no avail. Nor did devotion bring her the god's love. Becoming desperate, she herself took to asceticism like Shiva, and tortured her frail body. The rigorous course of her penances generated so much heat that Shiva could not sit in Kailasa. Disturbed in his meditation, he left his snow- and ice-covered mountain, searched for Parvati and appeared before her in the guise of a dwarfish Brahmin. He wished to know why she persecuted her tender body in so rigorous a manner. Parvati told him of her hopeless love for Shiva and the frustration that led her to asceticism. Assuming an amused expression, the Brahmin began to dwell upon the failings of Shiva, his frightening form, his persona smeared with ashes and adorned by serpents and his desolate and icy abode. He became so eloquent on the subject that Parvati could not stand it any longer and was about to pronounce a curse on him. On this, the dwarf metamorphosed into Shiva, and on his asking for her hand, the delighted Parvati gave up her asceticism and returned to her father's abode. Shiva duly approached Himavan for his daughter's hand, and the willing father gave her in marriage to him according to prescribed rites.

Rati, Kama's widow, attended the wedding and begged of the bride to request her Lord to regenerate her husband. Parvati took pity on the sorrowing widow and, at her intercession, Shiva permitted Kama to be reborn. Accordingly, the god of love was reborn as Pradyumna, son of Krishna and Rukmini. Parvati, reunited with Shiva, attained godliness. In all Shiva temples, she is also worshipped as Bhavani, the Mother Goddess.

Parvati is a dutiful wife and the domestic felicity enjoyed by Shiva and Parvati is a popular theme of the Hindu poet. In all Shiva temples, Parvati is also worshipped.

It is interesting to note that though the gods expressly desired a son to be born to Shiva for the destruction of Taraka, after his marriage they began to feel that the progeny of such lovers like Shiva and Parvati would be more tyrannous than Taraka himself. Hence they supplicated Shiva, and the god promised that he would not have any children by Parvati.

When Parvati came to know of this, in her anger, she cursed all the goddesses of heaven to become barren like herself. That, however, did not satisfy her maternal instinct. So one day, when Shiva was away, she moulded out of the oil and other substances used in her toilet, the form of a boy and breathed life into him. She called the young boy her son and asked him to guard her apartment. Soon after, Shiva returned and was surprised to see a stranger at the door to Parvati's room. He rudely asked the lad who he was, and this person as rudely replied that it was no concern of the intruder and that it was his duty to keep anyone away from a respectable lady's apartments. Words and blows followed, and the irate Shiva cut off the young god's head and sent it flying through the air.

Parvati now came upon the scene, and seeing the destructive work of her husband began lamenting her lost son, and this brought all the gods of heaven to Mount Kailash. Parvati would not be pacified by anything the gods said and she said that she wanted her son back. Vishnu now started a hunt for the lost head, but it could not be found anywhere in the fourteen worlds. So he cut off the head of an elephant he happened to find on the way, and grafted this head to the trunk of Parvati's son. Thus the origin of Ganesha, the elephant-headed deity of the Hindu pantheon.

Ganesha is an amiable god. He is pictured in art as a pot-bellied, short-legged god with an elephant's head and infinite wisdom. He rides on a mouse. As the Remover of Obstacles, he is worshipped by every orthodox Hindu before beginning any new undertaking. Born, independent of his father, Ganesha is his mother's favourite.

Ganesha was not, however, equal to the task of killing the demon Taraka, and for this purpose, another son was born to Shiva. Kartikeya or Kumara was also begotten in a mysterious way. The fire-god Agni happened to get 'the seed' of Shiva in a manner into the details of which, we need not go, and as he was carrying it across the Ganges, the precious possession fell in the river. From the seed, a baby hatched. Six princesses happened to see the resplendent baby on the bank of the Ganges and all of them wished to suckle it; the divine baby then opened six mouths and with commendable impartiality, sucked all the six of them. Hence Kumara is also known as Shunmukha, meaning 'having six faces'.

Kartikeya is the war god of the pantheon. He is said to be a bachelor and womanhater in some accounts, and the husband of

Devasena (army of the gods) in others. His main delight is war and he rides on a peacock. Bom independently of a mother, he is the favourite of his father. Kartikeya killed Taraka and liberated the worlds from his oppression.

Shiva's is a happy family. But as in all happy families, there are times when domestic quarrels take place and these happened in Shiva's house, too. One day, for instance, Shiva came home from his begging rounds with very little in the bowl. The voracious Ganesha and the hungry Kartikeya ate most of what was in the bowl, and Ganesha's rat and Kartikeya's peacock finished off the rest. The result was that poor Parvati had to go without a meal. She would not have minded it, if only Shiva had a good word to say to her. But he had just finished his long day and slept comfortably, completely oblivious to his wife's agony. Next morning Shiva got up late, and it looked as if that day too he would not get much to bring home for the wife and children. At this point, Parvati protested. One thing led to another, and Parvati told her husband that it was impossible for her to live with a person like him. If that was the case, Shiva told her, the proper thing for her to do was to leave him. Parvati took him at his word and, collecting her children, left for her father's house.

The sages now intervened and brought about a reconciliation. The reconciliation was sweet and emotional, and Shiva hugged his beloved so violently that he became 'one' with her. This was the origin of *Ardhanarisvara*, the bisexual figure often found in Shaiva shrines.

Another petty quarrel needs to be mentioned here. One day, Shiva was reading the scriptures to Parvati and explaining to her the import of the sacred lines, when she began nodding. Shiva was so exasperated by his wife's indifference to erudition that he cursed her to become a fisherwoman. Parvati immediately disappeared from Kailash and was born as a fishermaid. Shiva, however, could not get on without his wife and after sometime, managed to reclaim his wife from the fisher-folk.

It may be mentioned that in all these petty quarrels, reconciliation always follows. The point is that a permanent rupture between Shiva and Parvati is inconceivable!

Chapter 14

The Divine Feminine

The Shakta tradition in Hinduism offers a profound exploration of the divine feminine, positioning Shakti as the primordial power of the universe. This chapter delves into the worship of Shakti in her many forms and her significance in tantrik practices. By examining these practices and beliefs, we see how the feminine is venerated not just as an object of desire, but as an integral force of creation, transformation, and spiritual power, highlighting the complex interplay of women, power, and divinity in ancient Hindu thought.

The Shaktas are Hindus who consider Godhead to be essentially feminine. In the worship of the female deities, the outward decorum associated with the cult of the Lingam is not always maintained. In fact, most of the practices in Hinduism that appear objectionable to westerners are connected with the worship of the female in one way or the other. It is difficult to justify certain practices of the Shaktas; nor can one appreciate the hair-splitting arguments advanced by apologists of Shakta cults in defence of animal and human sacrifice and salvation through *Panchatattva* worship. Although the Aryas of the Rig Vedic age were not much into worshipping female deities, the worship of goddesses became important in the later period of Hinduism. This shift occurred probably through societies outside the periphery of the Aryas, which were incorporated into their religion during the post-Vedic period. India has had important female deities in its pantheon. Excavations at Mohenjo-daro show that the principal deities of the Indus Valley civilisation were goddesses and some of them were worshipped by the Aryas. In modern India, too, the worship of female deities is more widespread than that of gods in certain communities across the country.

An interesting feature of Hindu mysticism is that the active principle in the universe is always conceived as feminine. The Sankhya stream of Hindu philosophy provides a typical philosophical example of this view—the numerous Purushas or male entities are quiescent and free from activity till they get entangled with Prakriti or the female principle which is essentially dynamic. Similarly, Brahma, or the Supreme principle of *Vedantins* (arguably termed Hindu Monists), is *Nirguna* (without qualities) and is passive, while the attendant Maya, the female principle, is vigorously active and responsible for the visible world. This view is maintained in all Hindu mystic conceptions. The Hindus assert that the Trinity of all Creation, namely Brahma, Vishnu and Shiva, are themselves passive, but that the Shakti (energy) of a god is responsible for his activity. This Shakti is said to be feminine and is worshipped as the consort of the Divine One. A wider conception, mainly held by the Shaktas, is that the Shakti of a god is essentially the god himself and, apart from Her, the god has no existence. This view is further elaborated into an all-embracing Monism in which Shakti is said to be the Supreme Being, the all-in-all, identical with the Nirguna Brahma of the Vedantins. The Shaktas maintain that Shakti pervades all;

the entire universe is her emanation, that she is without form or qualities, vast and imperceptible, the creator, preserver and destroyer of the universe, all in one. But, it is difficult to worship Shakti in the abstract, and for the benefit of the spiritually less inclined, she is endowed with forms.

The most widely accepted form of Shakti is as the wife of Shiva. This distinguished position given to the consort of Shiva is in consonance with the greatness of Shiva who is the most widely worshipped deity of the pantheon. Shakti, the Goddess, has remained supreme; the rise of the Vaishnavas has been unable to replace her in favour of Lakshmi, the Goddess of wealth and prosperity, and the wife of Vishnu. However, it must be mentioned that in her wider aspect, Shakti encompasses not only the wives of other gods but even mortal women; the term is applied to everything feminine, including even the females of animals.

At present, Shiva's wife is worshipped all over India, from the Himalayas to Kanyakumari. One of her names is Himavati (daughter of the Himalayas) and another is Kumari. She has many names and many forms typifying the various aspects of the deity—some mild, tender and kind, others terrible, forbidding and devastating. The most commonly known names of Shiva's wife are—Durga, Devi, Uma, Sati, Parvati, Kali, Chinnamasta, Bhavani, Rudrani, Kamakshi and Meenakshi. Each of these names signifies a certain aspect of Shakti and is worshipped with appropriate rituals. Many temples can be found all over India dedicated to one or the other form of the Goddess. The most powerful strongholds of the Shakti cult are in Bengal and Assam where the worship is organised and systematised.

The Shakti cult represents Hinduism in its entirety. The Goddess is worshipped in all conceivable aspects including those that are considered objectionable by modern notions.

The most tender and appealing form of Shakti-worship is as the Divine Mother. The Christian conception of God as Father and men as his children does not adequately express the relation between human beings and the Divine. The father is a stern person who, in his dealings with children, is ruled by reason and duty, whereas the mother can overlook logic and duty in her affection. This is said to be typical of Godhead. God is not a judge or a taskmaster, but a loving mother who can please her child. The saint Ramakrishna Paramahamsa, the guru of Swami Vivekananda, was an ardent devotee of Goddess Kali and would often fall into ecstasy while contemplating the love of the Mother Goddess. Even Adi Sankara and Vivekananda found solace and joy in mother-worship, which all their learning, logic and wisdom could not give them. Both composed passionate songs in praise of the Goddess. Many enlightened Hindus of the present age are also Shaktas in this respect.

A sacred verse supporting the cosmic importance of Shakti and the universal nature of Her worship says:

> The Shaktas call her Mother, for she is the great Mother, the Mahadevi who conceives, bears and nourishes the universe sprung from her womb. This is so because she is the active aspect of consciousness, imagining the world to be according to the impression derived from enjoyment and suffering in former worlds. It is natural to worship her as Mother. The first mantra into which all men are initiated is the word 'Ma'. It is the first word and generally the last.

Moreover:

> Maheswaras call her Shakti, Sankhyas call her Paraprakriti, Buddhists know her as Tara, Charvakas call her Asha, Pashupatas call her Snata, Jainas call her Sri, the followers of

> Brahma know her as Shraddha, Vaidikas call her Gayatri, and the ignorant call her Mohini.

The powers of Shakti are thus described in the *Mahanirvana Tantra* when Shiva reveals her greatness to Shakti:

> Thou art the very Paraprakriti of Brahma, the Paramatma, and from Thee has sprung the entire universe. O Gracious One! Whatever there is in this world, of things which have motion and are without motion, from *Mahat* (the largest or greatest) to an atom, owes its origin to and is dependent on thee. Thou art the origin of all manifestations; thou art the birthplace of even us (members of the Trinity). Thou knowest the whole world, yet none knows thee. Thou art Kali, Tarini, Durga, Shodashi, Bhuvaneshwari, Dhumavati, Begala, Bhairavi, Chinnamasta, Annapurna, Vagdevi, Kamalalaya. Thou art in the form of all the Shaktis and thou pervadest the bodies of all the devas. Thou art both subtle and gross, manifested and veiled, though in thyself, formless, yet thou hast form. Who can understand thee? The helping of the worshipper, the good of the world and the destruction of the enemies, the gods; Thou doth assume various forms. Thou art four-armed, two-armed, six-armed and eight-armed and holdeth various missiles and weapons for the protection of the universe.

As Parvati or Uma, Shakti is the faithful wife of Shiva. This aspect of the Goddess has been described in the previous chapter.

As Kumari (virgin), Shakti is worshipped for her blooming beauty and virgin purity. Temples dedicated to this form of Shakti are few, but in domestic rites and petty ceremonies, Kumari holds a prominent place.

The most popular form of worship of Shakti is as Durga, the

destroyer of evil. She is fabled to have assumed this formidable form for the destruction of a demon called Mahishasura. The terrible combat between the Goddess and the demon in the form of a buffalo, who could be killed by no one but a woman, is legend, and is described in vivid detail in many Hindu scriptures. However, Mahishasura was not the only demon Durga destroyed. She is reputed to have killed Shumbha and Nishumbha, Chanda and Munda, and a host of other devils whom the devas feared. One of the greatest Hindu festivals, Durga Puja is celebrated in honour of Durga's triumph over Mahishasura. Till recently, it was customary to sacrifice a buffalo on the occasion, but enlightened Hindus have replaced the gory tradition with the cutting of a Kalabash or any other vegetable or fruit symbolical of the custom.

The aspect of the goddess which symbolises destruction as such is Kali, Bhavani or Chinnamasta. Hindus do not believe that destruction of evil alone is divine. The terrible and the destructive are as much part of Nature and, hence, of Godhead as the pleasant and the beneficial. It is not the wicked alone that die. Death is inherent in all life, essentially emanating from Godhead. The personification of this aspect of Shakti is commonly seen in the images of Kali or Chinnamasta. The idol of Kali is usually made of black granite, with blood-dripping tusks that protrude from her mouth; she is naked, but for a garland of human skulls hanging from her neck. In one of her hands, she holds a weapon, and in the other, the severed head of a victim. The image of Chinnamasta is peculiar and likely to appear as revolting to most. In one of her hands, she holds her own severed head, with the mouth drinking the blood spouting from the hewn neck.

Kali is popular, especially in Bengal and South India. Animal sacrifice is a common feature of all the shrines dedicated to the Goddess. The most famous shrines dedicated to the terror form of Shakti are the Kali temple at Kalighat (from which Calcutta takes its name), and the Kamakhya temple in Assam. A continuous flow of blood is kept at the altars of the goddesses all from sacrifices that are meant to appease the Goddess. It is feared that if the Goddess is not appeased, she might forcibly claim victims through epidemics, pestilence, famine and cataclysms.

However, the terror form of Shakti is not as important for the purpose of this book as the peculiar form of worship known as *Panchatattva*. Before coming to Panchatattva worship, the reader would have to bear in mind a few points about the beliefs of certain Shakta sects.

The Shaktas are broadly divided into *Dakshinamargis,* or right path worshippers, and *Vamamargis,* or left path worshippers. The Dakshinamargis worship Shakti publicly, whereas the Vamamargis insist on complete secrecy in worship. The Vamamargis are also known as Tantriks because they follow the scriptures called *Tantras*. The word 'Tantra' means a simple precept and is at times used to indicate a complicated device. In a broader sense, it is used to denote a large number of Hindu sacred books, but in its popular sense, it refers to only those books that lay down rules for worship of Shakti through Panchatattva.

The Tantriks maintain that the *Vedas* and other scriptures are meant for bygone ages and not for the present age of evil, known as Kali Yuga in Hinduism, or the age of the demon Kali. To try to understand this theory, it is essential for the readers to have some idea of the Hindu mythical cycle of time. The life of the world is divided into a number of *Maha Yugas* each consisting of four Yugas or ages. The first Yuga is known as *Satya Yuga*, or *Krita Yuga*, which is the age of the total sway of dharma or virtue in the world. In the second, *Treta Yuga*, virtue diminishes by a quarter; in the third age, *Dwapara Yuga*, evil becomes predominant; and in *Kali Yuga* (our own times), there is little left in the world that is not evil. A description of the miseries and wickedness of Kali Yuga is found typically in every *Purana*. People of this age are marked by their depraved tendencies. They love what is evil, and detest what is good; dharmic duty is neglected, with men developing an insatiable thirst for sensuous pleasures. Rulers persecute their subjects, and the subjects rise in rebellion against their rulers. Nations wage war on nations, and all are driven by violence. Brahmins forsake the study of the Vedas in their pursuit of pleasure and wealth, while low-born men usurp the thrones of virtuous and noble monarchs. Friendship degenerates into mutual exploitation; desire becomes the attachment between men and women.

Tantriks maintain that there is a certain fatality in this state of affairs. Human beings have fallen so low that they are rendered incapable of realising this. Hence, the Tantriks tell us that the high precepts of Vedic times are inapplicable to the men of Kali Yuga, who are so stupid that they can neither understand nor apply them. According to them, Vedic rites are meant for Krita Yuga, the *Smritis* (like the codes of Manu and Parashara among others) for Treta Yuga, and the *Puranas* for Dwapara Yuga. For Kali Yuga, the most important, in fact the only texts, to be followed with benefit are the *Tantras*. The focus of the Tantriks is to make *Tantras* attractive to people. Speaking of other forms of worship, the *Rudrayamala Tantra* mentions that pleasure and religious merit seldom go together. The *Tantras*, however, ensure both:

> Where there is worldly enjoyment, there is no liberation; where there is liberation, there is no worldly enjoyment. But in the case of the excellent devotees of Shri (a form of Shakti) both liberation and enjoyment reside in the hollow of their hands.

Not surprisingly, such a conception of worship would appear to Western religions, particularly to Christians, a deliberate degeneration of religion. But Hindu logic is highly subtle. It maintains that it is worse than useless to preach high ideals to a person incapable of understanding them. Yet, religious forces in man must not be ignored; every man is entitled to worship that is suited to his genius and limitations. Hence, various practices exist among Hindus that are all different from one another, yet are recognised as orthodox.

To make religion pleasant to the evil men of Kali Yuga, the Tantras prescribe worship by means of Panchatattva, or the five elements or fundamental principles. Tattvas also carry the rather gross nomenclature of the five *Makaras* (or simply M's), and in this categorisation, they are referred to as the Panchamakaras—*Madya* (liquor), *Mansa* (meat), *Matsya* (fish), *Mudra* (posture) and *Maithuna* (sexual intercourse).

The *Tantras* give detailed instructions for worship through the Panchatattvas. While rituals differ and precepts vary in detail, the most important is known as the *Chakrapuja* or worship of the various *chakras* (for a chakra worship in a shrine, the diagram of that particular chakra is drawn on the floor of the room where the worship is to be conducted).

Chakra rites are usually performed at night in the house of a wealthy Shakta, to ensure secrecy, or in the inner shrine of a temple inaccessible to the public. The place where the rite takes place is cleaned and consecrated for the worship, and a circular diagram with a prescribed radius is drawn. At the centre of the circle is drawn a *yantra* (a diagram of circular formations representing various gods and goddesses; yantras play an important part in all Tantric rituals and possess divine powers) where the host and his Shakti sit. Around them sit the guests, each beside his Shakti (the

Shakti has to be seated to the left of the Shakta in Chakrapuja).

The Shaktis, represented by living women, are of three types—*Sviya,* or one's own wife; *Parakiya,* or another man's wife; *Saddharani,* or common woman. Some texts ordain that Maithuna is permissible only with the Sviya, while others hold that there is no harm in Maithuna with any woman, as every woman is in effect the living embodiment of Shakti.

The first act in the rite is the placing of the *kalasha* or jar of wine, and the consecration of its contents. The jar is of given dimensions, but is big enough to hold a large quantity of liquor. It may be made of gold, silver, copper, bell-metal, crystal, stone or clay, according to the host's preference. A gold jar brings prosperity, silver emancipation, copper contentment, bell-metal nourishment, crystal love, stone fascination and clay, all in small proportions.

After filling the jar with wine, it is placed in front of the host and his Shakti on a jewelled altar enclosed in a mystic diagram. Incantations are now repeated to counteract the curse of Shukracharya[2] and turn wine into nectar. After the consecration of the jar and its contents, cooked meat, fish and gram are brought in large quantities. These are blessed by repeating incantations and by appropriate mystic gestures known as *Mudras.*

2 Shukracharya, the preceptor of the Asuras, was once tricked into drinking the ashes of his disciple Kacha. The Asuras had murdered Kacha, burnt his body, mixed his ashes with wine and presented it to the sage. Shukracharya brought him back to life using his knowledge of the Sanjivani, but cursed all intoxicants and prohibited their use when he learnt what he had done under the influence of the Asuras. Manu, and other law-givers, enforce prohibition of intoxicants on the three higher castes in general, and strictly on Brahmins.

Drinking may now begin. The devotee eats meat with the first cup, fish with the second, gram with the third, all of these with the fourth and anything he desires with the fifth. The *Mahanirvana Tantra* ordains that not more than five cups of wine must be drunk during the worship which is followed by sexual union. Here again, the *Mahanirvana Tantra* insists that a man should have Maithuna only with a Sviya or one's own wife. Excess in drinking is proscribed. The drinking rule for the Tantric rite is given as follows:

> They may drink until the sight or the mind is not affected. To drink beyond this is bestial. How is it possible for a sinner, who becomes a fool through drink and who maligns the *sadhaka* of Shakti, to say 'I worship the Adya Kalika?'

However, the *Mahanirvana* is one of the mildest of the Tantras and it is quite probable that the injunctions contained in this scripture are not always followed. In fact, the tone of the warning itself indicates that excess is not rare in *Kaula* (Tantric rites are also called Kaula rites because of its supposed noble nature; Kaula meaning either ancient or noble) rites. One of the objectives of Tantric rites is said to be the rising of the devotee above all sense of right and wrong, an ideal often emphasised in Hindu mysticism. We know for certain that the Tantric rites of Mahayana Buddhists were marked by much debauchery and exhortation for actions considered evil or sinful by society. Mahayana Tantriks even symbolically killed Buddha to show their complete emancipation from the binding sense of good and evil, which is believed to prevent a man from realising the Absolute Unity of Godhead. As Buddhism and Hinduism have borrowed much from each other, it is probable that Hindu Tantrik rites also ended up in excessive drinking and communal Maithuna.

This rite which appears strange not only to westerners but also to many Hindus, is supported by a sound philosophy. Apologists for it can be found outside the Hindu world as well. Of those who have justified it on various grounds, mention may be made of the English Knight who wrote under the pen-name of Arthur Avalon. He translated many Tantric texts and explained the true nature and meaning of this strange cult. Quoting Tarkalankara, a scholarly Hindu commentator on Tantric texts, Avalon says of the Panchatattva rite:

> By the poison which kills all animals, by that same poison, the physician destroys disease. The root of homoeopathy is to cure illness by that which causes illness. Amongst us too, there is the tradition that poison is destroyed by poison. What, then, is it that makes man sin and die before his time, the object of contempt to all? The first amongst these causes are wine and women; meat and fish are mere accessories. These five Tattvas are the primary cause of the terrible, incurable disease which is *Sansara* (worldly life). Man, under the influence of wine, becomes devoid of manliness, and worthless. The stupefying power of wine and woman is so great as to attract even the pious and wise and hurl them into the abyss of darkness and ignorance. Here, Shiva (the propounder of the Tantric system) prescribes poison which eradicates poison. We know, as other Sadhakas (seekers) do, that this homoeopathic system of Shiva is infallible and yields speedy results. He, who thirsts for wine or lusts after women, can be cured by this treatment within a short time. But the physician, that is the guru, must be experienced and skilful. A slight error in the administration of the poison may lead to fatal results. On this account, Shiva said that the path of the Kaula rite is more difficult than walking on the edge of a sword or to embrace the neck of a tiger. Here

> we give a popular or esoteric explanation of the Tattvas. But, if the esoteric meaning of these be also known, then it will be seen that in the matter of *sadhana* (spiritual or occult quest) they are absolutely necessary. No one who is not a *Tattva-Jnani* (Knower of First Principles) can master their esoteric meaning. On this account, Shiva has prohibited disclosing sadhana to ordinary people. We have seen people who claim to be Kaulas, but as a fact, they are no better than drunkards and libertines. O Reader, blame not Kulachara on seeing these erring men. A libertine and drunkard can never be a Kaula. The Kaula method is unique. He cannot be a drunkard and libertine. On seeing a woman, he sees his mother and *Ishtadevata* in her, and makes obeisance to her in either mind or body. The saints Gauranga, Nityananda and Advaita are brilliant examples of the true Kaula. In the *Mahabharata* and *Vishnu Purana*, it has been said that desire cannot be quenched by enjoying desired objects. On the contrary, desire flames up like fire when ghee is poured into it. This is very true. No one says that the drinking of poison will not kill. But the physician administers poison in such a wonderful way that it does not kill the patient; on the contrary, the poison in the body is destroyed. The way in which the guru administers the poison of wine and thus destroys the poison of *sansara* cannot be disclosed before the unworthy and is, therefore, prohibited by Shiva.

However revolting Kaula practices may appear, especially inside the sanctuaries of worship, their conduct in society is praiseworthy. The majority of Kaulas, no doubt inspired by Tantric doctrines, show a deep respect for woman as the visible representation of the Goddess. Tantriks have all along been bitter enemies of widow-burning, and many of the passages that praise women in law-books and epics of the Hindus are inspired by Tantric doctrines. Killing of women or even causing minor hurt to them is denounced as a heinous sin by Tantriks. They encourage widow marriages and maintain that women married to impotent men have the right to divorce and remarriage. The use of woman as a mere object of pleasure is also denounced by the Kaulas.

A good part of Tantric ritual consists of magic. The Yantras, and certain monosyllables, like *Hring* or *Kling*, are believed to possess terrific power if properly used. The power of mantras or spells is significant, and Tantric texts give elaborate instructions on how, when and where to repeat them and attain occult powers known as *Siddhis.* The best method of attaining Siddhi, or even liberation, is said to be to rouse *Kundalini,* the mystic force. In fact, Shakti herself lies coiled in the body of every person in the form of a serpent. Normally, Kundalini is dormant; she needs to be roused using a complicated realm and system of yogic exercises, aided by repeated chanting of mantras and performing mudras or mystic hand postures. One who rouses his Kundalini rises above the binding sense of time, space and causation. But, Tantric texts insist that the occult power obtained by the rousing of the Kundalini, or by means of spells, should not be used for evil purposes. The main object of rousing one's Kundalini is to enable an individual to work out his or her own salvation.

From the forgoing observations, it is clear that Tantric religion cannot be practised openly. Apart from the secret nature of Panchatattva worship which, for obvious reasons, cannot be publicly held, Hindu tradition holds that knowledge loses its magical power when made public. This convention is zealously and rigorously enforced to Tantric rites. The Kaulas maintain that open worship is meant only for the ignorant, and the elect always worship in secret. They speak of the Kaula system as noble and dignified like a high-born woman who displays her charms to her wedded husband only in secluded privacy, while the Shaivas, Vaishnavas and Dakshinamargis, who worship in public, are likened to prostitutes who practise their trade in the streets. For ensuring the secrecy of the system, the Tantras declare that no Kaula should acknowledge his true sect in public. The Kaula goes about the world as a Vaishnava or Shaiva, publicly worshipping in the shrines of these sects, and conforms to the practices of the sect he openly professes. But, he must always bear in mind that he is the favoured one of the goddess and, as such, above the sect he has accepted as a social convenience. The Kaula has a high opinion of himself and calls the followers of other persuasions, *pashus* (beasts), not possessing the saving knowledge of the Kaula doctrine. He is, however, aware that Shaivas and Vaishnavas hold the Kaula rites up to ridicule; some Shaiva works mention Tantric rites sarcastically. But the Kaula is not perturbed by these jibes. For he holds that a certain amount of accumulated merit in previous births is necessary to give an individual a leaning towards the Kaula doctrine and where this is wanting, a man, far from being attracted by the Secret Doctrine, is likely to be repelled by it.

The origin of the Kaula system is a much disputed subject. Hindus who do not believe in it maintain that it is foreign to Arya (noble) values and found its way to Hinduism through Buddhistic influences. During the decadence of Buddhism in India, Tantric practices were fairly common among the *Mahayana* sect, which later transmogrified into a third sect called the *Vajrayana*. Tara was the presiding goddess of Tantric rites among Buddhists in India, and some of the monasteries where her worship was instituted degenerated into dens of secret vice. The northern hordes who invaded India and were converted to Buddhism had strange cults and their influence was quite marked in the Mahayana sect. It is probable that these northern races introduced Tantric cults into Indian Buddhism. In Tibet, and among certain Central Asian Buddhists, Tantric practices are still common. The fact that the denizens of Assam and Bengal have a racial affinity to them and these two provinces are the greatest strongholds of Shakti cult at present, lends considerable support to the theory of the northern origin of Tantric rites.

The Tantrics themselves, like all orthodox Hindu sects, trace the origin of their rites and doctrine to the Vedas. But their view of the order of importance of the Vedas is different from that of other sects. They consider the Atharva Veda to be anterior and superior to Rig, Sama and Yajur, whereas the usually accepted order of priority is the reverse. The Atharva Veda contains much magic and many spells, together with deep and elevating doctrines. Some of the passages of the Atharva Veda may, however, be mistaken for Tantric precepts. Here are a few spells from the Atharva Veda for making impotent men virile:

> Play the bull, blow, increase and spread; let thy member increase limb by limb; with it smite a woman.
>
> Wherewith they invigorate one who is lean, wherewith they incite one who is ill with that, O Brahmanaspati, make thou his member taut like a bow.
>
> I make thy member taut like a bow-string on a bow; mount as it were a stag a doe, unrelaxingly always. (*Atharva Veda* VI. 5, ii, iii & iv).

Since goddesses are mentioned in all the Vedas and hymns are addressed to them, Tantriks do not find much difficulty in tracing the origin of their rites to the Vedas. However, they do considerably stretch the meaning of words so as to make them yield the desired sanction. The probabilities are that the magical rites mentioned in the Atharva Veda were elaborated into a system when the Hindu religious synthesis developed and Aryas assimilated the practices and beliefs of several non-Arya people.

Followers of the Tantra system have a legend that explains the origin of the principal shrines of their cult. The legend goes that Shiva, after killing Daksha, took the charred body of Sati in his hands and fell into a paroxysm of grief. Berserk with emotion, He started dancing with the body of Sati still in his hands—the terrifying and destructive cosmic *Tandava*. Such was the terrible rhythm of Shiva's *Tandava* that all the fourteen worlds trembled and all the creatures were about to perish. In this predicament, the terror-stricken gods supplicated Vishnu, the Preserver, to save the universe from impending doom. Finding no other method of stopping Shiva's dance, Vishnu took his flaming *Sudarshana Chakra* (discus) and sundered the body of Sati into fifty-one pieces, which fell from Shiva's hands. Mahadeva regained his senses and ceased his dance. The fifty-one pieces of Sati's body fell in different parts of the country, and a shrine sprung up over each piece. The *yoni* is said to have fallen in Assam where the Kamakhya temple stands today. Shaktism is said to have spread mainly from this place.

The Kamakhya Temple is one of India's most sacred and important Hindu shrines. The temple stands on the Nilachal hills, 40 kilometres from Assam's capital, Guwahati. The temple is also known as *Yoni-Sthana*. It is one of the holiest places in Assam and has been a pilgrimage site for thousands of years.

The Kamakhya Temple has an underground portion that houses a natural cave where Kamakhya Devi resides. The temple was erected by the Koch king Naranarayan in 1565, and destroyed by Kalapahar in 1572. King Chilarai of Koch Hajo rebuilt the temple. There are many secrets associated with the temple, and it is, therefore, considered one of the most sacred places for Shakta Hindus.

The Kamakhya Temple is where locals worship Goddess Kamakhya. Even today, the main worship is of an iconic *yoni* set in natural stone. A *Shakti Pitha* is an ancient temple dedicated to the Hindu goddess Sati and Parvati. It is one of the 51 *Shakti Pithas* (also called *Astha-pithams, or Astha-pithas*) and is one of the most important pilgrimage destinations for Tantric worshippers.

***

Chapter 15

Love as God

In Hinduism, devotional love is seen as the highest form of connection with the divine, where love for God transcends rituals, taboos, and asceticism. This chapter explores how the personification of love and mercy is embodied in deities like Krishna, whose interactions with his devotees reflect an intimate bond that goes beyond divine command to one of reciprocal affection. Devotion, love, and the role of women in society converge through the lens of divine love, revealing how sacred love challenges traditional norms and celebrates the transformative power of the heart over rituals.

Vishnu, as the Preserver of the universe, has held a unique position in the Hindu pantheon even in the heyday of Shaiva greatness, though His worship was not as widespread in ancient India as that of Shiva or his consort. The greatness of Vishnu as a universal benefactor and the god of love and grace was first preached by Ramanuja, a South Indian Brahmin in the twelfth century of the Christian era. His disciple, Ramananda carried his message to the north of the country, and soon the whole of India went through a vibrating change inspired by the new cult.

The gist of Ramanuja's popular teaching is that God, represented by Vishnu and his incarnations, is essentially the personification of love and mercy; the most effective way of approaching Him is through devotion and a humble heart and not through rituals, taboos or asceticism. Vishnu is much benign; rather than being the master of His devotee, He is more like his slave. One of Vishnu's many names is Bhaktadasa meaning the slave of the devotee; another name is Bhaktavatsala, meaning always affectionate upon His devotees. He cares not for caste or creed or what is offered to him, but is concerned only with the heart of the devotee and the intensity of his devotion. In love with the devotee, Vishnu forgets Himself and becomes the devotee's friend, companion, or even servant.

Rama, the seventh incarnation of Vishnu and the central figure of the epic Ramayana, is the god of devotion in popular Vaishnavism. For love, however, greater focus here would be on Krishna, the eighth incarnation of Vishnu, who is the central figure in the love cults of Vaishnavas.

On reaching a certain stage, the all-absorbing devotion to God becomes an intoxication which, to the ordinary people, may appear like a mania. In his ecstasy, the devotee often forgets himself and the world around him. Drunk with love of the Lord, he is likely to behave in a manner objectionable to the respectable.

Sages with sufficient devotion experienced these mystic joys and some of them actually behaved this way. Nothing could compare with this ecstasy and they could not describe their experience to others. But it was necessary that others should know the nature of this joy so that they too could become devotees of Vishnu and obtain liberation and bliss. In this predicament, Vaishnava mystics expressed their experience in terms of the greatest joy that ordinary mortals are incapable of understanding and experiencing. Now, there is no pleasure so eagerly sought after by men of the world as union with a beautiful, loving woman. Hence, Vaishnava poets often uttered the unutterable in terms of sex love.

This divine love is denoted by the Sanskrit word *Prema* as opposed to *Kama* or sensuous love. In common literature, however, the two words are indifferently used in both senses. Prema, in its true sense, stands for all-absorbing devotion to God, which leads to spiritual intoxication. In prema, the distinction between the devotee and the deity is often lost; it establishes complete equality or union between the two. Some advocates of prema even maintain, as already stated, that the deity becomes the slave of his devotee.

However, sexual symbolism in devotion is not peculiar to the Hindus. The Hebrew *Song of Songs*, the worship of Christ as the Divine Bridegroom by Christian mystics, and Sufism in Islam all indicate the same religious tendency. In Hinduism, the genius for pursuing an idea to its extreme end, aided by a vivid creativity, is unique. There is no restraint imposed on passion for speculation, either by the practitioner themselves or by pontifical authority, and many sound principles are often stretched to limits that the non-Hindu world might perceive as undesirable. The emotion of love in Hindus is no exception to this general tendency. One can find many offshoots of this basic human emotion which may appear as objectionable as the Panchatattva ritual.

Just as Shiva is the god of destruction and regeneration, Shakti of power, and Kama of sensous pleasure, Krishna, the eighth incarnation of Vishnu, is also the god of spiritual love. Vaishnavism gave a new interpretation to Krishna's *Lilas;* He became the most popular god of the Vaishnava world, stealing a march on the greatness of even Rama. Krishna is peculiarly suited to the genius of the common people. He did not preach asceticism as a means to salvation; on the contrary, for Him the world is a *karmabhumi* (domain of action) and the universe is said to be the *Lila* or play of Krishna. His own life on earth, depicted in the scriptures—the *Shrimad Bhagwat*, the Mahabharata and the *Brahmavaivarta Purana*—is so varied that every devotee has found in him a god after his own heart. In his childhood, Krishna was the darling of his folk in Gokul among whom he grew up, and to this day, Hindus experience a divine joy in reading about his sweet pranks as a divine child. As a young man, Krishna foiled his maternal uncle Kansa's innumerable attempts to kill him, and destroyed many demons and evildoers. He was also the heart throb of the young women of Braj where he lived and tended his flock. Reaching manhood, Krishna transformed into an invincible warrior and wise statesman, organising his people, the Yadavas, into a powerful community of formidable fighters. He fended off and defeated seventeen invasions of Jarasandha, the imperialist emperor of Magadha, who was out to destroy Krishna and the Yadavas and extinguish Mathura in revenge for Krishna's slaying of Kansa, the Magadhan emperor's son-in-law. The timeless, metaphysical *Shrimad Bhagavadgita*, a philosophical gem, contains, in a nutshell the entire conception of life and liberation. It was first revealed and spoken by Krishna to his cousin Arjuna, the Pandava prince and warrior. Adherence to duty is the greatest virtue preached in *Shrimad Bhagwat*. Krishna is one of the outstanding examples in Hinduism of a teacher who asserts that a well-lived worldly life, with adherence to dharma and performance of one's karma, is more noble than renunciation or asceticism.

Krishna, in his youth, is described as an attractive figure, slightly dark in complexion (hence the name Krishna), with a well-proportioned body and an incomparable fluteplayer. The young maidens of Gokul, the Gopis, loved him, longed for him and loved listening to the notes he played on the flute. The arcadian fields of Vrindavan, on the banks of the Yamuna, were the haunts of young Krishna. At midnight in spring, when the full moon shone and turned the blue waters of the Yamuna into a silvery sheet, Krishna stole into the mango groves on the banks of the river and played his flute. On hearing the call of the divine lover, the Gopis, leaving their husbands, parents and children, ran to the grove in sheer delight and danced and sang with Krishna.

In marked contrast to the other deities of the pantheon, like Shiva and Shakti, who represent the imposing and the powerful, Krishna is depicted in art as a playful young man of pleasing countenance, skilled in music, and well-adorned with beautiful garments and ornamental head-dress. He is usually represented as standing with one leg gracefully bent and the foot resting on the other, playing on a flute, as a rhythmic figure. He is generally pictured as the central figure among a number of Gopis, or alone with Radha.

The love of the Gopis for Krishna is symbolic of the intense devotion of a devotee completely absorbed in God. In his love for God, the devotee reaches a stage when no bonds, either of duty or mundane relationship, can keep the soul from the Lord. The Gopis' desertion of their husbands and parents for the pleasure of union with the Lord illustrates the soul's yearning for God to the exclusion of all other sentiments. A certain disdain for the trivialities of social codes can arguably said to be a feature of the true Vaishnava. While this guide to conduct has worked well for Vaishnavas whose love for God has been a guarantee against moral lapse, some so-called followers of Vishnu might have acted as they pleased. They lacked sufficient love for and devotion to the Lord.

It must be mentioned that the Hindus do not consider it degrading to give a sensuous interpretation to the Gopis' love for Krishna. Sex is not particularly irreligious; if an erotic sentiment is mixed up with the devotional, the Hindus consider it a legitimate union with God. Contemplation of Krishna from any angle is thought to be meritorious. Such being Hindu conceptions of devotion, it is not surprising that thinking of Krishna as also a hero of sensuous love should find a place in Vaishnavism. Some of the sects that worship Krishna have strong erotic leanings and their practices are condemned by others.

Like the Shaktas, Vaishnavas of the Krishna cult insist on making religion as pleasant as possible. But in place of Panchatattva, Vaishnavas advocate salvation through song and dance. Singing kirtans and dancing before idols of the deity is a peculiarity of all Vaishnava cults and many of the great saints of the sect expressed their devotion in song. Thyagaraja, the famous musician-saint from the south of India, whose kirtans in praise of Rama are considered masterpieces of classical music, and Jayadeva, the author of the famous *Gita Govinda*, a work which we will have to notice later, were notable examples. The Rajput princess Mirabai, who left her palace and her husband in search of Krishna, her Divine Lover, was also a great songstress. Her ecstatic songs expressing her eagerness to meet her lover, her impatience on his delayed arrival, and her overflowing emotions on meeting him, vibrate with divine passion. Her name and songs are household words among Vaishnavas, especially in northern India. Examples of sublime devotion will also be found in the works of Surdas, Tulsidas and Tukaram, all well-known Vaishnava poets and musicians.

But, all songs of Krishna and the Gopis do not breathe sublime mysticism. In Bengal, poems of mystic love often took a sensuous turn. In the works of Jayadeva and Vidyapati, the descriptions of the love scenes, quarrels and jealousies between Krishna and his beloved Radha, are hardly distinguishable from similar poetry describing the love of ordinary mortals.

Dance is an important feature of the Krishna way of devotion. Chaitanya, the saint who popularised Vaishnavism in Bengal was an ardent advocate of dance as expressive of devotion. He himself used to sing and dance before the idols of Krishna. Dance is in fact a common feature of all Hindu rituals irrespective of sectarian differences. Shiva is the arch-dancer of the pantheon and he is often worshipped by his followers as Nataraja or Lord of Dancers. Goddess Kali, too, dances after a triumph over her enemies. The dances of Shiva and Kali symbolise the rhythm in the universe or the terror-inspiring whirl of the worlds. Shiva usually dances solo; so does Kali. But the dances of the Krishna cult have high symbolism of love and Krishna seldom dances alone. He dances either with his favourite Gopi, Radha, or with a number of Gopis in his play known as *Rasa Lila*, one of the popular dances of Vaishnavas. In *Rasa Lila*, a number of Gopis dance—each with her beloved Krishna, the god having multiplied Himself for the purpose. Mathura, the birthplace of Krishna, is also the home of the dance which is organised on a large scale on festive occasions. Born in Mathura, Krishna lived there for a considerable period of his youth, after leaving Gokul and Vrindavan. During spring, for the pleasure of pilgrims, festivals are still held in the temples dedicated to Krishna in Mathura, in memory of his midnight revelries with Gopis. However, it is not Mathura alone that is associated with the cult and the dance. *Rasa Lila,* is today, a popular dance all over India.

It is interesting to note that in the love cult, Krishna is worshipped not with his wives but with his sweethearts from before marriage—the young, married and unmarried girls who grew up with him in Vrindavan, where he lived and tended the flocks of the *Gopas* (cowherds) in his boyhood. The following description of Krishna's sport with the Gopis extracted from the *Vishnu Purana* will give the reader an adequate idea of the activities of the gay, youthful god:

> Beholding the clear sky with the autumnal moon, and the air perfumed with the fragrance of the wild water lily, in whose buds the clustering bees were murmuring their songs, he (Krishna) felt inclined to join the women of the cowherds in sport. Thereupon with Balarama (his half-brother) he began singing sweet low strains in various measures such as the women loved; and they, as soon as they heard the music, left their homes and hastened to meet the Slayer of Madhu. One damsel gently sang an accompaniment to his song, another attentively listened to his music: one called him by the name and then shrank in bashfulness; whilst another, more bold and prompted by love pressed close to his side; one as she came out saw some of the seniors of her family and dared not venture farther than satisfying herself with meditating on Krishna with closed eyes and wholehearted devotion by which immediately all sin was expiated by regret at not seeing him; and others again reflecting upon the cause of the world, in the form of Supreme Brahma, obtained, by their sighing, final emancipation. Thus, encircled by the females of the cowherds, Krishna thought the lovely moon-light night of autumn suited the *Rasa* dance.

Krishna started dancing with the Gopis and when they were enjoying his company, he suddenly disappeared leaving them, as it were, in mid-air. The love-mad Gopis wandered all over the banks of the Yamuna calling him by name and crying pitifully. They could find him nowhere and in despair returned to the spot where he had left them and started singing his songs. Then, they saw the Protector of the three worlds with a smiling countenance coming speedily towards them, on which one cried out 'Krishna, Krishna', being unable to utter anything else. One liked to contract her forehead with frowns as if drinking with the bees of her eyes the lotus of Hari's face; another, shutting her eyes, meditated upon His form. Thereupon, Krishna coming amongst them conciliated some with soft words, some with gentle looks and some he took by the hand and sported in the stations of the dance. As each of the damsels attempted to remain close to Krishna, the circle of the dance could not be constructed. Thereupon taking each by the hand and when their eyelids were closed by the magic of his touch, Hari formed the circle. Then began the dance to the accompaniment of the music of clashing bracelets round the neck of Krishna: a girl proficient in the art of singing embraced him. The drops of perspiration from the arms of Hari were like fertilising rain which produced drops of dew upon the temples of the damsels. Krishna sang the melody that was suited to the dance. The damsels cried 'Bravo! Krishna!' as he sang. When leading, they followed him, when retracing, they met him; whether he went forward or backward they always followed him. While thus sporting with him, they regarded even moment of his absence as the separation of a myriad of years. And although prohibited in vain by their husbands and brothers, they went out at night to sport with Krishna, the idol of their love. Thus, the deity of unbounded prowess, the remover of all imperfections, assumed the character of a youth amongst the damsels of Braj, pervading their nature by his own essence like the wind; for even as in all creatures the elements of ether, fire, water, and air are comprehended, so also is he and in all.

Later, as the love cult of Krishna grew, Radha, one of the Gopis, was exalted to the position of the presiding goddess of the cult. She was the wife of Gopa Ayanaghosha, but her husband does not have a place in the cult. Radha was *the* beloved of Krishna; she adequately represents the passionate devotee, ceaselessly seeking him. Her jealousies, her anxiety at her lover's absence, her pangs on his separation are the favourite theme of song and dance among the Vaishnavas. Because of the unique position that Radha occupies in the cult, it is also called the Radha-Krishna cult.

The most popular Hindu work describing, in terms of amorous love, the soul's yearning, despair, sorrows and anxiety in the absence of the Lord, as well as its supreme joy in meeting Him, is Jayadeva's *Gita Govinda*. It is a drama which has Radha as the heroine, and is performed during religious festivals even today. In order to give the reader an adequate conception of the nature and trend of the Radha-Krishna cult, a brief summary of the drama is presented below.

Radha is introduced in the opening scene; she is described as jasmine-bosomed, reclining in a bower in the woodlands by the Yamuna. It is spring, the season of love, when the love-god Kama stirs feelings of love with his bow of luscious cane and shafts of flowers. The lovelorn Radha is waiting for Krishna, becoming impatient at the delay in his arrival. The appointed hour is past and Radha becomes apprehensive of his loyalty. For Vrindavan is full of lovely maidens and Krishna is a sportive lad. Radha calls for her maid, and both of them go in search of Krishna.

Radha's worst fears are confirmed when she sees Krishna

sporting with the other damsels, forgetting both his promise and Radha. The maid points at Krishna and tells Radha:

- See, lady! how thy Krishna passes these idle hours
- Decked forth in fold of woven gold, and crowned with forest-flowers
- And scented with the sandal, and gay with gems of price
- Rubies to mate his laughing lips, and diamonds like his eyes
- In the company of damsels who dance and sing and play
- Lies Krishna, laughing, toying, dreaming his Spring away

Radha sees Krishna and the fair Gopis. One of them takes his head and gives for a pillow 'tenderly outspread' and other girls fan him with the leaves and petals of roses. One lady leans over him and, whispering sweet words of love in his ear, kisses him, and Krishna, drawing her face to his, returns the kiss. Another, feeling jealous of him reclining on the bosom of her rival, pulls him away by the cloth and tries to lead him to the shade of a spreading mango tree laden with blossoms. A third damsel stops him and starts dancing with him in the *Rasa*, much to the delight of all.

Radha, burning with jealousy of her rivals, thus laments her misfortune:

> Yes; in habiliments becoming the goddess of love and with tresses waving like flowery banners, a damsel more alluring than Radha enjoys the conqueror of Madhu. Her form is transfigured by the touch of her divine lover; her garland quivers over her swelling bosom; her face, like the moon is graced with clouds of dark hair, and trembles while she quaffs the nectarous dew of his lips; her bright earrings dance over her cheeks which they irradiate; and the small bells on her girdle tinkle as she moves. Bashful at first, she smiles at length on

> her embracer, and expresses her joy with inarticulate murmurs while she floats on the waves of desire, and closes her eyes dazzled with the blaze of approaching Kama: and now this heroine in love's warfare falls exhausted and vanquished by the resistless Murari, but alas! In my bosom prevails the flame of jealousy, and yonder moon, which dispels the sorrow of others, increases mine. See again, where Murari sports in yonder grove on the bank of the Yamuna. See, how he kisses the lip of my rival, and imprints on her forehead an ornament of pure musk, black as a young antelope on the lunar orb! Now, like the husband of Rati, he fixes blossoms on her dark locks where they gleam like flashes of lightning among coloured clouds. On her breasts, like two firmaments, he places a string of gems like a radiant constellation; he binds on her arms, graceful as the stalks of the water-lily, and adorned with hands glowing like the petals of its flower, a bracelet of sapphires, which resemble a cluster of bees. Ah! see, how he ties round her waist a rich girdle illumined with golden bells, which seem to laugh as they tinkle, at the inferior brightness of the leafy garlands which lovers hang on their bowers to propitiate the god of desire. He places her soft foot, as he reclines by her side, on his ardent bosom, and stains it with the ruddy hue of Yavaca. Say, why do I pass my nights in this tangled forest without joy and without hope, while the faithless brother of Haldhara (another name for Balarama, Krishna's older brother) clasps my rival in his arms?

The distressed maid weeps for her mistress without uttering a word. Radha says:

> But why, my companion, shouldst thou mourn, though my perfidious love disappointed me? What offence is it of thine

> if he sports with a crowd of damsels happier than I? Mark, how my soul attracted by his irresistible charms, bursts from its frame and rushes to mix with its beloved. She whom the god enjoys, crowned with sunflowers sits carelessly on a bed of leaves with him whose wanton eyes resemble blue lilies agitated by the breeze. She feels no flame from the gales of Malaya with him whose words are sweeter than the water of life. She derides the shafts of soul-born Kama, with whose lips are like a red lotus in full bloom. She is cooled by the moon's dewy beams while she reclines with him whose feet and hands glow like vernal flowers. No female companion deludes her, while she sports with him whose vesture blazes like tried gold faints not through excess of passion while she caresses that youth who surpasses in beauty the inhabitants of all worlds. O gale, scented with sandal, who breathes from the regions of the south, be propitious but for a moment: when thou hast brought my beloved before my eyes, thou mayest freely waft away my soul. Love, with eyes like blue water-lilies assails me and triumphs; and while the perfidy of my beloved rend heart, my female friend is my foe, the cool breeze scorches me like a flame, and the dew dropping moon is my poison. Bring disease and death, O gale of Malaya! O god with five arrows (Kama)! I ask not mercy from thee: no more will I dwell in the cottage of my father. Receive me in thy azure waves, O sister of Yama (the god of death; Yamuna is Yama's sister), so that the ardour of heart may be allayed.

In despair, Radha returns to her bower, torn by anguish, seriously contemplating suicide. But she cannot keep Krishna off her mind. With all that he had done to her, all his 'perfidy', Radha still wants him desperately. As a last attempt to bring back the lover o her, Radha sends her maid to Krishna with a message of love.

The maid finds Krishna sitting alone and pensive on the river bank. The sport with the Gopis was over. Now, only Radha engrosses him. Overburdened with a sense of guilt in having broken faith with Radha, Krishna wails:

Radha, Enchantress! Radha, queen of all!
Gone lost, because she found me sinning here;
And I so stricken with my foolish fall,
I could not stay her out of shame and fear;
She will not hear;
In her disdain and grief vainly, I call.

The maid approaches the wailing Krishna and tells him that Radha is dying for a glimpse of him. The news is too good to be believed. Moreover, the guilty Krishna is not bold enough to face Radha. He begs the girl to go to Radha and tell her to come to him.

The maid, unable to persuade Krishna to go to Radha, returns to her mistress and tells her Krishna's plight. His conscience is stricken, she says, and the erring lad is unable to face her. Says the maid:

Yea, lady! In the self-same spot he waits
Where with thy kiss thy taught him utmost love,
And drew him, as none else draws with thy look;
And all day long, and all night long, his cry
Is 'Radha, Radha', like a spell said o'er
And in his heart there lives no wish nor hope
Save only this, to slake his spirit's thirst
For Radha's love with Radha's lips; and find
Peace on the immortal beauty of thy breast.

Radha is delighted to know that the prodigal is longing to

return home. But she would not go to him. Let the repentant sinner come to her and prove his sincerity; there is a touch of vanity too in her demand. Besides, 'the lotus seeks not the wandering bee, the bee must find the flower.' So Radha sends the maid back, asking her to bring Krishna with her.

The mission of the girl proves successful and Krishna comes to Radha. The proud lady, happy, yet jealous, upbraids the foolish wanderer. With folded hands and bent knees, Krishna begs for pardon. But Radha must have her say, especially, what she thought of the Gopi with whom he spent the night:

Krishna! My Krishna with the woodland wreath!
Return, or I shall soften as I blame;
The while thy very lips are dark to the teeth
With dye that from her lids and lashes came
Left on the mouth I touched. Fair traitor! Go!
Say not they darkened, lacking food and sleep
Long waiting for my face. I turn it—so
Go! Ere I half believe thee, pleading deep;
But wilt thou plead, when, like a love-verse printed
On the smooth polish of an emerald,
I see the marks she stamped, the kisses dinted
Large-lettered, by her lips? Thy speech withheld
Speaks all too plainly; go abide by thy choice!
If thou dost stay, I shall more greatly grieve thee;
Not records of her victory?—peace, dear voice!
Hence with that doe-like brow, lest I believe thee.

Radha goes on in this strain and Krishna interrupts:

Speak but one mild word and the rays of thy sparkling teeth will dispel the glow of my fears. My trembling lips, like thirsty Chakoras long to drink the moon-beams of thy cheek. O my darling, who are naturally so tender-hearted, abandon thy causeless indignation. At this moment the flame of desire consumes my heart; O! Grant me a draught of honey from the lotus of thy mouth. Or if thou art inexorable, grant me death from the arrows of thy keen eye; make thy arms my chain; and punish me according to thy pleasure. Thou art my life; thou art my ornament; thou art a pearl in the ocean of mortal birth: Oh! Be favourable now, and my heart shall eternally be grateful. Thine eyes, which nature formed like blue water-lilies, are become, though thy resent me like the petals of the crimson lotus: Oh! Tinge with their effulgence these my dark limbs that they may glow like the shafts of love tipped with flowers. Place on my head that foot like a fresh leaf, and shade me from the sun of my passion whose beams I am unable to bear. Spread a string of gems on those two soft globes; let the golden bells of thy zone tinkle, and proclaim the mild edict of love. Say, O damsel with delicate speech, shall I dye red with the juice of alactaca those beautiful feet which will make the full-blown land lotus blush with shame? Abandon thy doubts of my heart, now indeed fluttering through fear of thy displeasure, but hereafter to be fixed wholly on thee; a heart which has no room in it for another: none else can enter it, but Love, the bodiless god. Let him wing his arrows; let him wound me mortally; decline not, O cruel, the pleasure of seeing me expire. Thy face is bright as the moon, though its beams drop the venom maddening desire: let thy nectarous lip be the charmer, who alone has power to lull a serpent or supply an antidote for his poison. Thy silence afflicts me: Oh! Speak with the voice of music, and let thy sweet accents allay my ardour. Abandon thy wrath, but abandon not a lover, who surpasses in beauty the sons of men, and who kneels before

> thee, O thou most beautiful among women. Thy lips are a Bandhujiva flower; the lustre the Madhuca beams on thy cheek; thine eye outshines the blue lotus; thy nose is a bud of the Tila; the Chunda blossom yields to thy teeth: thus, the flowery shafted god borrow from thee the points of his darts, and subdues the universe. Surely, thou descendest from heaven, O slender damsel, attended by a company of youthful goddesses; and all the beauties are collected in thee.

Radha, half-pacified, tenderly reproaches him more out of self-pity than anger:

> Alas! alas! Go, Madhava, depart, O Kesava; speak not the language of guile; follow her, O lotus-eyed god, follow her who dispels thy care. Look at his eye half-opened with continued waking through the pleasurable night, yet smiling still with affection for my rival! Thy teeth, O cerulean youth, are azure as thy complexion from the kissed which thou hast imprinted on the beautiful eyes of thy darling graced with dark black powder; and thy limbs marked with punctures in love's warfare (nail and teeth marks), exhibit a letter of conquest, written on polished sapphires with liquid gold. That broad bosom stained by the bright lotus of her feet, displays a vesture of ruddy leaves over the tree of thy heart, which trembles within it. Ah! How canst thou assert, that we are one, since our sensations differ thus widely? Thy soul, O dark-limbed god, shows its blackness externally. How couldst thou deceive a girl, who relied on thee; a girl who burned the fever of love? Thy roves in woods, and females are thy prey: what wonder? Even thy childish heart was malignant; and thou gavest death to the nurse who would have given thee milk (the reference is to the destruction of Putana, a *rakshasi* by Krishna's enemy Kansa for

> the destruction of the divine child, who was preordained as Kansa's slayer. While she was feeding him her poisoned milk, Baby Krishna killed her by sucking her breasts hard). Since thy tenderness for me, of which these forests used to talk, has now vanished, and since thy breast, reddened by the feet of my rival, glows as if thy ardent passion for her were bursting from it, the sight of thee, O Deceiver, makes me (ah! must I say it?) blush at my own affection.

Radha relentlessly pursues the guilty Krishna in this manner, and the maid comes to the rescue of the persecuted lover. She asks Radha to forget and forgive:

> The lesson that thy faithful love has taught him
> He has heard;
> The wind of spring, obeying thee, hath brought him
> At thy word:
> What joy in all the three worlds was so precious
> To thy mind?
> My proud one! do not indulge in scorn,
> Ah! be kind.

The words of the maid were not without avail and the lovers were reconciled. The train now appear on the scene and the drama closes with a wedding song. Radha enters the bridal chamber to the music of the marriage song.

> Then she, no more delaying, straight,
> Her step a little faltered, but her face
> Shone with unutterable quick love; and—while
> The music of her bangles passed the porch
> Shame which had lingered in her downcast eyes,
> Departed shamed...and like the mighty deep,

Which sees the moon and rises, all his life
Uprose to drink her beams.

Jayadeva was aware that his song of divine love is capable of being misinterpreted in a mundane sense. Hence he tells us:

And this shadowed earthly love
In the twilight of the grove,
Dance and song and soft caresses,
Meeting looks and tangled tresses,
Jayadeva the same hath writ
That ye might have gain of it,
Sagely its deep sense conceiving
And its inner light believing;
How that Love—the mighty Master, all the stars that cluster
In the sky, swiftest and slowest,
Lord of the highest, Lord of the lowest
Manifests himself to mortals,
Winning them towards the portals
Of his Secret House, the gates
Of that bright Paradise which waits
The wise in love, Ah, human creatures!
Even your fantasies are teachers.
Mighty love makes sweet in seeming
Even Krishna's woodland dreaming;
Mighty love sways all alike
From self to selflessness. Oh! Strike
From your eyes the veil, and see
What Love willeth Him to be
Who in error, but in grace,
Sitteth with that lotus-face,
And those eyes whose rays of heaven

Unto phantom-eyes are given;
Holding feasts of foolish mirth
With these visions of the earth;
Learning love, and love imparting
Yet with sense of loss upstarting
For the cloud that veils the mountains
Underneath the Sandal mountains,
How as if the sunshine drew
All its being to the blue
It takes flight, and seeks to rise
High into the surer skies,
High into the snow and frost,
On the shining summits lost!

Such is the deeper meaning of this apparently lascivious song. The cult of *Prema*, like most other Hindu conceptions, has a gross as well as sublime aspect. Some of the sects have definite erotic leanings and their practices have been the target of attack by conservative Hindus. One such sect that obtained countrywide publicity is the Vallabha or Maharajah Vaishnavas. The sect was founded by Vallabha, a Telugu Brahmin born in 1470. Such was his religious precocity that at the age of 12 he preached a new cult. He traversed India twice, visiting all important centres of pilgrimage. He was an ardent Vaishnava and popularised the worship of Balagopal or the child Krishna. A pugnacious disputant, he was acclaimed as the greatest exponent of the Vaishnava school of thought by the then king of Vijayanagara.

Vallabha settled down in Banaras and married. He had two sons. Marriage and progeny did not, however, bring peace to his vigorously active soul and, at the age of 52, he became an ascetic, passing away shortly afterwards.

Though Vallabha died an ascetic, he was an advocate of what is known as the Pushti Marga or the path of comfort. The import of Vallabha's philosophy is that since man and God are but one, the needs of the flesh are not essentially different from the needs of the spirit. Probably the belief of the Kaulas that religion should be made pleasant to the degenerate people of Kali Yuga underlies the philosophy of Vallabha too. The goal of life, according to Vallabha, is to serve Krishna and imitate his sportive life.

The distinctive feature of the Vallabha sect is the extraordinary reverence and homage paid to the heads of the community called *Maharajahs* (great kings) who are descendants of Vallabha; hence the other name of the sect (Maharajah sect). The Maharajah, for the laymen and women of the sect, is not merely the representative of Krishna, but Krishna himself. The initiation ceremony of the sect is the *samarpana,* or absolute dedication of the member to the Maharajah in the role of Krishna. The initiate must take this solemn oath during the ceremony:

> Om! Krishna is my refuge. I, who suffer the infinite pain and torment of enduring for a thousand years of separation from Krishna, consecrate to Krishna my body, senses, life, heart and faculties, my wife, house, family, property and my own self. I am thy slave, O Krishna.

The dedication is harmless in principle and is characteristic of Vaishnavism in general, which emphasises the absolute surrender of the individual to the deity. But some of the practices of the Vallabha sect have led to much criticism. The *Rasa Lila* dance is a favourite ritual of the sect—the Maharajah dancing the role of Krishna and his female devotees those of the Gopis. Another feature of the extraordinary reverence paid to the Maharajah is the drinking of the water in which the Maharajah's feet have been washed.

Towards the latter half of the nineteenth century when Hinduism began assimilating modern ideas and undergoing regeneration, the sect of the Maharajah came in for much criticism. The editor of a newspaper made a vigorous attack on the sect in general, and one of the Maharajahs in particular, and this dignitary brought an action for libel in the Bombay High Court in 1862. The proceedings created a sensation all over the country and much dirty linen was washed in public. In the end, the defendants proved, to the satisfaction of the court, that the charges were real and not imaginary and the action was dismissed with costs. This decision caused much sorrow to the sect, but the power of the Maharajahs did not abate on that account. An excerpt from the judgement may be reproduced here, indicating what a British Judge of the High Court (Sir Mathew Sausse) thought of the practices of the sect:

> The Maharajahs have been sedulous in identifying themselves with the god Krishna by means of their own writings and teachings and by similarity of ceremonies of worship and address which they require to be offered to themselves by their followers. All songs connected with the worship of Krishna, which were brought before us, were of an amorous character, and it appeared that songs of a corrupting and licentious tendency, both in ideas and expressions, are sung by young females to the Maharajah upon festive occasions, in which they are identified with the god in his most licentious aspect. In these songs as well as stories both written and traditional, which latter are treated of a religious character in the sect, the subject of sexual intercourse is most prominent. Adultery is made familiar to the minds of all; it is nowhere discouraged or denounced; but on the contrary, in some stories, those

persons who have committed that great moral and social offence are commended.

With due deference to the moral sternness of a nineteenth century British Judge, it must be mentioned that singing of lascivious songs is not sufficient proof of moral lapse in a Maharajah. A Vaishnava saint may sing apparently lascivious song with as much reverence as a Christian divine may read the *Song of Songs*.

The Maharajahs are, after all, spiritual preceptors or Gurus, and it is seldom that a Guru abuses the confidence and trust of his followers. Besides, the disciples themselves will very soon lose respect for a Guru who is carnally inclined.

It is wrong to condemn the Maharajahs as morally lax. It is of course probable that some of the Maharajahs did not live up to the spiritual standard expected of men of their eminence. But, most of them are venerable individuals, enjoying the allegiance and confidence of a large number of educated, wealthy, cultured men and women. Further from the practices of the sect, one is inclined to believe that the Maharajahs assume an attitude of spiritual inaccessibility to their followers, and promiscuous activities are not at all helpful in maintaining this aloofness. It may also be mentioned that access to the Maharajah is considered spiritually elevating and only the elect are permitted the privilege of approaching or touching the Maharajah.

There were in the early twentieth century, at least over a hundred Maharajahs—all of whom claim descent from Gokulnathji, the fourth son of Vithalnath. Vithalnath was the son of Vallabha, on whom descended his father's authority. He was, like his illustrious father, a brilliant exponent of Vaishnavism. He resided in Gokul (Mathura), and was called Gokul Gosain; the latter being a corruption of *Goswamin* (lord of cattle), an epithet of Krishna.

Though many Maharajahs lived then in Mathura, they had the greatest following among the mercantile communities of Rajputana and Gujarat. The Maharajah of Nathdwara in Rajputana was a powerful dignitary in the cult and was acclaimed the chief of the Maharajahs. The temple of Nathdwara is believed to be the real abode of Krishna, having migrated from Mathura when the Muslim persecution of the city became intolerable for the faithful. The idol of the main temple of Mathura was smuggled to Rajputana and invested at Nathdwara during the days of distress under Mughal emperor Aurangzeb, who was known as the epitome of tyranny and religious intolerance and of his hatred of Hinduism and Hindus, as also for his temple desecrations and demolitions.

It may be mentioned that Swami Narayana, a Vaishnava Brahmin born in 1780, tried to bring about some reforms among the followers of Vallabha. But, being persecuted, he could not undermine the authority of the Maharajahs; all that he could do was to found a subsect called the Swaminarayana sect, which has nothing erotic in its teachings.

A sect that has much in common with the Maharajahs is the Radha Vallabhi founded by Harivamsa in the sixteenth century of the Christian era. The members of this sect give preeminence to Radha. Some scholars are of the opinion that they have nothing to do with Vallabha and are an independent sect to whom the misnomer Radha Vallabhi had been attached. Whatever their origin and name be, their practices had, like those of the Maharajahs, a strong erotic leaning. In their secret dances, men dress as women. They maintain that Godhead is essentially male and this world of illusion and all its creatures are female. The only true male is Krishna, and until a man identifies himself as a woman, he cannot enjoy the bliss of communion with Krishna.

Another peculiar sect of Vaishnavas that came into some prominence a few hundred years ago was the Sakhi Bhava. Its members are taught to regard themselves as *Sakhis,* or the female companions of Radha. To approach that character to the utmost extent possible, some of the Sakhi Bhava-infused devotees went to the length of assuming the female dress and wearing ornaments. They also feigned some physical conditions which are possible only to women.

Chapter 16

Temple Art, Devadasis and Bacchanalian Festivals

The phenomenon of reproduction and preceding sex activity led the ancients to believe in the efficacy of promiscuity as a fertilising agent of their fields. Spring and autumn, seasons during which the verdant earth puts on a vestment of gaiety and the animal and vegetable kingdoms are at their best, were particularly selected for celebration of festivals connected with the principles of regeneration.

In ancient Babylon, Egypt and Greece, there were temples dedicated to gods and goddesses of reproduction, and during the spring festivals in these temples, ordinary morality of society was given up in favour of licentious behaviour for the pleasure of the deities.

Hinduism is coeval with the religions of Babylon, Egypt and Greece though it has survived them.

Many of the goddesses of the Babylonian, Egyptian and Greck pantheon may still be found in Hinduism though known under different names. The ruins of the temples of North India show that the practice of sex cults were prevalent in many of them.

In almost all the great temples that have survived the ravages of middle ages the decorative art consists of erotic sculptures.

Some of these show coital postures illustrative of Vatsyayana's treatise on the subject ; a few even depict perverted practices and the sex activities of animals and birds. The great temple of Konarak, now in ruins, was particularly noted for its erotic sculptures.

The temple was dedicated to Surya the sun god. Sun temples are now few in India, but at one time, his worship was fairly widespread: and a characteristic feature of the architecture of temples declicated to the sun god is the erotic sculptures that form part of the decorative art.

In Vedic literature Surya appears as a chaste god, the bright and beneficient luminary. In the Puranic pantheon, he has, however, fallen from the high moral plane

Of the Vedic period and in some of the Puranas, may be found stories of his moral lapses. We have already noticed the story of his seduction of the fair maid Pritha and the circumstances which made her expose her first-born.

In another myth we are told that the sun god mated with a mare, and in a third that he and Varuna jointly produced on the celestial dancer Urvashi, the sage Agastya.

It is not, however, the sun god alone who delights in erotic art.

The famous temple of Jagannath in Orissa, the Khajuraho temples, and most of the imposing shrines of South India have erotic carving as forming part of decorative art. Apart from the fascination the mystic has always had for sex, the Hindu sculptor seems to have found in Maithuna (sexual union) an interesting motif.

It is a peculiarity of the erotic sculptures of the temples that they appear mainly on the outer shrines and not on the inner.

This circumstance has led some writers to believe that the idea emphasised is that the worshipper should be able to give free vent to his imagination outside the shrine and cast away all his lascivious thoughts before entering it. This is a modern interpretation inspired by the Western notion of the indecency of sex, and it is doubtful if this was the real intention of the builders of the temple.

The Hindus, as we have already seen, do not consider sex as something outside the province of religion, but on the contrary, emphasise the importance of the sex force in all their religious conceptions.

As such, its universality and greatness are probably indicated to the worshipper by means of art.

An objectionable institution associated with temple worship was Devadasi (slave of the god) which had been flourishing in all parts of the country till recently.

We have seen in a previous chapter that Hindu kings used to keep in their palaces numerous courtesans for pomp and for pleasure. Kings were after all, humans and it was but proper that gods should have greater pleasures and privileges. For the medieval Hindu, an idol was not a mere representation of a god, but the god himself in person and the idol was believed to have most of the needs of humans. Hence in public and private worship, idols were bathed, anointed with perfumes, fed and clothed. They had other needs too.

The devadasis were either courtesans bought by the temple trustees or children dedicated and given to the temple by some pious parents in keeping with some vow, and brought up by the priests.

The ostentatious duty of a Devadasi was to sing and dance before the idols at regular intervals. Fanning the idol, leading the procession when idols were taken out on ceremonial occasions were the special privileges of the Devadasis; in fact, in all temple ceremonials and pageantry imitating royalty, they played an important role. For these services they were paid by the temple either in cash or by endowments of lands.

This was not, however, the only source of income for the Devadasis. Most of them were no better than common courtesans and they plied their trade in their establishments which were situated not far from the temple itself. Pilgrims and sight-seers who visited shrines in large numbers during festivals often diverted themselves towards these establishments, presumably after their temple visit was done.

To appreciate this point fully, the reader must bear in mind that a temple was not exclusively a place of worship. Much of the social and political life of the community, especially in villages and small towns, centred round the temple. Social functions, political discussions and even business transactions often took place in the temple. To the temple was attached theatres, halls for discussion of religious and philosophical matters and for the meeting of the Panchayats for settling municipal affairs. It is not surprising then that in medieval India, courtesans, too, got themselves attached to some temples.

Some of the priests of the temples were not above exploiting public credulity in the matter of recruiting Devadasis for the gods. Abbe Dubois mentions a peculiar custom by which the Vaishnava idol of Tirupati recruited women for his seraglio:

While the image of Venkatesvara is borne through the streets on a magnificent car, the Brahmins who preside at the ceremony go about the crowd and select the most beautiful women they can find, demanding them of their husbands or parents in the name of Venkatesvara for whose service, it is asserted, they are destined. Those husbands who have not lost all common sense, understanding or at least suspecting that a god of stone has no need for wives indignantly refuse to deliver up theirs, and bluntly speak their mind to the hypocritical rogues. The latter, far from being disconcerted, proceed to apply to others who are better disposed, for some of the men are delighted at the honour conferred upon them by so great a god in condescending to ally himself with their family and do not hesitate to deliver their wives and even their daughters into the hands of the priests.

It is thus that seraglio of Tirupati is recruited. When the god takes it into his head that some of his wives are beginning to grow old or are no longer pleasing to him, he signifies through the priests his intention of divorcing them. A mark is branded on their thighs or breasts with a red-hot iron, representing the god Venkatesvara, and they receive a certificate showing that they have faithfully served a certain number of years as legitimate wives of the god, and are, therefore, recommended to the charitable public. Then they are dismissed, and provided with their certificates of good conduct, they go about the country under the name of Kaliyuga Lakshmis (Lakshmis of Kaliyuga). Wherever they go, their wants are abundantly supplied.

It need hardly be said that the institution, if it ever existed, has fallen into disrepute. At present, a Brahmin who goes to respectable pilgrims begging for wives for Venkatesvara will do so at the risk of his life.

The institution of Devadasis was popular in medieval India and some of the larger temples had hundreds of these women attached to them. The famous temple of Somnath which Mahmud of Ghazni destroyed had more than five hundred Devadasis in it. The temple of Jagannath in Orissa also harboured a large number of Devadasis.

At what precise date the institution was introduced as part of temple ceremonials cannot be ascertained with accuracy.

The absence of its mention in ancient literature shows that it originated in medieval times. The *Artha Sashtras* of Kautilya, comprehensive in all respects, does not mention temple dancers. The book lays down elaborate instructions on how to control prostitution in the city and in the palace, but does not refer to Devadasis or prostitutes in the temple.

The growth of Puranic religion brought the institution to the forefront. Several Puranas recommend that arrangements should be made to enlist the services of singing girls to provide vocal and instrumental music at the time of divine services. These singing girls were usually prostitutes, and we are pained to find that some of the Puranas should have gone to the extent of recommending the purchase of beautiful girls for their dedication to temples. The *Padma Purana* goes to the extent of saying that the best way to win *Suryaloka* (the heaven of the sun god) is to dedicate a bevy of prostitutes to a solar temple.

The solar temples were notorious for Devadasis. Huien Tsang who visited India in the seventh century of the Christian era observes that he saw a large number of dancing girls in the sun temple at Multan. In fact, the main attraction of the sun temples seems to have been their erotic art and the Devadasis. And it is creditable to the moral sense of the Hindus that few living temples of Surya now exist in present-day India.

The institution of Devadasis came in for a good measure of criticism by rightminded Hindus from very early times. The Muslim traveller Alberuni says that there was vehement opposition to the institution from a section of Hindus, but kings and nobles being in favour of it, the efforts of the opposing section to abolish the institution proved of no avail.

A tenth century inscription from Rajputana confirms the statement of Alberuni. It records the express instructions of a chieftain to his attendants that if the arrangement he had made about the services of dancing girls at different temples was interfered with by ascetics and Brahmins, they should at once be stopped. It is probable that kings and nobles derived as much pleasure from the Devadasis as the temple trustees and their gods, and hence the zeal of Puritanical sects were powerless against the powerful combination.

The contact with the British and the modern conceptions of religion considerably influenced public opinion in the matter and at present few Hindus of the better class will be found to uphold the institution. In fact, with the rise of modernism, a vigorous crusade against Devadasis was launched all over the country, and as a result, the institution was legally stopped in the Madras Presidency where the evil had assumed alarming proportions. Legal prohibition does not, however, mean the annihilation of the institution for priests and temple trustees had many subtle ways of retaining Devadasis under respectable pretexts. The most salutary factor in the matter is enlightened public opinion, and this is so much against the institution that few temples anywhere in India now retain Devadasis.

Coming to the subject of Bacchanalian festivals, it is good to remember that a certain amount of rowdyism and license is a common feature of festivals of every community in the world. When the occasion indicates excessive hilarity, drinking is usually indulged in and public rejoicings often burst forth into bad language and even violence.

Song, dance and noise play an important part in all Hindu festivities, and some of these have their origins in the fertility cults of primitive tribes. By far, the most important Hindu festival in which the Bacchanalian element is predominant is Holi. It is a spring festival which has for its presiding deities, Krishna and

Kama, the love gods of the pantheon. It is obvious that a festival in honour of the divine lovers cannot but have some sexual significance. The Holi festival usually falls in the fifteenth Hindu month of Phalgun, corresponding to February-March, and is eminently suited to the genius of the mob and the folk.

One of the important items of Holi celebration is the bonfire that is lit in the evening and kept burning for the whole night. The bonfire is symbolic of the cremation of winter and the birth of the joyous spring. According to popular belief, the bonfire indicates the destruction and cremation of the female fiend Putana who was killed by Krishna. Some Hindu scriptures, on the other hand, maintain that Shiva is the presiding deity of the festival and the bonfire symbolises the destruction by this god of a female demon named Holika. Whoever may be the victim of the symbolic bonfire, it is considered meritorious to abuse her on the occasion of her cremation, and those who take part in the festivities use vulgar language against the dead fiend.

In keeping with the expectation of the spring season which would shortly clothe the earth with flowers and plants of variegated colours, the Holi festival is celebrated as a festival of colours. Indian villages, towns and cities present a unique spectacle. Rich and poor, the respectable and rowdy, all universally besmear their clothes and faces with red, green and yellow powder and paste. Holi players collect in groups at street corners armed with packets of coloured powder and water-filled balloons, and forcibly besmear the clothes of passersby who happen to wear clean clothes. Children take great delight in thus humiliating the respectable. With syringes and bottles of coloured water, they waylay pedestrians, demand baksheesh and threaten colourful confusion in the event of non-payment.

Because of the infectious nature of all rowdyism, even

members of other communities join the fun. Sometimes, however, forcing members of other communities to take part in the festival leads to communal riots.

Hindu women in their own houses 'play Holi' by sprinkling coloured water among themselves and on near male relatives. It is permissible to fool the elderly and the respectable on this day. Something of the spirit of April first, is a feature of Holi. Respectable women, however, strictly keep to their houses and do not move outdoors, for obvious reasons.

The cult of the vulgar is often pushed to extremes by drunken merry-makers. The abuse on Putana, Holika, the two devils, extends to persons who have absolutely no connection with this enemy of the gods.

In South India, some festivals in honour of goddesses are sometimes marked by obscene language. This writer had, some years back, occasion to witness the celebrations of the Bharani festival of Malabar, held in honour of Kali and she has her principal shrine at what was once known as Cranganoor in old Cochin state. For the Bharani festival, pilgrims from all over Malabar congregate there. Every pilgrim brings with him a cock to be scarificed at the altar of the goddess and each village sends out a large number of pilgrims. After the bird is sacrificed at the altar, the pilgrim gets it back on payment of a small fee and the flesh is cooked near the shrine and eaten; to wash down the meat, the pilgrims provide themselves with a good stock of arrack, a liquor distilled from the juice of the coconut palm.

Until recently, it was considered the sacred duty of every pilgrim to sing obscene songs, from the time he left his home on the pilgrimage till he returned. One of the diversions of the pilgrims at the shrine was the listening in and appreciation of competitive singing of songs by celebrated poets of the land.

Embrace
From Sculpture, Amraoti: 2nd Century AD

Toilet
Drawn after finds at Begram: 2nd Century AD

Photo: E S Mahalingam

Shiva And Parvati In An Amorous Pose
Vellore Temple: 17th Century AD

Radha And Krishna In A Grove By The Jumna
From a Pahari Painting: 18th Century AD

Radha And Krishna In A Grove By The Jumna
From a Pahari Painting: 18th Century AD

I have had occasion to listen to some of these, and it must be admitted that quite a number of these are works of genius possessing considerable literary merit. But unfortunately, they are unprintable. These peculiar notions of pleasing the goddess were not approved of by enlightened Hindus. Public opinion against the singing of vulgar songs became too strong to be ignored, and thankfully, the Maharajah of Cochin by a public proclamation finally prohibited the practice.

KAMA, GOD OF LOVE

He is the most handsome god of the Hindu Pantheon and enjoys perpetual youth.

A Loving Couple
From an Orissan temple sculpture:
11th Century AD

A Fond Mother With Her Child
From sculpture, Bhuvanesvar,
Orissa: 11th Century AD

Couple

Karla Caves, 1st Century BC

Dancers

Karla Caves, Bombay State: 1st Century BC

Lata Veshtika Embrace
From Mathura: 2nd Century AD

A Lady With A Mirror
Belur Temple, Mysore: 12th Century AD

Vellore Temple: 17th Century AD

Photos: E S Mahalingam

Gandharva Or Celestial Musician

Dancers

Lovers

Rajarani Temple, Bhuvanesvar, Orissa: 10th Century AD

Couple

Karla Cave, 1st Century BC

Belur Temple, Mysore State: 12th Century AD

Photos: A K Banerji

An Exquisite Dance Pose

A Dance Pose Of The Aggressive Type

Pahari Painting: 17-18th Century: Coomaraswamy's Collection

Photo: K Arunachalan

The Bashful Bride
Venu Gopal Temple, Srirangam. S, India, 16th Century AD.

Utka
She who waits alone for her lover in a lonely place.

Swadhina Patika
She who has her husband under control. The happiest of Nayikas, her husband is her slave.

Pahari Painting: 17-18th Century: Coomaraswamy's Collection

Abhisarika
She who goes forth alone at night to meet her lover: The figure on the tree is a witch and serpents trail the Nayika's path but she is dauntless.

Vasaka Saya
One who has received news of her lover's return from abroad and comes out to meet him. The crow on the roof on the left is announcing his return and the maid is putting everything in order.

Pahari Painting: 17-18th Century: Coomaraswamy's Collection

Vasaka Saya
She meets her lover who has returned from abroad.
The maid is preparing the bed for the lovers.

Abhisarika Or One Who Forth To Meet Her Lover
The Abhisarika journeys through a forest in a night of rain and lightening to meet her lover.

Pahari Painting: 17-18th Century: Coomaraswamy's Collection

Abhisarika

After the perilous journey through the dark night she has reached her lover.

Abhisarika

The joyful welcome by the lover of the bold Abhisarika who has reached her lover's home after a dangerous journey in a stormy night. The lover holds up his hands in approbation and wonder.

Rajput School: 17th Century AD, Prince of Wales Museum, Bombay

Sorath Ragini
The melody for Royal Lovers

The Final Look Of Satisfaction
Rajput School; 17th Century AD, La Peinture Indienne, Stchoukine

Marriage Of Shiva And Parvati
Khajuraho: 11th Century AD

Shiva And Parvati On Mount Kailas
Khajuraho: 11th Century AD
Chhattarpur State Museum

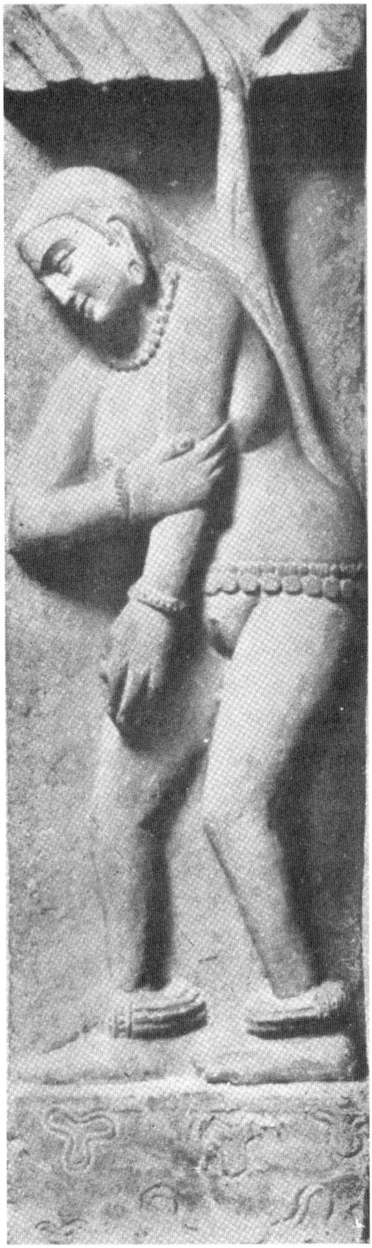

Bathing Beauty
Mathura: 2nd Century AD

Photos: E S Mahalingam

A Dance Pose
Halebid, Mysore: 12th Century AD

Bliss
Vellore Temple: 17th Century AD

Deccani Lovers
From Sculpture, Ellora: 8th Century AD

Hindustani Lovers
From Sculpture, 2nd Century AD
Provincial Museum, Lucknow

Royal Lovers
From Ajanta Paintings: 2nd-6th Century AD

Feminine Fashions

Hairstyles and jewellery in ancient and medieval India

A Woman Of No Distinction

A Maid Servant

A Noble Woman
From sculpture, Barhut: 2nd
Century BC

Southern Style
Penakonda, Madras: 9th
Century AD

An Apsara Or Celestial Courtesan
From Sculpture, Bagh Cave:
7th Century AD

A Prince And His Consort
From Ajanta Paintings:
2nd-6th Century AD